BEYOND REALISM

Turgenev's Poetics
of Secular Salvation

BEYOND REALISM

*Turgenev's Poetics
of Secular Salvation*

Elizabeth Cheresh Allen

Stanford University Press   Stanford, California
1992

Stanford University Press
Stanford, California
© 1992 by the Board of Trustees of the Leland Stanford Junior University
Printed in the United States of America

CIP data appear at the end of the book

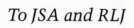

To JSA and RLJ

Acknowledgments

Various stages in the research and writing of this book were generously supported by the Mrs. Giles Whiting Foundation and a Morse Fellowship awarded by Yale University. I am grateful to the editors of *Russian Literature* and the *Occasional Papers* of the Kennan Institute for permission to use portions of Chapter 5 that appeared in somewhat different form in those publications.

Acknowledging the individuals who contributed, perhaps more than they know, to the preparation of this monograph is not merely a professional obligation but a personal pleasure. First among them is Robert Louis Jackson, whose inspired—and inspiring—teaching and writing on Turgenev drew me ever deeper into the subject, and who ceaselessly encouraged me to trust my own judgment in exploring it. I am immeasurably indebted as well to Gary Saul Morson for his invaluable suggestions during the course of my work, and for the unfailing moral support that kept renewing my energies. I am also deeply grateful to William Mills Todd III and Caryl Emerson, who generously gave various stages of the manuscript painstaking and insightful readings that resulted in the revision or clarification of several crucial concepts. Many thanks go to Cathy Popkin for exceeding the norms of both collegiality and friendship with her patient willingness to listen and respond to those concepts as they were cast and recast. Special gratitude must additionally go to Victor Erlich, the scholar and teacher who first convinced me that my ideas about Turgenev were worth pursuing.

I owe further debts of gratitude to other colleagues for their most timely words of advice and encouragement: Thomas J. Carew, Michael G. Cooke, Donald Fanger, Laura G. Fisher, Joseph W. Gordon, David Lowe, Amy Mandelker, Dale Peterson, and Riccardo Picchio. Those debts extend as well, at Stanford University Press, to Helen Tartar, who graciously gave me the benefit of her rare intelligence and experience over many months, and to Karen Brown Davison, who provided exemplary copy editing. I will always be grateful to the kith and kin who for years have granted me more tolerance than I deserve, and never more so than while they awaited the conclusion of this work: Theresa D. Christensen, Sidney and Barbara Cheresh, C. Roland and Dorothy Christensen, I. Richard and JoAnn Savage, Mark and Phyllis Allen, Kirsten Allen Foutz, and Hadley Allen.

Finally, I thank my husband, James Sloan Allen, for his surpassing help and guidance at every step along the perilous path of scholarly writing, and for reminding me at every turn that there is, after all, life beyond literature.

E.C.A.

Contents

Note on Translations
and Transliteration

All translations of Turgenev's works are my own, following the
Soviet Academy of Sciences' second edition of I. S. Turgenev,
Polnoe sobranie sochinenii i pisem v tridtsati tomax, ed. M. P.
Alekseev, et al. (Moscow, 1979–86). Spaced ellipsis points (. . .)
indicate portions of Turgenev's text that I have intentionally
omitted. Closed suspension points (...) indicate breaks in Turgenev's own text. Volume and page number are noted in paren-
theses after each translated quotation. Passages from other texts
not written in English are quoted wherever possible from standard English-language translations, as cited in the notes.

For the sake of readers who do not know Russian, titles of Turgenev's works and names of familiar characters are rendered as
most commonly found in English translations. The standard English spelling of well-known Russian names—Tolstoy, Chekhov, Bakhtin—are also used. Other Russian names and terms
are transliterated according to the modified Library of Congress
system.

BEYOND REALISM

Turgenev's Poetics
of Secular Salvation

Introduction:
The Critics' Turgenev

At the pivotal point in Ivan Turgenev's masterly novella *First Love*, there occurs an incident emblematic of Turgenev's entire artistic vision. The narrator recalls an evening, years earlier, when he stood gazing at the bedroom window of the young woman he loved with an adolescent passion:

The small, slightly convex panes of the little window dimly shone with a weak light falling from the night sky. Suddenly, their light began to change... Behind them—this I saw, saw clearly—carefully and quietly a whitish curtain was being lowered down to the windowsill—and then remained motionless.

"What is all this?" I asked myself aloud, almost involuntarily, when I returned to my room. "A dream, chance, or..." The imaginings that suddenly came into my head were so new and strange I could not even articulate them. (6: 351)

He had seen without seeing and known without knowing: his beloved had entered into a clandestine liaison with his own father. The next day "an unusual sadness" descended upon him, he remembers, "as though something in me had died" (6: 351). Something in him *had* died—the blind innocence of youth, the beneficent ignorance of reality.

The incident thus marks an epiphany for the narrator, but it should for the reader as well, for it is vintage Turgenev. Phrased with rhythmic restraint, lapidary care, and evocative ambiguity, conveying only a suggestive action in an otherwise still and silent scene, it nonetheless portrays a moment of concentrated dramatic intensity. Indeed, the very understatement, the unruffled quietude of the scene's surface, betokens the tempestuous emotions underneath—in both the lover's desire and disillusionment. The whitish curtain thus reveals while concealing.

Because he could so compellingly invoke this combination of disclosure and disguise, Turgenev was lionized in his own day as the equal, if not the superior, of his fellow authors Dostoevsky and Tolstoy. At his death in Paris in 1883, Turgenev was celebrated as one of Europe's preeminent literary figures; the cultural lights of Paris gathered at the Gare du Nord to memorialize and bid him farewell as his body was entrained for its return home. On the occasion, Ernest Renan eulogized Turgenev as an extraordinary Slavic genius "whose exquisite works charmed our century." "No other man," Renan declared, "has been so much the incarnation of a whole race. A world lived in him, spoke through his lips."[1] A decade later, the cultural critic Max Nordau would place Turgenev's works above Tolstoy's because "Tolstoy does not possess the splendid sense of artistic proportion of Tourgenieff, with whom there is never a word too much, who neither protracts his subject nor digresses from his point and who, as a grand and genuine creator of men, stands Prometheus-like over the figures he has inspired with life."[2]

Yet in the past century, Turgenev's reputation and renown have diminished. Although lip service is still paid to Turgenev as a contributor to the so-called Golden Age of Russian literature, his works cannot be said to enjoy anything like the sweeping admiration they once inspired. Here we have what might be deemed the mystery of Turgenev: Why have his works lapsed into relative obscurity while those of his two famous compatriots have become classics of the Western literary tradition? Addressing this mystery, Robert Louis Jackson adduces several plausible explanations, aptly labeling them a "treasury of cliches": "Turgenev's novels are period pieces; he is a conduit only for studying his class and culture; he was indecisive and weak in character; he is a writer with poetic sensibility and style, but with nothing to say."[3]

Intentionally or not, commentators since the turn of the century have tended to promulgate just such assessments of Turgenev's artistic achievements. On the whole, they fall into two groups, each of which has damned Turgenev not so much with hostile criticism or even faint praise as with imbalanced praise. And in so doing, they bear responsibility for the deterioration of Turgenev's reputation and for creating nothing less than myths about the nature and value of Turgenev's art.

The first group, which has dominated the discussion of Turgenev's works both in Russia and in the West, contains those scholars who give a ritual nod in passing to the formal virtues of Turgenev's prose fiction as they hasten to focus on its social and historical content. They extol the precision and vividness with which Turgenev portrays the mid-nineteenth-century life of both rural landed gentry and peasants—their appearance, their customs, their environment, their conflicts. Taking some of Turgenev's extraliterary commentary as a clue to his literary goals, they often appreciatively affix the label "realist" to Turgenev's narratives. This label, though—which they regularly point out Turgenev himself did not reject—gave rise to the myth that Turgenev devoted himself solely to the objective recording of the contemporary ways of life he witnessed.

The second group is typified by imaginative writers, including Henry James, Thomas Mann, Joseph Conrad, Ernest Hemingway, William Dean Howells, Virginia Woolf, and Somerset Maugham, to name but a few. Distinctive and superb stylists themselves, they cared more for Turgenev's mastery of form than for his historical subject matter. Lauding Turgenev's stylistic perfections, they commended what Woolf called "a simplicity so complex,"[4] which distinguished for them his skillful orchestrations of sound, word, and image. Yet this kind of admiration also contributed to the decline of Turgenev's literary standing. It is as if these readers encountered in Turgenev a crystalline image that, as Nietzsche remarked in *The Birth of Tragedy*, while seeming "to invite us to pierce the veil and examine the mystery behind it," possessed a "luminous concreteness" that "nevertheless held the eye entranced and kept it from probing deeper."[5] For in praising so lavishly Turgenev's genius in the artful manipulation of literary forms, they have directed too much attention to the surface and have discouraged the ambition to "pierce the veil"—or to raise the "whitish curtain"—and explore the realms beyond. Thus they have fostered the myth that there is little within to explore, that Turgenev is in essence an aesthete who pursues art purely for its own sake and who is not to be compared in psychological insight to the greatness of Dostoevsky or Tolstoy.

This monograph attempts to demythologize Turgenev criticism. Readers should not turn to Turgenev merely to find transparent narratives of nineteenth-century Russian life or simply to enjoy pure samples of polished prose. They should read him for his singularly Turgenevan virtues, which are equal to, albeit different from, those of Dostoevsky and Tolstoy.

The monograph therefore addresses both the form and the content, the surface and the substance, of Turgenev's narratives in order to uncover the unique literary patterns that cohere in an intricate, imaginative vision of art and human existence. Moreover, it discloses that this vision is informed by a complex, enduring set of ethical principles largely neglected by Turgenev's critics. And yet nothing is more central to an appreciation of Turgenev's unique accomplishments as an artist and thinker than his ethical ideals.

Part I examines the ethical and aesthetic values of the tradition with which Turgenev's works are most frequently associated—realism—and charts the course for looking beyond it to discover other characteristic values, particularly the ethical ones, that identify and unify Turgenev's art. Part II analyzes Turgenev's poetics, that is, the distinctive orchestrations of space and time, the language, the types of narrative voice, and the characterizations he deploys to dramatize his ethical beliefs. Taken together, these beliefs are subsumed under the label "secular salvation," in the sense that they are derived from a faith in redemption, not by the grace of a divine being, but by the rational and creative powers of a human being.[6] The Conclusion shows how Turgenev faltered in his last novel by compromising his ethical and aesthetic principles, yet once again affirmed those principles in his final creations, prose poems.

To avoid the fully explored and no longer highly productive critical paths to Turgenev, this study relies almost exclusively on Turgenev's prose fiction. It does not rely on many of his extraliterary writings, including his self-assessments, which have been given much weight in other critical studies. But the time has come, indeed it is long overdue, to focus on what Turgenev *actually* wrote without regard for what he *said* he wrote. The words, lines, and passages quoted herein have thus been selected not merely because they are central to an interpretation of individual works—although they are discussed as such and used to offer interpretations often diverging from traditional ones—but, more important, because they represent consistent, distinctive intellectual and artistic patterns that inhere throughout those works. As a result, their discussion is not organized chronologically; the point here is to elucidate what remains constantly Turgenevan, from the first narrative to the last.

Hence if read properly, as works of neither a detached observer nor a disinterested artist but of a profound psychologist and moralist in his own right, Turgenev's narratives will be understood to be as relevant to modern readers as they were to his contemporaries, if for other reasons. For the ethics and poetics distinguishing them are rooted in a conception of human nature familiar to the present, one that holds human nature to be frail, vulnerable to insidious forces ready to exploit every weakness. At the same time, these narratives rigorously insist that, however weak, human beings must continue to struggle, even at the cost of conventional morality, to achieve the only form of redemption possible in a secularized world—self-redemption. Thus Turgenev is disclosed to be at once more complex and more creative, more modern and more moral, than many readers have hitherto recognized.

Beyond Realism

I

The Ramifications of Realism

In the winter of 1857, Ivan Turgenev, at that time the most renowned Russian author in Europe, wrote an admonishing letter
to his sometime friend, sometime foe, Lev Tolstoy. Turgenev
had learned that his compatriot was undergoing one of what
would become repeated bouts of spiritual torment, during
which Tolstoy desperately sought some sense of coherence and
calm in an otherwise conflict-ridden existence. From Bougival,
France, where he had taken up residence so as to be near his
adored songstress, Pauline Viardot, Turgenev hastened to warn
the passionate Tolstoy of the dangers of adopting some rigidly
codified and narrow intellectual program or system while in
quest of spiritual equanimity:

> God grant that your mental horizons may grow wider every day! Sys-
> tems are only dear to those who cannot take the whole truth into their
> hands, who want to catch it by the tail. A system is just like the tail of
> the truth, but truth is like a lizard; it will leave its tail in your hand and
> then escape you; it knows that within a short time it will grow an-
> other.[1]

Having made his own attempts in previous years to capture "the
tail of the truth" by subscribing to one intellectual program after
another, Turgenev, nearing the age of forty, had come to concede
the futility of such endeavors.

Yet ironically, literary historians and critics addressing the
works of these two authors have nonetheless discerned more
"system" in Turgenev than in Tolstoy. Most conclude—although not always approvingly—that Tolstoy's artistic genius,

coupled with the psychological and religious conflicts that beset him, led him to avoid relying on one systematic philosophical or aesthetic ideology.[2] By contrast, the majority of historians and critics, from his own day to the present, have deemed Turgenev an adherent of one and only one aesthetic system: realism. According to this standard critical line, Turgenev is certainly a superlative writer, as long as his works are judged within the parameters of this dominant literary mode of nineteenth-century prose. To such critics, Turgenev's aesthetic priorities thus appear clear and well-established, headed by the "realist" desire to depict social, political, and historical reality of the moment—in Turgenev's case, the reality of mid-nineteenth-century Russia—objectively and accurately.[3]

The main impetus for the traditional view that Turgenev's literary aspirations and achievements were elementally and unshakably rooted in the system of realism—Turgenev's rejection of systems notwithstanding—comes from an admittedly impressive source: Turgenev's extraliterary writings, or at least some of them, regarding his literary intentions. For, ignoring his own advice, Turgenev did claim more than once to think of himself as a "realist" like his French friends and self-proclaimed *réalistes* Alphonse Daudet and brothers Jules and Edmond Goncourt, as well as Gustave Flaubert, who rejected the label but achieved his renown as its preeminent practitioner.

The most explicit assertion of this self-definition appears in a letter Turgenev wrote to an admirer in 1875: "I shall say briefly that in the main I am a realist, and above all interested in the living truth of human physiognomy; to everything supernatural I am indifferent."[4] Borrowing a phrase from Shakespeare, Turgenev vowed elsewhere to record "the body and pressure of the times"[5] (9: 390), avoiding invention and keeping his own emotions, personality, and ideas as removed from his works as possible. An acquaintance recalled Turgenev more than once stressing the necessity of a novelist's professional disinterest by averring that "the main thing in composing a novel is to cut the umbilical cord connecting one's characters with one's own person."[6] Thus he maintained that reality, not his imagination, provided the matrix for his artistic efforts. Turgenev told another correspondent that he never invented anything, insisting that he always began a story or novel with the "images" of actual things or people, not with "ideas."[7]

In these and similar statements, Turgenev denied the possibility that any overarching abstraction, artificial imagery, or original inspiration guided his artistry. To be sure, he did grant, in 1880, in an introduction to a collection of his novels, that "reality should not be simply reproduced, but has to be transfigured and presented in 'artistic images' " (9: 396). These images, though, are transfigured only in the sense that they are rendered in what Turgenev called their "concentrated reflection," that is, in a focused and intensified manner. Still, they remain to his mind not imaginative creations but careful recreations of extant phenomena, mirroring reality and nothing but reality.[8]

To most of his contemporary readers, Turgenev fully lived up to his self-assessment—and the system called "realism." What, after all, such readers maintained, did Turgenev write about most often and most successfully but the realities of the social and political life of nineteenth-century Russians? As early as 1848, Vissarion Belinsky, the most influential Russian literary critic of the day, applauded Turgenev's "successful physiological portraits" and "gift of observation, his ability to comprehend and evaluate truly and quickly every occurrence, with the instinct to discern its causes and effects"[9] and to express all this in his narratives. Similar evaluations of Turgenev's merits as a realist followed from every quarter. Guy de Maupassant hailed Turgenev for "turning away from all old forms of the novel in order to render life, only life, slices of life, without intrigue and without coarse adventures."[10] And Henry James declared that Turgenev "belongs to the class of very careful writers" whose "line is narrow observation,"[11] as a result of which, "his manner is that of a searching realist, his temper is that of a devoutly attentive observer, and the result of this temper is to make him take a view of the great spectacle of human life more general, more impartial, more unreservedly intelligent, than of any novelist we know."[12]

It is certainly no surprise that modern Soviet critics have also followed this interpretive line and found in Turgenev a herald of the "literature in the service of society," extolling him, in the words of one such critic, as "an artist of life, a social novelist, composing the carefully crafted history of the social development in nineteenth-century Russia,"[13] because, as another explains, "he sees as a poet and feels as a citizen."[14] Playing out this line, study after study and article after article from Soviet presses account for every facet of Turgenev's creative practice by reference to realism.[15] To the Soviets, Turgenev, more than Dostoevsky or Tolstoy, is nineteenth-century realism's standard-bearer.

And twentieth-century critics in the West have generally sounded the same refrain. For example, in his extensive study *Ivan Tourguénev et les courants politiques et sociaux de son temps*, the French critic Henri Granjard lauds Turgenev especially for being a "poet" turned "citizen," who therefore became the "meticulous chronicler" of Russian society, "the novelist who proposed to bring to life before his readers the cultivated Russian society of the nineteenth century."[16] According to Granjard, Turgenev patriotically, almost heroically, served his native land by reporting the details of the daily life of a people with whom Western readership at that time had little or no familiarity. In Granjard's view, so convincing were Turgenev's portrayals of that life that they practically single-handedly confirmed the reality of Russia's existence to Europe.

Attuned more to aesthetic than political virtues, the American commentator Edmund Wilson nonetheless equally prizes Turgenev's realism. Claiming that, as authors go, "Turgenev is not one of the great inventors"[17] but that his "realistic habit of mind" endowed him with keen powers of observation, Wilson finds a saving grace in Turgenev.[18] This habit of mind led Turgenev to embark "by the middle eighteen-fifties on a deliberate and scrupulous study of the social situation in Russia."[19] And this study, carried out in novels and short stories, was consistently successful, Wilson holds, because, unlike his contemporaries Dostoevsky and Tolstoy, Turgenev was "the expert detached observer, rather than the searching psychologist of the phenomena of Russian life."[20] Turgenev's literary triumph lies, therefore, in the precision and breadth of his descriptions of

Russian reality rather than in their depth. Nevertheless, Wilson divines in those descriptions unsurpassed realistic achievement.

Wilson's admiration for Turgenev's triumph as a realist is thoroughly shared, and the singularity of that triumph elaborated upon, by the British scholar Richard Freeborn, whose monograph *Turgenev: The Novelist's Novelist* (borrowed from Henry James's summary appellation for Turgenev) has served for thirty years as the preeminent critical study in English devoted to Turgenev's art. Freeborn insists that the greatest strength of Turgenev's narratives lies not simply in their realism, but in the unself-consciousness of that realism. Turgenev has the remarkable ability, Freeborn declares, to allow "the story to tell itself," as it were, and thereby to permit "the reality of the portrait" to "grow of its own accord" into "pictures of real life which are true to life and acceptable in terms of a reality every man can experience."[21] Hence Turgenev's works give the impression of "a reality . . . not of Turgenev's making which indeed surprises Turgenev as much as it may surprise and delight the reader."[22]

Freeborn therefore elevates Turgenev's achievement above that of realism of the *"tranche de vie* variety,"[23] as he puts it, in which an author self-consciously depicts coarse, unpleasant, even hideous forms of human experience in order to manipulate the reader's emotional responses. By contrast, the unself-conscious artlessness of Turgenev's realistic imagery, plots, and characters renders Turgenev infinitely more credible as "the dispassionate observer of the social scene" and "the chronicler of his age"[24] who succeeded "in giving the reader a picture of reality that is universally acceptable,"[25] as a self-conscious realist could not have done. For Freeborn, Turgenev is truly the realist par excellence.[26]

Thus, Turgenev-qua-realist has become a commonplace of literary criticism. Like all commonplaces that are too readily accepted, though, this one is due, even overdue, for review. Such a review is particularly important, because this label has slowly evolved from a term of sincere celebration to one of subtle derogation, becoming a kind of conceptual albatross hung, as it were, from the neck of Turgenev's narratives. The appellation of realist, unmodified and unmitigated, has arguably deprived those works of the attention of critics and readers alike, relegating the novels and stories to relative obscurity, even oblivion. It conveys the impression that Turgenev indeed fulfilled the allegedly realist goal of capturing the historical, political, social, and economic reality of a particular place at a particular time, but a place and a time in which the twentieth century is no longer very interested.

As sensitive a reader as Osip Mandelstam gently but firmly records such a dismissive reaction to Turgenev's works as early as 1925, when he noted that "in my youth I already knew that the tranquil world of Turgenev was lost, never to be recovered."[27] And even as admiring a commentator as Freeborn acknowledges the dismissal implicit in this response when he observes that Turgenev's focus on contemporary "ideological or sociopolitical issues . . . may tend to detract from the popularity of his novels . . . for it dates them to an epoch which has little direct relevance to the present."[28] Moreover, it may be that readers nowadays have come to accept Oscar Wilde's claim that "no great artist ever sees things as they really are."[29] If Turgenev the realist sees Russian "things as they really are," such reasoning would have it, he must not have been a "great artist" at all.

The relative lack of popular and critical attention accorded Turgenev's works during the late twentieth century can undoubtedly be traced in large part to just such dismissive conceptions as these. Explicitly or implicitly taken to largely belong to realism, these works must be outdated in subject and outmoded in style. But the time has come to consider whether the reason for this lack of interest resides wholly in the works alone. Some of the lack of interest may be the result of the conception, or misconception, of realism itself. As a category of aesthetic and historical understanding, realism has arguably been subjected to more variation, imprecision, and downright confusion in its use than comparable categories such as Romanticism or Modernism. Thus any further discussion of Turgenev's relation to realism must be prefaced by an analysis of the difficulties, both historical and current, besetting realism in general, and by the offer of a potential resolution of those difficulties. Only then can acceptable conclusions be drawn about the nature and value of viewing Turgenev's narratives strictly as works of realism.

This discussion and the conclusions drawn from it must themselves be prefaced by a brief orthographic and lexical note. The conventional practice of writing the word "realism" with a small "r," when referring to the artistic movement of the nineteenth century, will be abandoned in the remainder of this study. Instead, this word, used in this way, will be written with a capital "R." As a lexical corollary of this practice, the word "Realist," also with a capital "R," will be exclusively employed to denote those artists or works that exemplify the movement of Realism. The attributive form often employed interchangeably for this purpose, the generic term "realistic," will still be written with a small "r," and will refer to that infinite variety of qualities or experiences signaling what people take to be reality. These new orthographic conventions bring the advantage of creating practices consistent with those already used in the common capitalization of the words "Romanticism" and "Romantic" when referring to the artistic movement and its exemplars, and in the noncapitalization of the word "romantic" when referring to the infinite variety of qualities or experiences that people take to be marked by some attribute of romance.[30]

The capitalization of Realism and Realist symbolizes an effort to achieve the clarification and refinement of the definition of Realism itself, thereby reestablishing its utility as a critical concept. This effort is not undertaken lightly, but is made in full awareness of the warning sounded by one student of the subject that any attempt "to formulate a concept of realism which will serve the purposes of the history of the arts courts the alternative dangers either of falling victim to a philosophical naivety which accepts without question an everyday conception of reality or of becoming lost in cerebrations which end by allowing the whole concept to disintegrate."[31] Nonetheless, such an attempt is justified if it will enable the precise use of an all-but-indispensable critical term, yet a term that has fallen into such semantic disarray as to become all but useless. Indeed, the semantic value of the term has deteriorated to the point where, as one commentator on the contemporary critical scene has observed, "even responsible scholars seem to use words like 'reality,' 'objectivity,' and 'realism' almost ingenuously, as if in the hope that they won't be noticed."[32] Others, at the opposite extreme, have become not ingenuous but cavalier. C. P. Snow, for example, blithely asserts in his book on this subject that he does not need to define "realism" because most people would agree on the works and authors that fall under its rubric.[33]

The trouble is that most people, or at least most students of Realism, do *not* agree on the works and authors that fall under its rubric. Snow, for example, welcomes Dostoevsky and Tolstoy into the Realist fold, whereas Erich Auerbach, author of the magisterial study *Mimesis: The Representation of Reality in Western Literature*, categorically refuses to do so. George Levine, in *The Realistic Imagination*, offers Jane Austen and Joseph Conrad as the beginning and end of Realism's heyday in England, but does not admit Defoe, Richardson, or Fielding into the canon, although Ian Watt's seminal analysis of Realism, *The Rise of the Novel*, hails the latter three as the wellspring of Realism's development. Harry Levin includes Balzac, Zola, and Proust as exemplary practitioners in *The Gates of Horn: A Study of Five Realists*, despite their much more typical identification with, respectively, Romanticism, Naturalism, and Modernism. And Auerbach himself finds a brand of Realism in Homer, Cervantes, and Virginia Woolf, authors to whom very few others would attach the label Realist.

The evidently disparate criteria for admission into the Realist domain have fostered an unfortunate relativism in endeavors to actually describe Realism, albeit a relativism cloaked in the guises of flexibility and tolerance. Levin exemplifies this tendency by approvingly citing the words of the painter Fernand Léger, who declared that "every epoch has its own realism, invented more or less in relation to the preceding epochs."[34] Levine also participates in this relativistic trend by asserting that because Realism as a "historical impulse" was "particularly vulnerable to social, scientific, and epistemological transformation, its actual embodiments were polymorphous."[35] Thus he concludes that "realism exists as a process,"[36] whereby "what realism may be at any moment depends both on what it has been and on what the culture expects it to be."[37] Even Donald Fanger, who provides the felicitous compromise formulation of Realism as both "moment" and "mode" in his study *Dostoevsky and Romantic Realism*, makes passing reference to "realism (or realisms)."[38] This phrase tacitly, if inadvertently, concedes that the term Realism nowadays is possessed of no definitive substance at all.

Such a conclusion is shared—and most forcibly articulated—by Roman Jakobson. In his essay "Realism in Art," Jakobson excoriates historians of literature who have been, as he says, so "slipshod with respect to scholarly terminology" that Realism has developed "multiple meanings," which have become "hopelessly confused."[39] Yet he does not blame the critics alone, since, as he rightly points out, "classicists, sentimentalists, romanticists in part, even the 'réalistes' of the nineteenth century, in large part the decadents, and finally the futurists, the expressionists, etc., have often affirmed with insistence that fidelity to reality, the maximum verisimilitude, in a word realism, is the fundamental principle of their aesthetic program."[40] Thus Jakobson complains that artists and critics alike have found in the vast semantic reaches to which Realism has been stretched a license to label almost anyone and any work of art Realist. For Jakobson, the concept has therefore lost all semblance of conceptual shape and might as well be scrapped altogether.

An equally impressive student of the subject, René Wellek, has drawn the same conclusion, although on diametrically opposed grounds. Wellek rejects Realism as a useful critical term not because it has become a hopelessly broad concept, but because it has been an impossibly narrow one all along. Wellek argues in *Concepts of Criticism* that Realism is "an ideal type which may not be completely fulfilled by any single work,"[41] because the goal to which it aspires is beyond the scope of art. In the attempt to "give a truthful representation of the real world . . . dispassionately, impersonally, objectively,"[42] as one early partisan, Champfleury, mandated, Realism became subject to highly formalized "conventions and exclusions" that forced literary works to betray their artistic inspiration and to descend into "journalism, treatise writing, scientific description, in short, into non-art."[43] To Wellek, then, Realism is an excessively demanding concept at best, an aesthetically destructive one at worst, and one better abandoned by all concerned.

Jakobson and Wellek together create a kind of conceptual double bind for those who might still dare to invoke the term Realism. But whether "empty and harmless," as Jakobson might deride it, or "rigidly exact and menacing,"[44] as Wellek might denounce it, to them Realism is an essentially worthless concept. So then why not accede to such exceptionally informed judgments and jettison it for all time? Why not conclude, paraphrasing Wilde, that as an aesthetic and historical category (Wilde says as a method) realism is "a complete failure"?[45]

With all due respect to these judgments, it would be a mistake to declare Realism a failure as a conceptual category and abandon its use altogether. Despite the semantic fog in which Realism, with or without a capital "R," now founders, the continued, albeit clarified and refined, use of the concept is still justified for two compelling reasons. First, the term is absolutely entrenched in literary discourse. Not even the imprecations of voices as mighty as those cited have succeeded in banishing Realism from the realm of criticism. Clearly, both a need and a desire to use the term exist and should be satisfied, not denied. Second, the confusion into which the term has lapsed and the antagonism its manifold uses have aroused derive from essentially the same mistaken assumption about the nature of Realism. By correcting this mistake, it is possible to revitalize the concept of Realism, to determine its true character, and to validate its distinction as a literary mode most characteristic of one cultural historical moment.

The mistaken assumption leading so many commentators astray is based on the conviction that Realism utterly rejects its provenance, that is, the philosophical tradition from which the term was obtained.[46] In Western philosophy, "realism" refers to a Platonic belief in the metaphysical "reality" of ideas or of abstractions removed from material, physical actuality, the very actuality that literary Realism purportedly labors to portray. George Bernard Shaw captured this opposition between the two species of Realism with anachronistic abandon when he proclaimed that "the Real has always been a hard bird to catch. Plato did not succeed in getting it under his hat until he had divested it of everything that is real to the realists of noveldom."[47] As Shaw's quip implies, literary Realism is generally assumed to espouse a physical rather than a metaphysical conception of reality.

It is this assumption that has led to most of Realism's troubles. Time and again, a description of Realism has been wrongly connected to some physical conception of reality—an understandable connection to be sure, given the etymological affinities of "Realism" and "reality." Thus virtually everyone who has ever employed the term, as theoretician or practitioner, has felt obligated to relate literary Realism to the nature of reality itself. The British author of the meditation *On Realism*, J. P. Stern, for example, records his own sense of just such an obligation by posing the rhetorical question, "How can you say anything sensible about realism unless you have first defined what reality is?"[48] It is such a sense of obligation, in no small part, that led to the conclusions about Realism mentioned earlier: since *reality* can variously be construed as either too relative or too diverse to encapsulate in one definition, Realism must likewise be so relative or so diverse as to preclude its own single, specific definition.

However well-intentioned the ambition to link a conception of Realism to a conception of reality may be, it is misguided, for Realism is not sufficiently distinguished by a descriptive vision of what human life *is* like—infinitely too many such visions exist. Yet a definition of Realism becomes possible as soon as it is sought not in an idea of the real but in an image of the ideal. In fact, it is an image of the ideal, specifically a normative or prescriptive ideal of human life—that is, what human life *should* be like—that truly distinguishes works of Realism. Realism cannot be wholly comprehended, then, until it is recognized not to have drifted as far from its philosophical forebears as has often been assumed, because in fact, literary Realists, if not in all ways close to the metaphysical realists, are at least not far from their equals as moral idealists.[49]

The normative ideal that unites and identifies works of Realism is primarily distinguished by a system of ethics. To be sure, the notion that Realism is inspired at least to some extent by an ethical impulse has been suggested by a number of critics, who have basically discerned two types of ethical impulses. Stern, in compromise fashion, finds both, and labels them (1) descriptive and (2) evaluative, attributing a revelatory ethic to the former and an admonitory ethic to the latter.[50] The descriptive exposes the ills of contemporary existence by meticulously documenting them—engaging in what Levin, for one, identifies as "a searching and scrupulous critique of life,"[51] especially life in a complex, often urban, society. The evaluative disabuses its characters, and hence its audience, of any illusions about human perfectability, in order to inculcate tolerance for human fallibility—in Levine's words, to "extend the limits of human sympathy."[52]

Although by no means patently wrong, observations such as these, like many discussions of Realism itself, tend to be couched in terms so vague, relative, or general as to fail to distinguish Realism from other sorts of prose fiction, and they leave too many questions unanswered. The claim that the ethical goal of Realism is to increase sympathy for fellow mortals or to reveal the defects of human nature and society provides no means of discrimination between works of Realism and the vast majority of novels. From *Don Quixote* and *The Princess of Clèves* to *The Trial* and *Ulysses*, novels have portrayed a solitary individual with whom the reader learns to sympathize and who is in some way at odds with organized society; historically, this is the stuff of which the novel is made.

Thus to say that the ethics of Realism serve to repair deficient human sympathies or to encourage the criticism of defective human societies is not to go far enough; one further step is required to disclose Realism's identity. This step is made with the understanding that Realist ethics depend less on what they criticize than on what they prize in human nature and society. They thereby follow in the Aristotelian tradition, which derives its conception of the Good from a conception of human nature. According to this tradition, the Good is what fulfills or completes human nature and thereby facilitates the development of the best possible human being. The Realist conception of human nature perceives human beings as inherently incomplete and eternally struggling to overcome forces, both internal and external, that divide and disintegrate their psyches. (The psychological affinities of Realism to Romanticism here suggest themselves.)[53] Realism thus posits as an ethical ideal the achievement of psychic wholeness, or at least integration, and integrity. This ideal weds psychological unity, which entails the absence of conflict between intellect and emotion, to moral integrity, which ensures the absence of conflict between intention and action.

According to Realist ethics, ideal unity and integrity cannot be achieved independently, through the isolated efforts of the individual. They can be achieved only by the affiliation of one individual with another, that is, through some form of social interaction. But that interaction cannot occur in society as a whole, which is too large and stratified, nor in urban society, which is too impersonal and dehumanizing. The social interaction that enables the individual actively to pursue integration and integrity occurs, according to the ethics of Realism, within the smaller social group known as the community.

As envisaged by Realists, the ideal nineteenth-century community, located in the countryside, is a highly personal, humane realm, where life is filled with emotion, intimacy, and engagement. Most residents of a relatively homogeneous village community, by contrast to the residents of a city, are bound by common history, common traditions, common interests, often even by kinship, for the authentic community valued by Realism has developed organically, growing over time to incorporate new generations of its founding families. Communal members thus tend to share a worldview, a set of assumptions about meanings and values, that enables them to negotiate differences of opinion or interest that arise. Prominent nineteenth-century thinkers such as Comte, de Tocqueville, Taine, Arnold, and Ruskin also hailed the community thus conceptualized, and lamented the thought of its dissolution; the nineteenth-century German sociologist Ferdinand Tönnies, detecting the passing of even the possibility of such communities, made a well-known theoretical distinction between the benign traditional rural community, the *Gemeinschaft*, and the destructive depersonalized urban society, the *Gesellschaft*.[54]

Just such a *Gemeinschaft* is represented in Courbet's *The Burial at Ornans*, which depicts the entire village assembling at the graveside of one of its members, whose identity is undisclosed and unimportant—all mourn for the loss of any.[55] A community like that cannot be constituted arbitrarily, say, by residing in the same boardinghouse, as do the inhabitants of Madame Vauquer's establishment in Balzac's *Father Goriot*, for instance. Nor can it be created artificially by unanticipated circumstances like the storm confining sailors to the ship in Conrad's *Nigger of the Narcissus*. Although groups such as these may temporarily assume some attributes of a Realist community, cooperating to achieve certain goals, the assertion of self-interest by one or more individuals inevitably leads to the disruption of the new and therefore fragile communal cohesion: Balzac's boarders eventually move out, Conrad's surviving sailors move on.

But the legitimate, active pursuit of self-interest cannot truly threaten the community as conceived by Realism, for the supreme interests of the individual and of the community are reciprocal, often virtually inseparable. And they are eminently moral: together, the individual and the community seek to fulfill human nature, in concert they strive to develop the best possible human being. Individuals alone may be deceived about their true interests, or about the best way to gratify those interests, but the Realist community is not; it serves as a moral repository of strength, support, and counsel for all individuals, since it can draw on collective wisdom accumulated through generations of experience, as individuals cannot.

Indeed, the values cultivated by this community are the ideals of the individual as well: wholeness and integrity. The community manifests its espousal of these values by approving and assisting acts evincing such qualities as responsibility, cooperativeness, sympathy, and generosity, all of which bind its members in a moral compact of trust. Just such a compact is advocated in the famous seventeenth chapter of George Eliot's *Adam Bede*, where the narrator digresses to summon the reader to adopt these values with the admonition that "fellow-mortals, every one, must be accepted as they are . . . ; it is these people—amongst whom your life is passed—that it is needful you should tolerate, pity, and love."[56] The expression of these feelings at once ensures the continued coherence and integrity of the community as a whole and draws the individual out of narcissistic self-absorption through exposure to self-enriching emotions and events unattainable in isolation. Thus life in a community brings each member closer to becoming the best possible human being while benefiting all other members as well.

The Realist community therefore serves as both model and matrix for the psychological and moral growth of the self. The greater the psychic investment in and integration into the community, the closer the self comes to completion—and to liberation. Literary critic Stephen Marcus has noted this effect of communal life as envisioned by George Eliot, for example, remarking that participation in a community group "increases one's freedom, since it allows one to express himself more fully, to realize himself; that is to say, it permits further articulation and differentiation" of each member than would be possible to achieve in solitude.[57]

To be sure, this is not to suggest that most narratives rooted in Realist ethics represent communities as heavenly associations based on perfect tolerance, always able to adapt to each individual's needs and to forgive each individual's failings in pursuit of fulfillment. These are not Utopian visions of idyllic co-operatives, joyfully joined together in unconflicted pursuit of universally agreed-on goals. Realists repeatedly reveal a tempered awareness of the limits, drawbacks, and even defects of communal life. Specific members are shown to be flawed and foolish, stubborn and selfish; specific attitudes and actions are observed to be small-minded and superficial, the products of ignorance, poverty, or prejudice. Few characters are more so than the awful Aunt Glegg in *The Mill on the Floss*, for instance, and yet even she offers the errant Maggie Tulliver shelter when others have turned her away. In Realist communities—to quote the title of the chapter in which Aunt Glegg's offer is made—"old acquaintances," no matter how unsympathetic, "are capable of surprising us" with the expression of hitherto latent sympathy for other communal members.

To Realists, the far greater enemy of the individual is always society at large, particularly in its urban incarnation, since it is unrelenting in its impersonal demands for success, and merciless in its inhumane punishment of failure. By contrast, the members of a Realist community can always potentially comprehend and excuse failure, can rescue lost souls cast out by society, bestowing a kind of secular salvation on miscreant individuals that they cannot procure elsewhere.[58]

Thus the exponents of Realism ethically embrace their ideal of the community as the only way to redeem the individual from psychological incompletion and spiritual incarceration. In so doing, the ethical program of Realism implicitly accepts the dictum of the liberal religious thinker Lamennais, "Man by himself is but a fragment of being, true being is collective being."[59]

In order to convey the ethical ends of Realism—the achievement by every individual of "true being" in psychological wholeness and moral integrity—and the ethical means to attain this end—social integration into a congenial community—Realist narratives employ what might be termed "realistic" poetics. "Realistic," defined in general earlier as that infinite variety of qualities or experiences signaling what people take to be reality, in this connection means that which cultivates verisimilitude, or "the illusion of the real," as Maupassant put it. This illusion is often obtained by relying on a specific set of poetic devices: ordinary language, contemporary settings, extensive references to actual historical events and quotidian details, typical, often middle-class, characters, and a consistent point of view (though not necessarily that of an impersonal narrator; see Chapter 5).

Realist narratives convert "realistic" poetics into "Realist" poetics when they deploy these poetics to promote the ethical ends and means of Realism.[60] That is, they manipulate elements of "realistic" poetics so as to convince the reader that engagement in communal life is good. Inspired by the ideal of "true being" as communal being, these narratives embody their authors' desire to persuade their readers to become integrated into a community. They do so by portraying a picture of communal life that is not merely familiar, historically accurate, typical, and plausible, but one that is actively inviting. Realist poetics do not alienate the reader from social experience, as realistic poetics can readily do by depicting hideous or horrifying objects, events, and individuals appearing in social contexts; rather, Realist poetics invite the reader to partake of communal life, to encounter fundamentally familiar objects and events in a world peopled by fundamentally similar individuals. These poetics do insist on an elemental plausibility so that the reader can first accept the possibility of participation in a community and then be convinced to welcome it. They thereby draw the reader through the text, as it were, toward engagement with actuality as the reader has reconceived it. Thus the ethics and poetics of Realism couple to convince the reader not so much that Realist literature mirrors life, as is often supposed, but rather to convince the reader that life mirrors Realist literature.

This clarification and refinement of the ethics and poetics of Realism should not be understood as setting forth absolute prescriptive criteria for assigning narratives to a rigid Realist canon. Rather, these are standards and practices that should be viewed as normative concepts or ideal types that few narratives embody in all respects. For instance, some literary works endorse Realist ethics without relying primarily on Realist poetics, just as others engage a highly realistic poetics without Realist ethical intentions. The ethics and poetics of Realism as defined here thus serve as parameters or as spectra on which narratives can usefully be placed to determine their relation to "pure" Realism, to one another, and to other literary movements.

For example, Flaubert, whom most readers would likely classify as a Realist, ranks high on the scale of realistic poetics but quite low on that of Realist ethics. His novels *Madame Bovary* and *Sentimental Education*, although informed by poetics that meet the criteria of verisimilitude—familiarity, typicality, historicity, plausibility—do not endorse the ethical ends of Realism, for they in no way paint an attractive portrait of communal existence. Indeed, the community Emma Bovary inhabits, as personified by its success story, Homais, is appalling in its moral vacuity. This is not to say that Flaubert had no ethical vision of his own, as the prosecutors of *Madame Bovary* alleged,[61] but that that vision adopts art, rather than the community, as the ideal, the source of moral sensibility and the arbiter of moral worth. Hence Flaubert is far from a full-fledged or pure Realist, and the same is true of such other oft-named Realists as Theodore Fontane and Benito Pérez Galdós, who similarly extol the ability of art, rather than community, to establish and affirm moral values.

Most historical novels, frequently affiliated if not wholly identified with Realism, also employ realistic poetics without Realist ethics. Walter Scott's *Heart of Midlothian*, for example, elaborately reproduces the particularities of the Scottish judicial and penal system, as well as highland farm life and folkways, yet the ethical principles guiding this overtly didactic novel elevate individual conscience and will above communal judgments of right and wrong. Although relatively benign, the community members herein follow rather than direct the moral course that Scott delineates in this narrative. A similar pattern affirming individual moral inclinations over social mores is found in the historical novels of Victor Hugo, Alessandro Manzoni, and Elizabeth Gaskell, all of which nonetheless recreate the language, activities, and artifacts of their historical time. Thus these authors should not be considered proponents of pure Realism, even though they largely partake of the same poetics.

Still other authors who employ these poetics while subscribing to a non-Realist ethical code are those identified with Naturalism. The Goncourt brothers and Emile Zola in France, Thomas Hardy and George Moore in England, and Theodore Dreiser in the United States, to name the most prominent, stake a claim to utter impartiality, objectivity, and impersonality in their detailed depictions of social life. Accepting Hippolyte Taine's famed assertion that "vice and virtue are products, like vitriol and sugar," they seek to illustrate dispassionately what they take to be the biological and economic forces determining moral decisions and individual destinies. In so doing, they betray an underlying ethical conviction different from that of Realism, because although they often represent communities, they do not invest them with the moral authority and redemptive power over the individual that the Realists assign to communal groups. On the contrary, they treat both individuals and communities as essentially powerless against the strength of invariant laws of nature; only scientific study of these laws can impart some measure of control over human existence. The ethical aim of the Naturalists is therefore to expose the workings of the basic principles governing all of life. Literature thus becomes a laboratory for moral experiments in human character conducted with the aid of realistic poetics, but without the inspiration of Realist ethics.

At the opposite pole from authors who endorse realistic poetics but not Realist ethics are those whose works manifest the Realists' faith in community without wholly relying on the verisimilitudinous language, characterizations, historical references, and quotidian details that typify Realist poetics. The novels of Charles Dickens, for instance, ascribe ethical supremacy to the community, but do so with outsized or unusual characters participating in outlandish, implausible plots. In *Great Expectations*, Joe, a village blacksmith and brother-in-law of the main protagonist, Pip, personifies almost comically in his simplicity and sincerity the merits of the rural communal life: warmth, kindness, generosity, and forgiveness. Yet Pip's subsequent true remorse at his indifference to Joe upon receiving money from an anonymous benefactor and moving alone to London, as well as his painful realization that he has undervalued the humble but humane life Joe leads, underscores the moral dignity Dickens attributes to the values acquired only in the rural community.

Dickens further dramatizes the contrast between the humanity bred in the countryside and the inhumanity cultivated in the city in the characterization of the legal clerk Wemmick. Employed by the attorney who administers Pip's financial affairs, Wemmick comports himself and treats Pip in radically different ways in the commercial, public setting of the urban law offices and in the domestic, private setting of his suburban home. At work Wemmick behaves dispassionately and impersonally, acknowledging Pip's existence only by coldly advising him to invest in "portable property" so as to avoid inconvenient emotional entanglements. At home, though, Wemmick conducts himself as a devoted son to his infirm father (whom he affectionately refers to as "the Aged Parent," or "Aged P.," for short), and as a loyal friend to Pip in time of need. The same kind of contrast drives the plot of "A Christmas Carol," where Ebenezer Scrooge's heatless and heartless office has its antithesis in the warm hearth and home of Bob Cratchet. For Dickens, the intimate familial domicile, community-like in the readiness of its emotional embrace—in Tönnies's terminology, the *Gemeinschaft*—is the matrix of spiritual attachment and enrichment, whereas the public, professional business world, utterly depersonalized in the expanse of its emotional aridity—the *Gesellschaft*—is the matrix of spiritual deformation and death. As exaggerated as the poetics used to describe that death may be, the ethics motivating that description can rightly be deemed Realist.

Another group of narratives marked by the ethics of Realism but not much by its poetics is the one ordinarily classed under the heading "socialist realism." Indeed, "communist realism"— with a deliberately small "c"—would be more accurate, because socialist realism overtly attempts to foster the ideal of a relatively homogeneous, cooperative community as the model of social life. Despite the inevitable occasional conflicts among individuals, communes comprised of peasants or workers are extolled as the best possible source of material and moral sustenance for all their members. To promote this communal ideal, though, the poetics of socialist realism often deviate from those of pure Realism: they depict stereotypical characters instead of typical ones, they present artificial and unbelievable plots instead of historically or logically plausible ones, and they manufacture numerous details for the ideological mill instead of drawing them from ordinary experience. Thus it is fair to conclude, although some commentators have questioned the wisdom of doing so, that socialist realism should definitely be linked to Realism proper—but it should be linked through an ethical connection, not an aesthetic one.

If at one end of Realism's spectrum are narratives that employ realistic poetics without espousing Realist ethics, and at the other end are those that endorse Realist ethics without engaging realistic poetics, in between are those that to varying degrees embrace both Realist ethics and Realist poetics. The novels of Stendhal and Dostoevsky, for instance, adopt both, albeit to a limited extent. Each author engages in the Realist ethical advocacy of community more indirectly than directly, concentrating his focus more on the ethical failures of protagonists who pursue illusions of autonomous fulfillment regardless of any social constraints or consequences. Thus does Stendhal explore the moral complexity and culpability of Julien Sorel in *The Red and the Black*, Fabrizio del Dongo in *The Charterhouse of Parma*, and the eponymous Lucien Leuwen in their pursuit of self-aggrandizing fame and fortune, particularly in urban environments. Stendhal also disparages the hypocrisy and vacuity of the moral standards accepted in the pseudocommunities inhabited by the bourgeoisie purely to advance selfish rather than shared interests, implicitly contrasting these ethical deficiencies with the decency of characters such as Madame de Renal, the journalist Gauthier, and Clelia Conti, nurtured in familial or communal groups that define satisfactions as reciprocal and achievements as acts beneficial to others as well as to oneself.

In sketching these differing social and moral milieus, Stendhal favors subtle poetics of contrast and contradiction. (André Gide once commented that the point of view in each line of Stendhal's fiction is perpendicular to that of the preceding line.) These poetics transmit both the image and the ideal of communal integration less coherently and thus less convincingly than do the more constant narrative styles of other Realist authors; Stendhal's famous metaphor of the novel as a mirror reflecting the mud and the stars tellingly omits mention of the ordinary matter that exists in between the filth and the firmament. Nonetheless, his meticulous depiction of the conflicts and dilemmas that beset his protagonists when they abandon communal values legitimately brings Stendhal into the ranks of Realists.

The narratives of Dostoevsky also exhibit a complex relationship to Realism, since Dostoevsky's ethics at once esteem communal participation, particularly if grounded in common religious or spiritual convictions, and anticipate individual transcendence of any communal relationship in a final communion with a divine spirit.

Hence protagonists who in one way or another prize familial and communal affiliations, including Son'ia Marmeladova in *Crime and Punishment*, Prince Myshkin in *The Idiot*, and Alesha Karamazov in *The Brothers Karamazov*, provide a moral center around which the other characters are ranged. By contrast, characters who defiantly despise social integration and traditional moral values, such as Rodion Raskolnikov, Nastas'ia Filippovna Barashkova, and Ivan Karamazov, are psychologically devastated, their lives destroyed through their defiance. Yet the communal connections forged and sustained in these novels are treated more as means to instinctively engendered, individually achieved spiritual regeneration than as ends in themselves. Moreover, Dostoevsky's poetics, which intensely and unflinchingly detail extremes of goodness and evil, both attract and repel the reader, for they make communal engagement appear at once desirable and dangerous. Thus Dostoevsky's novels manifest distinct affinities to both the poetics and ethics of Realism while representing distinctive departures from both as well.

In comparison to the novels of Stendhal and Dostoevsky, the novels of Jane Austen and Anthony Trollope come closer to the center of the spectrum setting forth the ranges of Realist ethics and poetics. Austen and Trollope both represent protagonists who, no matter how well-intentioned, go astray when they set up private moral standards as superior to traditional communal values. Elizabeth Bennet and Charles Darcy in *Pride and Prejudice*, Mary and Henry Crawford in *Mansfield Park*, and Emma Woodhouse in *Emma*, as well as Septimus Harding in *The Warden* and Alice Vavasour in *Can You Forgive Her?*, all base pivotal decisions on the conviction of their superior moral understanding and rectitude. Subsequently they all discover the errors and inadequacies of their limited individual perceptions and interpretations of events, coming to regret their failure to accept the wise insights of a moral vision achieved and approved collectively. Although more irony and satire inhere in these works than in those of other authors who use Realist poetics to promote Realist ethics, on the whole Austen and Trollope belong not far from the midpoint of Realism's reaches, for both display to readers the psychic and moral benefits of some mode of communal existence.

Perhaps not as thoroughly persuaded of the virtues of the *Gemeinschaft* as Austen and Trollope, Honoré de Balzac nonetheless also extols the virtues he finds there over the vices he believes promoted in the *Gesellschaft*. Employing poetics to that end, Balzac thus also merits placement close to the center of Realism. Especially in the segments of *The Human Comedy* comprising *Scenes from Private Life*, *Scenes from Provincial Life*, and *Scenes from Country Life*, Balzac exhaustively explores the moral frameworks that communities erect for their members. Notwithstanding the pettiness and cupidity he finds in many inhabitants of these rural locales, Balzac also finds a redeeming sincerity and generosity of spirit, qualities he does not discern among most city dwellers. It is Eugene's provincial sisters who sacrifice their savings to aid their debt-ridden brother in *Father Goriot*; it is the daughter Marguerite, brought up to value family obligation above personal gratification, who salvages the Claes family business and reputation in *The Search for the Absolute*; it is David and Eve who find marital happiness by adapting to the limited life of the small village in *Lost Illusions*. Thus Balzac attributes a redemptive resourcefulness to those characters who evince the decency and humanity that only communal cohabitation can impart.

Tolstoy's most famous novels come closer still to the ethical and poetic core of Realism. In both *War and Peace* and *Anna Karenina*, communal existence is shown to offer the only hope for psychological satisfaction and spiritual fulfillment. Pierre Bezukhov and Konstantin Levin find the emotional equanimity they have sought for so long only when they stop striving to find meaning for their lives in philosophical and existential experiments undertaken on their own and settle into married lives with extended familial and communal ties encircling them. And Tolstoy employs poetics, as cogently analyzed by Gary Saul Morson in *Hidden in Plain View: Narrative and Creative Potentials in 'War and Peace'*, that violate readers' traditional literary expectations by emphasizing the unplanned and the ordinary (or "the actual and trivial," as Lionel Trilling observes),[62] thus effectively giving readers a sense of participation in authentic, common human experience that more conventional narratives cannot impart. The very effectiveness of Tolstoy's deployment of Realist ethics and poetics to draw readers into that experience in his great novels is only underscored by the palpable abandonment of both in his last novel, *Resurrection*. Coupling stereotypical characterizations and dogmatic narrative digressions with religious ideology, Tolstoy offers little incentive therein for communal engagement, and loses much of his power to attract readers to such engagement as a result.

Compared to the narratives mentioned thus far, those of George Eliot perhaps come closest to fully uniting Realist ethics and poetics. Taking as a fundamental precept the conviction voiced in *Adam Bede* that "men's lives are as thoroughly blended with each other as the air they breathe,"[63] Eliot installs an indispensable, vital relationship between individuals and their communities at the moral heart of her narratives. She repeatedly illustrates the need to appreciate and increase communal cooperation and trust alongside the dangers of allowing communal bonds to atrophy. Eliot places her characters in rural communities such as the Milby parish in *Scenes from Clerical Life*, Hayslope in *Adam Bede*, St. Oggs in *The Mill on the Floss*, and Middlemarch, in order to make manifest the high costs of social isolation, particularly when that isolation is prompted by a belief that individual satisfaction can more readily be obtained alone than through communal participation. Amos Barton, Maggie Tulliver, Romola, Silas Marner, Daniel Deronda, and Nicolas Bulstrode suffer deeply—and in some instances die—for their certainty that they are right to pursue their own desires independently, divorcing themselves from the communities in which they have spent their lives, only to discover their tragic self-deception.

Eliot effectively conveys the centrality of community to individual well-being by means of poetics that prize concreteness and particularity. She painstakingly delineates the smallest detail of daily life—the type of ribbon on a bonnet, the style of carving on a sofa leg—to reflect her conception of the interrelatedness of individual parts to wholes, be they whole objects or whole communities. Eliot's narrators maintain a consistent stance of sympathetic comprehension toward both the parts and the wholes they address, whether through expository narration or digressions aimed directly at the reader to encourage a sense of shared values. And Eliot's characterizations at once reveal distinct differences and a shared connection to some community with which each character must reach an acceptable accommodation or from which each must escape, though escape inevitably brings misfortune. Thus her poetics achieve the Realist ethical goal of inviting readers to appreciate social involvement and to develop communal attachments of their own. Eliot's works are therefore as close to pure Realism as any yet.

It should be noted that other students of Realism have certainly remarked the prominence of the idea, if not the ideal, of community in Realist novels. They tend to argue—although their precise terminology differs—that such narratives portray tyrannical communities ruthlessly imposing moral order to counter the potential for social disorder posed by naturally impassioned and independent individuals indifferent to collective well-being.[64] Thus this interpretation holds that communities seek to repress or oppress human nature rather than enhance it, as they stifle self-expression and self-gratification with demands for self-sacrifice. But this is largely a late twentieth-century, heavily Freudian-influenced interpretation. For the community was seen by many influential thinkers of the nineteenth century as a source of identity and refuge in an increasingly urbanized, mechanized, and depersonalized world. They became virtually haunted by the specter of individualism, the philosophical endorsement of the solitary soul in unrestricted quest of self-centered success. Hence the nineteenth-century authors who adopted Realist ethics and poetics did so not out of fear *of* the individual, but out of fear *for* the individual. Their efforts were meant not to thwart but to aid the reader in attaining complete self-fulfillment the best way they thought possible—through adherence to an authentic, vital, humane community.

This rethinking of Realism not only facilitates a reconsideration of Turgenev's relationship to Realism but necessitates it, for nowhere in Turgenev's narratives is there represented any coherent community whatsoever. No group of mature individuals with shared interests and values, bonded together by ancestry, tradition, or common goals, ever occupies center stage. This is particularly striking considering Turgenev's reputation as the "chronicler of his age"—if true, his "age," in Russia at least, had no organic communities. It had at best, according to Turgenev's representation, communities manqué, either artificial or anomalous. With the exception of the Kirsanov extended-family gathering at the very conclusion of *Fathers and Sons*, the few collections of people presented are either accidentally assembled, as are the Russian expatriates and tourists temporarily gathered at Baden-Baden in *Smoke*, or they are banded together only by the lack of alternative social options, as is the "society" collected around Marfa Timofeevna in *A Nest of Gentry*, which includes animals and outcasts.

Even as primary a communal unit as the nuclear family almost never appears: where there are married adults, more often than not there are no children; where there are children, at least one parent is absent, usually deceased. In *Rudin* and in *A Nest of Gentry*, the husband/father is dead; in *Fathers and Sons*, the Kirsanov wife/mother is dead too, as well as the parents of Anna Odintsova and her sister Katia, and the Bazarovs' only son has left his parents' home, returning in effect just to die. The shorter works admit the same pattern of incomplete familial structures: Vera's father in "Faust" is deceased; the title character in "Asya" travels with her half brother, since her parents are also deceased; Susanna in "The Unhappy One" has lost both her parents as well, and is forced to lead a miserable existence with her stepfather and stepbrother. In the rare instances where both parents are actually living with their natural children, irremediable differences between family members show that the unit exists in name only, without substantive ties. The Stakhov family in *On the Eve* exemplifies precisely this sort of nominal connection, since the parents, particularly the father, have little comprehension of or sympathy for their daughter's passionate nature.

Even more striking, though, is the absence of communal or familial closeness in the narratives treating the peasantry. Surely images of collective activity, of convivial intimacy, of familial comfort should appear somewhere among all the stories depicting peasants who inhabit isolated villages and estates— but such images do not appear. An occasional pairing of father and son, husband and wife, or friendly acquaintances can be observed, but instances of genuine group endeavor or exercise of judgment, although occasionally referred to, never dominate a Turgenevan tale. As Eva Kagan-Kans has acutely noted, the peasants Turgenev introduces to his reader tend to live on the fringe of their village or else dwell in solitude, physically and spiritually alienated from any community.[65]

This simple but significant absence of any representation— much less affirmation—of community inevitably brings into question the traditional close association of Turgenev with Realism. One conclusion is obvious: Turgenev's ethics differ fundamentally from those of pure Realism. Whether or not one agrees that he endorses some specific moral authority in his narratives, it must at least be conceded that the communal associations extolled by Realist ethics do not assume such authority; they hardly appear to exist at all. This study argues that Turgenev does indeed conceive of a moral authority other than the community, and Chapter 2 traces the nature of that authority. Subsequent chapters demonstrate that as a result of his subscription to an ethical vision divergent from that of Realism, Turgenev employs poetics that also repeatedly diverge from those of Realism, for he regularly engages in manipulations of language, narrative perspective, and characterization that do not encourage the reader's active commitment to social engagement. Rather, he frequently invokes poetics that discourage such engagement and instead promote the maintenance of a protective psychological distance from intimacy of any kind. Thus another conclusion becomes inescapable: Turgenev must not be categorized as in essence a representative Realist.

This study is not the first to reach the conclusion that Turgenev is not judged aright when he is judged a Realist. A number of critics have explored Turgenev's narratives with an eye to establishing his affinities to cultural and literary movements other than traditional Realism. For instance, some commentators, such as Mikhail Gershenzon and Dale Peterson, argue that if Turgenev is a Realist at all, he is a kind of psychological Realist, who records his subjective impressions of reality rather than registering objective reports.[66] Other scholars, including Galina Kurliandskaia, Marina Ledkovsky, and Andrzej Walicki, maintain that Turgenev's distinguishing aesthetic and philosophical ties are to Romanticism.[67] A third set of critics, led by Edward Garnett, André Maurois, and Leonid Grossman, finds Turgenev's narratives committed neither to the social concerns of Realism nor to the intense emotional explorations of Romanticism but to the tranquil harmonic meditations of Classicism.[68] Then there are scholars, such as Walter Koschmal and Peter Brang, who find in Turgenev manifestations of every modern aesthetic movement—Neo-classicism, Romanticism, Realism, and even Symbolism.[69]

Each of these schools of critical thought draws support for its conclusions from various passages in Turgenev's correspondence and various comments made by Turgenev to acquaintances, for his protestations of Realist objectives were only a portion of the self-analyses he proffered his contemporaries. Yet all these discussions of Turgenev as something other than a pure Realist, however reasonably argued and well documented, are forced somehow to fragment Turgenev's literary achievement by focusing on only a portion of his narratives, or on a few facets of a portion of them. The title of Marina Ledkovsky's study, *The Other Turgenev*, is therefore emblematic of these discussions. To claim that Turgenev's aesthetics are not primarily those of a Realist—or at least are not primarily realistic—has been for the most part to treat them in piecemeal fashion, ignoring some works in order to stress others, and implicitly denying any over-all consistency, any constant distinctiveness and distinction to those works as a whole. At the very most, these discussions encourage agreement with Victor Terras's ultimate conclusion on the subject: Turgenev's aesthetic program is fundamentally eclectic.[70]

And it must be conceded that Terras's conclusion is correct—but only if applied to Turgenev's extraliterary statements about his art, as well as those about political, social, and cultural issues of his day. For Turgenev's letters and comments to acquaintances reveal that his opinions and self-evaluations shifted in accordance with the Zeitgeist. The eminently plausible story of Turgenev agreeing with one side of a good argument until he heard the opposing side and then completely reversing his position suggests a geniality of temperament and a flexibility of mind that could account just as well for the alterations, inconsistencies, and even contradictions to be found in his nonfictional prose.

But the Turgenev who sat down at a writing desk to compose prose fiction was a different Turgenev. He was, as it were, the "true" Turgenev: a self-assured literary master with a consistently recognizable style bespeaking adherence to a unified, remarkably stable aesthetic program. The narratives he produced are not marked by eclecticism—which is really to say by no aesthetic program at all—but by uniquely Turgenevan ethics and poetics that distinguish and bind those narratives together. If there is an "other" Turgenev, it is the one who quite self-consciously wrote about his literary ideas and processes in varying and at times even antithetical terms.

Thus the tradition of Turgenev scholarship on the whole, in endeavoring to confirm his connection to one "-ism" or another, has relied perhaps too much on ultimately unreliable evidence—the "other" Turgenev's self-reports. Not that this "other" Turgenev had no insights into the creative process; if anything, he may have had too many, influenced by too many "good" arguments. Nor are scholars wrong to perceive in Turgenev's narratives signs of the influence of dominant cultural movements; Turgenev certainly did not create in a vacuum. But their perceptions, however admiringly couched, add up to a portrait of Turgenev's works as aesthetically derivative, more conventional than creative. It must be concluded, therefore, that such scholars have not wholly successfully isolated the Turgenevan ethics and poetics that at once assimilate components of those cultural movements and add to them the unique attributes that characterize and distinguish Turgenev's prose fiction.

This conclusion leads to another, that to accomplish the successful isolation of those ethics and poetics one must abandon concepts of periodization. But to date, only a few scholars have discussed Turgenev's art without reference to such concepts. S. E. Shatalov, Nina Kauchtschischwili, and Robert Louis Jackson have made the most notable attempts to observe and to explain the constants in Turgenev's art without reference to such concepts, the constants that render this art distinctive, and distinctively Turgenev's.[71]

In fact, to liberate Turgenev's art from the confines of period classification—and most especially from the parameters of Realism—is to follow the most productive intellectual path in formulating a truly comprehensive interpretation of that art. This interpretation is one that will elevate Turgenev's art above all systems—just as Turgenev himself once recommended.

2

The Creation of Noncommunal Ethics

To formulate a comprehensive interpretation of Turgenev without reliance on concepts of periodization, it is useful, oddly enough, to turn to a critic who largely discounts his artistry: Mikhail Bakhtin. In his wide-ranging critical writings, Bakhtin refers to Turgenev rarely, usually just in passing, and never with compliments.[1] In *Problems of Dostoevsky's Poetics*, for instance, Bakhtin offers several unflattering comparisons of Turgenev's narratives to Dostoevsky's. Lauding Dostoevsky for perfecting the "polyphonic" novel and "dialogic" mode of discourse, which provide multiple narrative points of view and constitute "a huge step forward not only in the development of novelistic prose . . . but also in the development of the *artistic thinking* of humankind,"[2] Bakhtin generally dismisses Turgenev's literary talent.

He contends that Turgenev (along with Tolstoy, Goncharov, and other Russian authors whose art Bakhtin treats as more straightforward and simply crafted than Dostoevsky's) created characters "of the usual type,"[3] wrote dialogues that "unfold in old, uniplanar forms,"[4] and relied almost exclusively on a "monological" mode of discourse, that is, on the "simple compositional device" through which a narrator gives voice to a single point of view. Frequently, Bakhtin finds, Turgenev's narrators therefore merely speak just as "Turgenev himself would have spoken."[5] The dialogic mode was beyond Turgenev's interests or powers: "To refract his own thoughts in another's discourse was something Turgenev did not like to do, and did not know how to do."[6] Even when Bakhtin discerns something admirable in Turgenev's narratives, such as a "prose lyric of spiritual and emotional quest"—of the kind he finds so compelling in *Notes from Underground*, for example—he undercuts the praise by noting that Turgenev's "quest" yields a "peculiar sort of lyric, analogous to the lyrical expression of a toothache."[7]

For one so sensitive to the subtlest shifts of tone in Dostoevsky's narratives, Bakhtin is surprisingly deaf to much in Turgenev's works but a dull and enduring moan—or at least is strikingly uninterested. To be sure, Bakhtin is so taken by Dostoevsky's extravagance and manifest complexity that it is no wonder he finds Turgenev's comparative restraint and formality both superficial and simplistic. Still, Bakhtin does not so much err in these critical observations themselves as in the conclusions he draws from them. His perception that Dostoevsky and Turgenev are very different kinds of artists, indeed that Turgenev's art is almost the polar opposite of Dostoevsky's, has merit (although he pushes both conclusions too far.)[8] But when he denies to Turgenev's art most of the aesthetic subtlety and psychological penetration that he so admiringly ascribes to Dostoevsky's, he misjudges.

This misjudgment notwithstanding, the value of Bakhtin's perception resides in its logical extensions: if Dostoevsky's art can be said to be based on a poetics of conflict, excess, and extremity, Turgenev's art can indeed be said to be based on a poetics of reconciliation, limitation, and moderation. If Dostoevsky's linguistic and narrative structures are marked by dissonance, disjunction, and imbalance, Turgenev's are marked by consonance, conjunction, and balance. If Dostoevsky endeavors to expose the tormenting dilemmas inherent in human experience, Turgenev endeavors to conceal, if not the dilemmas themselves, then at least their torments.

By highlighting these facets of Turgenev's art, even if unintentionally, Bakhtin's reading of Turgenev thus at the very least paves the way for an understanding of Turgenev's art based on aesthetic, psychological, and philosophical grounds unconfined by any restricting historical label, especially that of Realism. By suggesting that Turgenev's aesthetics are diametrically opposed to Dostoevsky's, Bakhtin sets in relief definitive attributes of Turgenev's artistry independent of affinities to particular cultural movements (without denying that such affinities do certainly exist).

To be sure, these attributes—orderliness, limitation, moderation, and the like—have not gone unnoticed.[9] But their definitive role in both Turgenev's ethics and poetics has yet to be fully understood. Still another step toward that understanding can be taken, though, by pursuing the insights of one of Bakhtin's philosophical forebears, Friedrich Nietzsche.

At the beginning of his pioneering meditation on art, culture, and psychology, *The Birth of Tragedy*, Nietzsche draws a now-famous distinction between two types of art and artistic inspiration. The one he identifies with the refined form and psychic economy of dreams: "In our dreams," he says, "we enjoy an immediate apprehension of form, all shapes speak to us directly, nothing seems indifferent or redundant."[10] In a bit of fanciful mythologizing, Nietzsche links dreams with Apollo, who "reigns over the fair illusion of our inner world of fantasy,"[11] and labels the art of that "fair illusion" Apollonian. The other type of art and inspiration he identifies with the formless ecstasies and instinctual extravagances of drunkenness: in this state, man runs "the whole outrageous gamut of nature . . . and strides with the same elation and ecstasy as the gods."[12] Linking this art of ecstasy with Dionysus, the Greek god of wine, revelry, and instinctual release, Nietzsche labels this art Dionysian.

The parallels between Nietzsche's concept of the Dionysian and Bakhtin's conception of Dostoevsky's art are unmistakable. Nietzsche's claims that Dionysian art brings the "suspension of all the ordinary barriers of existence"[13] are echoed in Bakhtin's contention that Dostoevsky's "carnivalistic" art rejects "the laws, prohibitions, and restrictions that determine the structure and order of ordinary, that is, noncarnival life."[14] Nietzsche's discovery in Dionysian art of "the original Oneness,"[15] wherein "indiscreet extravagance revealed itself as truth, and contradiction, a delight born of pain, spoken out of the bosom of nature,"[16] resonates in Bakhtin's assertion that Dostoevskian literature has "its essence, its deep roots in the primordial order and the primordial thinking of man."[17]

But unlike Bakhtin's inclination to dismiss the opposite of Dostoevsky's art—that is to say, Turgenev's—Nietzsche does not write off the opposite of the Dionysian tendency. Rather, Nietzsche notes approvingly that the Apollonian artist, whether sculptor (whose god Apollo was), painter, musician, or writer, will always keep in mind "a discreet limitation, a freedom from all extravagant urges, the sapient tranquillity of the sculptor-god."[18] And by so doing, this artist will produce works that present "illusions of fair semblance"[19] whose visual forms can be apprehended and enjoyed immediately, like sculpture or the economical images of a dream that conceal more than they reveal of any disorderly forces beneath them. At their best, Nietzsche concludes, these Apollonian illusions exert salvific power, as they "overcome individual suffering by the glorious apotheosis of what is eternal in appearance: here beauty vanquishes the suffering that inheres in all existence, and pain is, in a certain sense, glossed away from nature's countenance."[20]

Nietzsche detects the origins of tragedy, which he takes to be the highest form of art, in the fusion of the Dionysian and the Apollonian tendencies of art. But he devotes a greater portion of this early study to the Dionysian because on balance he conceives of it as the more substantive of the two tendencies. Nietzsche consistently equates the Apollonian, however pleasurable, with illusory dreams and external appearances rather than with moral, psychological, and metaphysical realities. For he finds the Dionysian tendency rooted in what he believes to be the elemental chaos and tragedy of human life—and indeed, his conception of the Dionysian has alerted many observers to forceful impulses toward irrationality in art, culture, and the human psyche. He evidently deems the Apollonian tendency less significant because its function is really to deceive individuals "as to the universality of the Dionysian event"[21] by providing "a thin veil hiding . . . the whole Dionysian realm"[22] from those who demand a semblance of rationality and order superimposed on irrationality and disorder.

Nietzsche therefore implies that manifestations of the Apollonian are artificial, even deceptive, created mainly to serve individuals too squeamish or cowardly to confront directly the basic turmoil immanent in all human experience, an implication latent in Bakhtin's assumption of Turgenev's monological simplicity and controlling authorial interventionism. Thus Nietzsche anticipates Bakhtin's lesser appreciation of Turgenev—as well as Bakhtin's exaltation of Dostoevsky—by denying to the Apollonian tendency the elevating force of truth that he ascribes to the Dionysian.

Yet Nietzsche, like Bakhtin, underestimates the aesthetic and ethical possibilities of the art of control and appearance. Departing from Nietzsche's provocatively vague and insufficiently explored notion, one can conceive of a type of art, not merely a tendency, worthy of being called Apollonian, one that accomplishes more than superficial, cosmetic concealment of hideous truths. This type of art does not simply veil elemental, chaotic experience from view; it mandates the aesthetic transformation of that experience into harmonious, tranquil, and orderly images. And this transformation alters not only form but substance, so that a different kind of experience—a new experience—is consciously created by the artist. Apollonian art, therefore, does *not* assert that the harmony, tranquillity, and order it presents are objectively true to life. It embodies an original conception of life, a subjective conception envisioned by the artist irrespective of whatever reality (whether hidden or overt) may inhere in the world beyond art, for this harmonious, tranquil conception of reality is generated by the artist's imagination and hence is admittedly a fabrication, even a deliberate untruth. Nonetheless, by virtue of its ordered coherence and comprehensibility, this conception can provide meaning to life, whereas disordered, incoherent, incomprehensible reality cannot.

Nietzsche himself says something about this creative capacity of art in the aphorisms compiled as *The Will to Power*. There he asserts, for example, that "we possess art lest we perish of the truth."[23] He does not explicitly associate this redemptive power of art with the Apollonian tendency, though; he attributes this power to art in general, asserting that, amidst the hideous chaos of reality, "we have need of lies in order to conquer this reality, this 'truth,' that is, in order to live—That lies are necessary in order to live is itself part of the terrifying and questionable character of existence. . . . To solve it, man must be a liar by nature, he must be above all an artist."[24]

This evocation of organized untruths as a valid mode of combating anarchic truths in the modern struggle to survive recalls Ibsen's notion in *The Wild Duck* of the "life lie"—the falsehoods that give individuals reason to live. Although Nietzsche here accords to all art the capacity in effect to construct a life lie, his conception of art in *The Will To Power* best fits Apollonian art, since it is Apollonian art that "lies" in denying the Dionysian "truth," constructing a carefully controlled, equable, and endurable version of existence to supplant uncontrolled, inequable, unendurable reality. Apollonian art thus serves not only aesthetic but ethical ends, in that it deliberately aims to influence its audience, altering modes of both perceiving and living. It seeks to demonstrate ways in which the human will can impose order on events and thereby instill coherence and significance in otherwise incoherent and insignificant lives. Indeed, Apollonian art offers a reason to live by embodying the possibility of remodeling and thereby rescuing lives perched on the brink of chaos.

Apollonian art must not, therefore, be equated with aestheticism, the self-indulgent cultivation of refined beauty without regard for any moral effect on the beholder as long as there is a yield of pleasure. Apollonian art constitutes an explicitly morally inspired model of perception and interpretation; it proclaims the ethical superiority of human choices that grant control over life. Nor can it be equated with Classicism, despite their common emphasis on the aesthetic values of harmony, balance, and order, for Classicism entails a belief in the inherent, mathematically describable order of things, a faith in the ultimate reality and purity of form. Apollonian art, by contrast, posits no such fundamental orderliness; instead it openly affirms the precedence of artificially, artfully ordered ideation in encountering and representing experience, irrespective of whatever the objective reality of that experience may be.

The aesthetic affinities between Turgenev's art and the Apollonian are obvious to any reader cognizant of the manifest measure, balance, and harmony of Turgenev's works. Indeed, as noted above, most Turgenev critics regard these affinities, albeit not so labeled, as the dominant properties of Turgenev's aesthetics. But the underlying cause of these affinities, and the extent of their import, are not so manifest, and have not been widely recognized. Jackson, for one, succinctly remarks the Apollonian qualities in Turgenev's prose, finding "classical beauty, harmony, measure"[25] at its core. He maintains that Turgenev's aesthetic principles "are those of the fine artist, the painter or sculptor for whom the painterly or plastic values, 'clarity of lines,' are of supreme importance,"[26] and he further argues that these qualities derive from Turgenev's belief in "the existence of a determining subsurface reality"[27] consisting of "a real order and beatitude in nature."[28]

But Turgenev was more Apollonian even than this. He did not necessarily so much "follow nature"[29] in his aesthetics of harmony and order as impose those aesthetics, for Turgenev demanded ordered surfaces irrespective of what lay beneath. He once said in a metaphor comparing nature and art: "Remember that however subtle and complex the inner structure of some tissue in the human body, the skin, for example, nonetheless its appearance is comprehensible and homogeneous."[30] To Turgenev, the skin on the surface will always be smooth, "comprehensible and homogeneous," not because the underlying substance necessarily is inherently so, but because he must have it so. In his art, if needs be, Turgenev will even homogenize nature itself, insistently imparting a balanced order to both the natural and the human portraits he paints. And if this kind of surface order that the skin ensures must be invented and imposed, so as to conceal the tangle of tissue beneath, so be it. To fully comprehend Turgenev's art is therefore to comprehend it first as Apollonian, that is, as art that insists on the installation of con-

straints in the representation of all human experience, regardless of any inherent, elemental unconstraint. It is time to realize
how thoroughly, for Turgenev, faithfulness to reality was subordinate to faith in creativity. Like Nietzsche, Turgenev knew
that human beings might all too easily "perish of the truth," and
that acts of imaginative creation might well afford the sole
source of salvation.

To view Turgenev's art as Apollonian is to reconceive the features, meanings, and implications of that art, the most important of which have to do with the play of Turgenev's moral imagination. As it turns out, the significance of that play can most
easily be revealed by examining an unremarked yet recurrent
phenomenon portrayed throughout his works: Turgenev's characters love narratives. They are ever eager to hear stories. They
revel in recitations. With the exception of one arguably over-
protective mother and her obedient daughter,[31] they refuse to
participate in any other activity when the chance to listen to or
to read a narrative presents itself, never turning down an opportunity to serve as an audience for another's tale. In "The Unhappy One," for instance, listeners have evidently extracted a
"promise" from which they will not excuse the narrator to tell
them about his acquaintance with the title character, Susanna,
even though he professes reluctance to recall "difficult days" (8:
61). In *First Love*, friends of Vladimir Petrovich virtually im-
plore him to regale them with the story of his earliest passion.

Even an oft-repeated tale is greeted with avidity. The opening
of "The History of Lieutenant Ergunov" is exemplary: "That
evening Kuzma Vasilevich Ergunov told us his story again. He
repeated it accurately once a month, and we listened to it each
time with new pleasure, even though we practically knew it by
heart in all its details" (8: 7). Short story after short story opens
with someone's offer to narrate a series of events—an offer
never declined. Stories that commence otherwise nonetheless
often imply that the same offer has been made and accepted, as
for instance at the outset of "The Little Quail," where the narrator states, "I was about ten years old when that which I will
now relate to you happened to me" (10: 118). Although "our" re-

sponse is not explicitly recorded, clearly no objection to the narration is anticipated.

In both the novels and short stories, plot development often pauses as one character stops to tell another a story. No one resists, even when a tale is told about the experiences of someone other than the teller. No voice objects on the grounds that the narratives proffered might come secondhand, mediated and therefore potentially misconveyed by a separate consciousness. Thus, for example, the narrator of "Asya" happily hears about this girl's past not from her own lips but from those of her half brother, Gagin. Elena Stakhova in *On The Eve* listens eagerly to the life story of the Bulgarian exile Insarov as told not by him but by their friend in common, Bersenev. And no less self-consciously rigorous a scientist committed to objective observation and analysis than Bazarov in *Fathers and Sons* unhesitatingly allows his friend Arkadii to iterate the personal history of Arkadii's uncle, Pavel Petrovich.

Why do Turgenev's characters love stories so? Or, to be more precise, why does Turgenev so repeatedly accentuate the attractiveness of narratives and then exploit that attraction as a device to facilitate further exposition? Many authors use the same technique as a way of setting the stage or as a pretext for introducing material otherwise outside the temporal or spatial scope of a given narrative. But the frequency of its use and the alacrity and intensity of the reception Turgenev accords to narratives signify more than a mere device. They suggest that Turgenev divines in narratives an irresistibly gratifying experience. It can only be that this is the experience of art—and Apollonian art at that.

The distinct satisfactions of Apollonian art for Turgenev's fictional listeners and readers derive initially from the psychic security this art offers. This security is manifested in two ways. First, psychic security is provided by presenting events as constrained and organized, by molding them into harmonious shapes comforting in their coherence. Unlike the unconstrained, random, often shapeless flood of occurrences encountered in ordinary actuality, the flow of narrated events presented by Turgenev's eminently responsible narrators is so evenly tempered as to prevent any image of disruption from intruding and upsetting the audience.

Second, psychic security is created by affording the audience a sense of distance from those narrated events. This is possible because Apollonian art clearly marks itself as an artistic creation and not as actuality; Apollonian narratives are fiction, not fact. Thus each member of the audience is free to respond to a story without regard for the implications or consequences of that response in reality. As the psychoanalytic literary critic Norman Holland points out, "It is precisely the conscious knowledge that we are dealing with unreality that makes it possible for us to relax, to suspend our disbelief," whereas "conversely, during the time we think fiction is real, we are tense, sometimes even to the point of displeasure."[32]

The psychic security afforded by Apollonian art in turn affords Turgenev's fictional audiences the opportunity to use the narratives as models of how to respond imaginatively to real-life experiences. For Turgenev does not confer the benefit of security on the presentation of stories merely to provide a ready avenue of escape from reality. Through this conferral he expands the receptivity of his audiences, he increases their willingness to learn new modes of response to the arduous demands of actuality. They learn both by observing and by assessing characters' creative reactions to specific situations and then by observing and assessing their own reactions to those situations, all the while remaining utterly unthreatened. Turgenev thereby demonstrates that encounters with narratives can provide enhanced awareness of safe psychic ground on which to base original, imaginative responses to life.

These effects of Apollonian art collaborate to give Turgenev's narrative-loving characters the singular Turgenevan satisfaction—the satisfaction embodied by the image of the individual exercising control over experience. The narrative act of assembling a collection of events into an artfully ordered sequence gives a meaning to those events that they would lack in their actual random and meaningless disorder, a disorder of unorganized accidents that depresses and defeats the human spirit. The

Apollonian artistic response to such disorder, even while distorting or denying its actuality, attests to the superiority of the human spirit over any situation, however depressing or dehumanizing it may be, for that spirit, by producing works of art, demonstrates its ability not just to recreate or reform circumstance—and thus be dependent on it—but to create circumstance independently, to instill form where there was none. Turgenev's characters love narratives because they love the sensation of control over experience that the act of creation conveys.

Turgenev not only represents this love as inherent in his fictional characters, but attributes it to his actual readers as well. Assuming that they too are drawn to the sensation of control over experience, in one way or another he deliberately marks his works as narratives. Specifically, he employs meta-literary devices signaling that his works are indeed literary creations produced by a single imagination, not factual reports recorded by an objective observer. One of his favorite devices is the subtitle, particularly one that calls attention to the fictionality of the piece to come. Thus, for instance, he attaches the subtitle "Excerpt from an Unpublished Novel" to the short story entitled "The Master's Private Office," "A Story in Ten Letters" to "Faust," "A Fantasy" to "Phantoms," "Excerpt from the Notes of a Dying Artist" to "Enough," and "A Story by Petr Petrovich B." to "Punin and Baburin." And although not formally subtitled, both *A Nest of Gentry* and *Smoke* are labeled "A Narrative by Ivan Turgenev" on their title pages.[33]

In addition to or instead of subtitles, Turgenev often introduces narratives with dedications or epigraphs, both of which, as highly conventionalized forms, emphasize the literary nature of what follows. For example, *First Love* is dedicated to P. B. Annenkov, *Fathers and Sons* to the memory of V. G. Belinsky, and "The Song of Triumphant Love" to the memory of Flaubert. "The Song of Triumphant Love" also has an epigraph from Schiller; "Three Meetings" opens with an unattributed Italian quatrain; "Faust" takes as its epigraph a line from Goethe; "Phantoms" begins with a quotation from the Russian poet Fet; *Spring Torrents* uses a verse epigraph said to be "from an ancient romance" (8: 255).

And when Turgenev does not use these formal devices as reminders that his works belong to the realm of literature, he exploits other means. For instance, he often constructs a frame that expressly depicts a narrator telling the framed narrative, as in "Andrei Kolosov," "Asya," "The Dog," "King Lear of the Steppe," "Knock... Knock... Knock!," and "The Watch." Otherwise, Turgenev has the narrator either directly address "my reader" or "readers"—this regularly occurs in *A Sportsman's Sketches* and all of the novels, as well as in such short stories as "Three Portraits" and "Brigadier"—or else employ such colloquial or idiosyncratic language as nearly to force the reader to recognize that a narrative is being conveyed. Thus time and again Turgenev invites his audience to witness the expression of an inventive mind deliberately molding experience into literary form.

This explicit invitation to his readers presents only the most obvious evidence of a fundamental feature of Turgenev's creative process: it is guided by principles that are ethical as well as aesthetic. Granted, as Wayne Booth has elaborately argued, all narratives imply values having to do with such attributes as complexity and simplicity, intimacy and distance, etc., and put the reader in the position of having to judge the moral value of the characters and actions portrayed.[34] Yet the values that Turgenev's narratives communicate have gone too long unrecognized, for Turgenev is typically viewed as morally neutral, or at most moderately liberal.

Oscar Mandel represents the former view—and takes issue with the latter—in an essay entitled "Molière and Turgenev: The Literature of No-Judgment." Mandel here contends that in *Fathers and Sons*, for instance, Turgenev discloses "the actual consequences" of "two contradictory points of view" but allows "no moral decision" to be reached about those consequences. "This is not to say that the moral issues are irrelevant or uninteresting" to Turgenev, Mandel continues, but that "the resulting work has the prophetic greatness of being not indifferent, but modestly inconclusive."[35] Mandel finds that this moral inconclusiveness pervades all of Turgenev's major works, a finding implicitly or explicitly shared by those critics who deem Turgenev an uninvolved, objective reporter of nineteenth-century Russian life.

Other critics, such as Henri Granjard, Edmund Wilson, Isaiah Berlin, and Leonard Schapiro, find evidence of a more specific and positive moral stance in Turgenev's narratives. Prompted in part no doubt by their own generally liberal leanings, they see in those narratives a consistent criticism of the abuse of the underclasses by the Russian landed gentry and autocratic government. Yet even these critics discern a certain faintness in Turgenev's ethical sensibilities, since they concede that these liberal value judgments are more often implied than expressed.[36] Overall, most commentators have tended to share Freeborn's conclusion that Turgenev was "more concerned to make man real than make him better."[37]

Instead of declaring Turgenev distant or constrained in expressing his ethics, though, his readers should consider the possibility that distance and constraint are actually central tenets of Turgenev's ethics. For what may appear to be moral impartiality or diffidence is actually a moral commitment to a distanced and constrained vision of experience itself. Careful readings of his narratives reveal that Turgenev couples imaginative creativity with aesthetic constraint in a moral imperative. He imparts order and limitation, balance and harmony to his narratives not merely as aesthetic ends in themselves, but as means to an ethical end. This end can be summed up as the guidance of the reader toward the development of the best possible self, which Turgenev defines as the one most capable of enduring the trials of life with equanimity, of surviving setbacks with dignity and integrity. This self will be the most sufficient unto itself, the most autonomous, the least dependent on other people or outside circumstances. It will be the most able to govern itself and its circumstances by imposing its perceptions and interpretations on the experiences it undergoes. And this self will therefore be the least vulnerable to injury and the least susceptible to suffering. It should be, as it were, a "composed" self, in the two senses of "composed." The Turgenevan ideal self should be composed emotionally, that is, calm, controlled, undisturbed by internal or external vicissitudes. This ideal self should also be composed imaginatively, that is, consciously shaped to attain emotional equanimity and moral integrity.

The ethical means Turgenev advocates to develop the best possible self derive from several related psychic phenomena. One is consciousness, or more specifically self-awareness, which enables the individual to marshal psychic energy in the quest for autonomy. Another is rationality, which facilitates the dispassionate direction of that energy into self-constructive rather than self-destructive channels. A third is will, the union of intellect and emotion, which enacts the conscious, rational choices promoting self-control and self-sufficiency. And a fourth is creativity, particularly artistic creativity, which draws on consciousness, rationality, and will to instill an aesthetic order in the perception and interpretation of events that fosters the emotional and ethical well-being of independent individuals.

Turgenev invokes all these means to promote his ethical ends both within his narratives and among his readers. His art exhorts all individuals to engage their consciousness, their rationality, their will, and their creativity in order to achieve the psychological composure and moral composition that Turgenev places at the core of his ethics. Above all, then, in a manner of speaking, he encourages characters and readers alike to become the artists of their own lives.

An incident emblematic of Turgenev's ethical vision occurs in the narrative "The Execution of Tropmann." Overtly didactic—its introduction declares it "a lesson to others" (11:131)—this record of Turgenev's attendance at the guillotining of a notorious criminal offers an explicit protest against capital punishment. But it also depicts an epiphanic moment of ethical revelation made possible by an act of creative perception. Verbs of perception, especially visual perception, abound in the narrative, as Turgenev describes his impressions of the night preceding the execution. The verb "I saw" begins all but one phrase of the paragraph presenting Tropmann's final moments: "I saw the executioner rise . . . I saw Tropmann . . . I saw him stopping . . . I saw him appear above . . . I saw him falling forward" (11:149). Mesmerized by the spectacle before him, it is as though Turgenev cannot tear his eyes away from the proceedings. Yet at the climactic moment, the actual beheading, he does just that: "I turned away and began to wait" until the execution was over. He is unable to watch. For this inability, Dostoevsky excoriated Turgenev: "Man on the surface of the earth," Dostoevsky declared in reaction, "does not have the right to turn away and ignore what is taking place on earth, and there are lofty, *moral* reasons for this: *homo sum et nihil humanum*, etc."[38] Dostoevsky condemned what he took to be Turgenev's combination of elitism and cowardice in refusing to witness man's most extreme form of inhumanity to man. But Dostoevsky failed to take notice of what Turgenev does *instead* of watching the execution; moreover, Dostoevsky failed to comprehend why Turgenev does what he does instead.

What Turgenev does is look at something—or more precisely someone—else: "Before me stood a sentry, a young red-cheeked fellow... I just had time to see him looking intently at me with dull perplexity and horror." Turgenev studies the fellow: "I even had time to think that that soldier probably hailed from some godforsaken village and came from a decent, law-abiding family and—the things he had to see now!" (11: 149). By looking away from the inhuman, bestial act of slaughter—Turgenev says the fall of the guillotine blade sounded "just as though a huge animal had retched"—Turgenev can maintain his sanity, his identity, his very humanity. He can perceive himself as separate from the bloodthirsty mass of the crowd; he can extend his individual sympathy to a single fellow being. Turgenev knows that "the things" this fellow being "had to see" will eventually render the sentry inured to the horror of such activities, will inevitably make him less humane, less human—and hence less moral—just as directly observing the moment of execution would have made Turgenev.[39]

For Turgenev, the refusal to watch an offensive deformation and destruction of life therefore follows from a moral obligation. Such sights undermine self-affirmation and lessen self-control, when the development and preservation of the best possible self are preeminent moral mandates in Turgenev's fictional universe. Indeed, when seeing itself entails exposure to limitless disorder, not seeing—or reenvisioning what is seen within ordered limits—may offer the only possibility of self-preservation at all.

Thus instead of turning to some transcendent religious belief at a horrifying moment, as Dostoevsky might do, Turgenev summons up an alternative vision of experience, one that he himself creates. In this instance, he imagines a past life and a set of present emotions for a total stranger. In other words, he envelops the stranger in a narrative, and in so doing, separates himself from the grisly proceedings around him. This is the only means of self-preservation and self-assertion Turgenev can muster under the circumstances, the only act of independent self-affirmation he can undertake. And this act alone keeps him from becoming as ruined psychologically as the guillotined man is destroyed physically. Lacking faith in an ultimate sacred order that imparts meaning to events, Turgenev creates his own order and thereby espouses his own faith, a faith in aesthetic inventiveness that brings the only salvation Turgenev can envision—secular salvation.

To be sure, salvation in Turgenev's fictional universe is a limited concept, which is appropriate enough, since Turgenev portrays salvation as attainable only within limits. It is not represented as ultimate transcendence of all earthly ills enabled by an act of divine deliverance. Secular salvation is achieved not by acts of contrition and atonement that inspire redemptive intervention in human lives by an omnipotent deity, as religious salvation is often conceived. Instead, it holds out the promise of rescue from what Turgenev considers secular damnation—the loss of lasting psychological integration and consistent moral integrity. Turgenev's type of salvation is obtained by acts of individual volition. As even the most religious of Turgenev's characters, Luker'ia, in "Living Relics," asserts, "Each person himself must help himself" (3: 333). She really means that each person alone must save himself, must find salvation independently. Only in this way are there created and conserved distinguishable, delimited selves capable of redeeming solitary individuals not from death, but from the suffering begotten by the devastating dilemmas of life.

The illustration of the moral imagination required for secular salvation offered by "The Execution of Tropmann" suggests that Turgenev could have echoed Dostoevsky's sweeping boast that "nothing human is foreign unto me." But he would not have meant the same thing by it. Turgenev prizes what is human no less than Dostoevsky does; Turgenev simply has a conception of human nature that is quite different. Dostoevsky embraces an extremely broad conception of human nature, of what capabilities and behaviors qualify as "human." He therefore eagerly explores the irrational and immoral, as well as the more benign, tendencies of the human spirit. At the same time, Dostoevsky retains an abiding faith in the moral capacity of that spirit to achieve goodness and transcendence, a belief characteristic of many nineteenth-century thinkers. By contrast, Turgenev entertains a much narrower conception of human nature. He displays doubts about humanity more typical of the twentieth century than the nineteenth. Turgenev senses that the conditions of human existence are too complex, too powerful, too impersonal to allow the human spirit to transcend them thoroughly. For Turgenev, human nature does well to survive and sustain itself at all.

As Turgenev represents human nature in his works, he contributes to a venerable tradition—going back at least to the Stoics in the West and continuing through Freud—that dwells on the susceptibility of human beings to suffering. Within this tradition, the goal of human existence is to minimize pain, not to maximize pleasure. As Turgenev partakes of this conception of human nature, he manifests particularly strong affinities with Freud, whose theory of human nature and civilization is built around the idea that "life is too hard for us," a sentiment voiced in various ways by many of Turgenev's protagonists.[40] Declaring that "the intention that man should be 'happy' is not included in the plan of 'Creation,' "[41] Freud prescribed a psychological life in civilization in which the avoidance of pain was paramount. The sources of pain Freud economically reduced to three: the external world, other people, and the body. All strategies of life then amounted for him to defenses against these enemies of psychic well-being.

Turgenev's psychology, and the ethics derived from it, anticipated Freud in that Turgenev too could be said to have reduced
the sources of suffering to three, not so different from Freud's:
nature, other people, and the irrational. Turgenev's fiction can
thus be read as a cautionary tale about the threats these sources
of suffering pose to human nature, and how human beings either
succeed in defending themselves or fail to do so. These cautions
are communicated in both the substance and the shape of Turgenev's works; their most sensitive readers would therefore respond by acquiring insights into how they might effectively defend themselves against pain as well, and thereby become the
best human beings they can.

In Turgenev's works, nature confronts the individual with the
promise of physical suffering. The natural cycle from birth to
death that every living thing must follow inevitably ensures
that every individual will suffer, early or late, the torments of
physical deterioration. Turgenev's narratives are well known for
their images of natural beauty, but those narratives also abound
with images of organic disease and decay. Fatal illnesses beset
young and old—Aleksandra Andreevna in "The Rural Doctor,"
the narrator of "Diary of a Superfluous Man," Insarov in *On the
Eve*, Zinaida in *First Love*, and the title character Iakov Pasynkov, to name a few. Fatal accidents befall still others—Luker'ia
in "Living Relics," the peasant Maksim in "Death," Bazarov in
Fathers and Sons. With notably few exceptions, it is not man,
nor man's malevolence, that leads to the demise of most of Turgenev's characters—they generally suffer and die from natural
causes.

Turgenev adds to his acknowledgments of the physical pain
caused by natural degeneration repeated observations of the
psychological pain caused by human consciousness of both the
inevitability of that degenerative process and the indifference
with which nature allows humans to undergo it. The most emblematic and chilling moment of this agonizing awareness can
be found in "My Neighbor Radilov," one of *A Sportsman's
Sketches*, where the title character reports witnessing a fly
walking across the eyeball of his wife's corpse (3: 55). He cannot
bring himself to express the appalled despair this sight arouses,

but this same despair—and horror—at nature's ineluctable claims alongside its elemental disregard for human beings are explicitly articulated by the narrator of the prose poem entitled "Nature." In this work Turgenev personifies nature as "a magnificent woman in a flowing cloak of green," engaged in a dialogue with a narrator who reproaches her for failing to exalt human beings above her other "children." Believing that nature should be chiefly concerned with mankind and "how to lead it to the greatest possible perfection and happiness"—the ultimate moral goals—and not with lesser beings, the narrator asks, "But aren't we, people, your favorite children?" To which the figure of nature replies:

> "All the blades of grass are my children," she declared, "and I equally worry about them—and equally destroy them."
>
> "But goodness... reason... justice...," I cried out again.
>
> "These are human words," intoned the iron voice. "I know neither good nor evil... Reason is not a law to me—and what is justice? I have given you life—I will take it away and give it to another, to worms or to people... it's all the same to me..." (10: 165).

Plagued by this awareness of natural suffering and nature's indifference to that suffering, Turgenev's characters must live with an irremediably unhappy consciousness. It is true, as Jackson observes, that some of those characters may well bear the blame for this condition, for by "placing himself at the center of the universe," the Turgenevan protagonist "anthropomorphizes nature" and then "bewails her indifference to him."[42] However, the intensity of such unhappiness betokens more than misplaced expectations. It bespeaks a respect for and a commitment to consciousness itself as a definitively human attribute. Yet it is a consciousness that must turn against itself in the knowledge of its own inescapable doom. Turgenev thus underscores the difficulty of evading the pain caused by nature in the quest for psychological well-being.

Besides nature, Turgenev represents other people as a principal threat to psychic well-being. Although Freeborn, for one, asserts that Turgenev prizes society above the individual, the evidence points to the opposite conclusion.[43] Turgenev's fiction includes remarkably few scenes portraying socially complex groups, and those that are portrayed tend to be peopled by idiosyncratic or even antisocial characters. Turgenev accords no social segment favorable treatment. Like Tolstoy, he depicts the aristocratic and other monied strata of society as morally bankrupt. (The well-born, predatory Varvara Pavlovna Korobina in *A Nest of Gentry*, for example, is a spiritual sister of "la belle Hélène" in *War and Peace*, as each connives to seduce and dominate a decent, if naive, male.) But unlike Tolstoy, Turgenev repeatedly suggests that even social aggregates that are small, rural, and poor by comparison to the urban upper classes pose threats to the individual, for they tempt the self to indulgence in effortless, mind-numbing, spirit-deadening sameness. Thus, to take several disparate examples, neither the peasants collected at the Kolotovka inn in "The Singers," one of *A Sportsman's Sketches*, nor the inhabitants at Ipatov's in "A Quiet Place," nor the neighbors at Dar'ia Mikhailovna's in *Rudin*, nor the Russian travelers at Baden-Baden in *Smoke* evince any signs of constituting a coherent community capable of supporting, much less ennobling, its members, despite their being mostly acquaintances of long standing. Rather, these social assemblages exist out of boredom and habit. And their lack of social coherence actually gives rise to antisocial behavior: the inn's customers get disgustingly drunk, Ipatov's sister-in-law commits suicide, Dar'ia Mikhailovna's neighbors and the Russian émigrés argue more than they agree.

Almost nowhere does Turgenev represent a group that can provide psychological strength and moral support for the self. The only significant exceptions prove the rule: one, Marfa Timofeevna's cozy "establishment," comprises "five beings, almost equally close to her heart"—a bullfinch, a small dog, an angry cat, a nine-year-old orphan girl names Shurochka, and a middle-aged widow named Nastas'ia Karpovna (6: 56). Despite the affection that binds these stray beings together, they hardly constitute a human society. And the other, the extended Kirsanov family in *Fathers and Sons*, is formed only in the novel's epilogue; it has no place within the body of a Turgenevan narrative.

Even social relationships between two individuals, whether entered into as a romance or a friendship, are generally exposed as doing more damage than good. Many commentators have remarked the dangers of love in Turgenev's fictional universe, taking as a representative statement the parting words of the narrator's father in *First Love*: "Fear a woman's love, fear that happiness, that poison" (6: 362). The father's words are well advised: love brings upheaval, agony, despair, and sometimes even death to almost all of the characters who experience it. The father himself is reduced to tears, begging his wife for money to help the woman he hopelessly loves; Liza in *A Nest of Gentry* forsakes her home and family forever, withdrawing to a convent when she learns she cannot marry her beloved; Insarov in *On the Eve* contracts his fatal illness by going about in inclement weather on behalf of the woman he wants to marry; Masha in "A Quiet Place" and Susanna in "The Unhappy One" commit suicide when they realize they can never be united with the men they adore; Aratov in "Klara Milich" dies in hopes of reuniting his spirit with that of his deceased inamorata. The gratifications of love—if they occur at all—are short-lived. The afflictions of love—which always occur—are enduring.

Love, according to Turgenev, has the power to wreak such havoc precisely because it plays deceptively on human psychological and moral vulnerabilities. It appears to offer an opportunity to achieve self-satisfaction and self-enhancement, but it actually entails self-deprivation and self-degradation, because the intimacy created by love requires an expenditure of energy that would otherwise be devoted to self-preservation, and the diversion of that energy makes the self susceptible to any malign forces waiting to attack, be they forces of nature or of stronger personalities. Hence the individual in love can readily be drawn into self-betrayal and self-destruction. The portrait of love painted in Turgenev's works, like that of social life in general, exposes the frailty of a human psyche in need of succor and protection and yet unable to obtain them from others.

Even characters represented as friends provide little psychic support for one another. They tend instead to voice criticisms or complaints—in *Rudin*, Lezhnev castigates Rudin's glibness;

in *A Nest of Gentry*, Mikhalevich condemns Lavretskii's passivity; in *Fathers and Sons*, Bazarov reproves Arkadii's filial deference. Such reproaches, although well meant and often justified, offer little constructive assistance to the recipient, who is often left merely hurt or confused. The closeness of friendship thus recurrently makes for more, not less, pain, for increased, not decreased, uncertainty and insecurity in Turgenev's bleak social vision.

To be sure, some of Turgenev's characters value companionship—for example, both Liza Kalitina in *A Nest of Gentry* and Tat'iana Shestova in *Smoke* appreciate the company and counsel of an elderly aunt. Nonetheless, at a moment of romantic crisis each emotionally withdraws from the older woman, shielding herself from kindly but hurtful intrusions that can only heighten already intense unhappiness. Each young woman deems herself better off psychically when physically alone. A number of other characters reach the same conclusion, whether in an emotional crisis or not—among them, Kas'ian and Luker'ia in *A Sportsman's Sketches*, and Iakov Pasynkov—preferring to distance themselves from other people, finding it easier to sustain an autonomous and secure sense of self in a secluded existence.

Yet in Turgenev's fictional world, solitude itself does not suffice to ensure autonomy and security. Even when psychically sheltered from the external threats posed by nature and other people, the conscious self is subject to threatening irrational impulses and desires from within. The forces of irrationality—instinctual appetites and self-deceptions—oppose the rational self-control essential to an autonomous identity, for they subvert the constraints so carefully contrived by the self to preserve that identity. And when those irrational forces are disguised by being repressed in the unconscious, their expression becomes even more unpredictable, more subversive, more uncontrollable.

Time and again Turgenev's protagonists must consciously grapple with their irrationality. They repeatedly find themselves tempted to gratify an urge that they cannot rationally and morally justify. And more often than not they are unable even to ar-

ticulate fully the urge they seek to combat, at least while under
its sway, for in their morally inspired effort to resist it, these
characters have merely suppressed or repressed what they feel,
thereby intensifying its insidious, deceptively veiled influence.
Thus, on the one hand, Aleksei Petrovich in "The Correspondence," Litvinov in *Smoke,* and Sanin in *Spring Torrents* all deny
their strong physical attraction to a woman other than the one
to whom they have committed themselves, yet they find themselves increasingly unable to fight that attraction even as they
proclaim their determination to do so. Eventually they all succumb. On the other hand, the narrators of "Andrei Kolosov" and
"Asya," the eponymous Rudin, and Fustov in "The Unhappy
One" all experience involuntary fear of commitment to a
woman of their acquaintance despite a strong attraction to her.
Hence as soon as they proclaim their devotion, they emotionally withdraw, only later to regret that withdrawal. In both sets
of circumstances, irrational forces succeed in subverting the rational will of the individual, diminishing and even demolishing
self-control, and thus striking at the core of that individual's
self-sufficiency and independence.

In his view of the irrational, therefore, Turgenev is again far
removed from Dostoevsky, who finds in human irrationality the
potential for redemptive goodness no less than for uncontrollable evil, symbolized, for instance, by the seemingly unjusti-
fied kiss of forgiveness the prostitute Liza bestows on the seemingly unforgivable Underground Man. To Turgenev, by contrast,
human irrationality has no redemptive value whatsoever; it
only condemns human beings to demoralizing decadence.

Acutely sensitive, then, to the variety and strength of the
forces marshaled against the self—the forces of nature, society,
and irrationality—Turgenev is also acutely attuned to the variety and strength of the protective devices employed by the ego,
or the rational conscious self, in its own defense. Indeed, his
works reveal Turgenev to be a veritable poet of the psychic defense mechanism. He understands and sympathizes with the
mental maneuvers to which human beings resort in their need
to minimize pain—denial, projection, sublimation, etc.—as

perhaps none of his literary predecessors or contemporaries ever did. Even more distinctively, Turgenev discerns moral value in these mechanisms, which are so often dismissed or derided as psychic means to further self-serving, immoral intentions. But Turgenev presents self-protection as a prerequisite to moral development: if there is no ego, no self, there can be no endurance, no survival, no best possible self to preserve. Thus Turgenev, staunch champion of the ego, displays not only comprehension and compassion but ethical conviction in his portrayals of the ego's efforts to defend and thereby save itself when no other source of salvation obtains.

This is not to say that Turgenev denies or excuses the individual when these efforts go awry. Although, as observed earlier, his palpable compassion for such individuals has often led readers to accuse him of a lack of moral values altogether—or at least with refusing to articulate any—Turgenev consistently measures his characters against the specific moral standards of self-preservation. Steadfastly, if subtly, he lauds their moral triumphs and deplores their moral lapses in quest of secular salvation. Yet Turgenev knows that those lapses may be unavoidable, so difficult and demanding is this moral task. He also knows that the very defenses mounted against assaults on the integrity of the self may themselves cause harm, and he condemns that harm, albeit without altogether morally condemning the characters who employ them.

Moreover, he grasps that at times it may be difficult to discern why such harm occurs. He admits into his narratives periodic uncertainty about whether harmful acts are performed unintentionally or intentionally, at times leaving unclear whether moral wrongs result from incapacity and weakness of self or from capacity and strength of self. He renders ambiguous whether damage is done from the inability or the unwillingness to act otherwise—or from both.[44] His narratives are consequently infused with dramatic tension engendered by the difficulty in distinguishing between moral inspiration and immoral impulse, between conscious choice and unconscious desire. Indeed, most of the characters Turgenev creates want to be good; in the main, a conscience accompanies consciousness in the composition of the Turgenevan psyche. These characters make repeated, manifestly moral efforts to create their best possible self. But achieving goodness, successfully creating that best self, often proves far more difficult than anticipated. In all cases, though, as he illustrates these efforts—sometimes successful, sometimes not—Turgenev exhibits a profound sensitivity to moral complexities, demonstrating with extraordinary humanistic empathy that ethical ends can be correct even when the means adopted to achieve those ends are misguided.

It is typical and illuminating of Turgenev's literary psychology and morality that the most common of the defenses he represents is rationalization. The bulk of Turgenev's protagonists are past masters of rationalization, which is an attempt to elevate varieties of subjective self-interest or desire to the level of objective, rational judgment, and hence to render acting on them morally justifiable. Morally unjustifiable motives may thereby be cloaked in a guise of decency, since a response to objective conditions beyond individual control may constitute a moral obligation, as the indulgence in subjective desire may not. Rationalization is therefore a distinctly self-defensive mechanism, unconsciously inspired to obviate the unwelcome guilt engendered if such desire is consciously conceded. At the same time, this mechanism may well allow unidentified impulses to subvert self-protective sensibilities by turning the powers of reasoning to immoral purposes. Thus the act of rationalization, to which Turgenev was supremely sensitive, epitomizes the Turgenevan moral dilemma—attempts at self-protection may actually imperil self-preservation.

In *Spring Torrents*, for instance, Sanin rationalizes paying continued court to an exceptionally attractive woman who will seductively enthrall him and thereby destroy his chance for a happy marriage. Although dancing attendance on this woman keeps him apart from his fiancée, Sanin tells himself that he has no other way to attain the financial security to get married. He therefore persuades himself to do as this woman commands, thinking, "But there is nothing to be done! One must drink the vial to the dregs—get dressed, go to dinner, and thence to the theater" (8: 357). Unaware of how powerful is the physical at-

traction, he tries to convince himself that he acts not out of desire but out of necessity. Yet he betrays the fact that he is rationalizing, rather than simply behaving rationally, by his feelings
of amorphous guilt toward his fiancée: "A thousand times he
mentally begged forgiveness of his pure, chaste little dove, although he could not accuse himself of anything in particular"
(8: 357). Sanin senses that he is pursuing a course disastrous for
both himself and his beloved, but his unconscious urges prevent
him from clearly articulating that course and thereby turning
away from it when he still might have the will to do so. Thus
Sanin follows his seductress until he is cast aside, miserably embittered and alone. Here is the bitter paradox of rationalization:
its morally inspired, self-justificatory efficacy leads to immoral
self-deception and thence to emotional and existential disaster.

Turgenev accordingly condemns self-deception as a matrix of
self-destruction. Yet he complicates his moral position by refusing to condemn all forms of deception. One form he does not
wholly condemn, for example, is lying. And many of Turgenev's
protagonists tell lies. Indeed, some weave an extensive fabric of
dissemblings around their emotions or actions. But instead of
rendering them morally suspect or reprehensible for doing so,
Turgenev grants them an aura of virtue. To be sure, their deceptions are all of a kind—the kind Nietzsche would have placed
in his oxymoronic category of "honest lies."[45] These are conscious, deliberate misstatements by one individual with the
clear intention of deceiving another. Self-deception plays no role
in honest lies; such lies are the product of an individual will attempting openly to serve its own conscious interests.

Turgenev approves the "honest" lies told with moral intent—
those intended to spare their audience from direct confrontation
with a truth too painful to bear. They also aid their authors in
their efforts to safeguard themselves from hurt or humiliation,
thereby preserving a secure sense of self that the truth could undermine. Thus, for instance, in *A Nest of Gentry*, Liza Kalitina
tells an honest lie when she informs her aunt that nothing is
wrong, although Liza has just learned that her plans to be married cannot be realized. Likewise, when Tat'iana Shestova in
Smoke assures her traveling companion that she only has a cold,
whereas she has actually been crying over the dissolution of her

engagement, she too tells an honest lie. Each young woman deliberately falsifies the report of her condition, seeking to shield her sorrow from someone who would be terribly saddened by that sorrow. Additionally, each gains some time, gathering her psychic strength to cope with the loss of the love and future happiness around which she has built a strong sense of self. Now each must build a new sense of self, the self that each morally aspires to be. Thus psychological need coincides with ethical impulse.

Turgenev can therefore be said to admit a category of behavior that might be termed "moral mendacity." Actions that belong to it receive more than Turgenev's tolerance and sympathy; they win his approbation. In Turgenev's psychological and moral universe, the sacrifice of one type of integrity—public honesty—in order to sustain another type of integrity—private wholeness—is no sacrifice. It is a legitimate mode of self-defense. As long as the individual will is engaged in a conscious effort to create a strong self or to preserve one through the creation of a new image of experience, conventional moral standards may be violated with impunity, indeed, with nobility. Hence, anticipating Ibsen and Nietzsche by three decades, Turgenev has the narrator of *A Nest of Gentry* aver: "Without deceiving oneself, one cannot survive on earth" (6: 136). To Turgenev, contrivance can be a virtue.

The nobility of moral mendacity and contrivance inheres not only in the creation of the self, but in the creation of narratives as well. For narratives are themselves a kind of honest lie, requiring as they do the willful imposition of a new, ordered image of experience that deliberately alters or belies disordered actuality. And narratives lie, so to speak, for a moral purpose—to provide models of the benefits of such lying to their audience. They demonstrate the value of refusing to perceive what reality is in order to conceive of what reality should be if the individual self is to survive. It is this demonstration, finally, that explains why narratives play so important a role and are so eagerly embraced within Turgenev's fictional universe.

To the extent, then, that the preservation of the self constitutes a moral end of Turgenev's fiction, the relationships in that fiction between Goodness, Beauty, and Truth must be reconsidered. Most critics have argued, albeit with differing emphases, that Turgenev's narratives embody Truth Beautifully, and that it is Good to do so. Garnett, for instance, advances this argument in his impassioned defense of Turgenev against scholars who, in Garnett's words, "having themselves never seen or felt in nature's life those shades of 'truth' which Turgenev's poetical vision reveals to us, imagine that such have no 'real' existence," because these scholars "mean by 'truth' something both more photographic and commonplace, something more striking or more ordinary in the 'lighting,' something observed with less beautiful shades of feeling, less exquisitely stamped and recorded in classical contours."[46] To Garnett, Turgenev's art provides its audience with the perfect union of Beauty and Truth, and is therefore Good, because it brings into view hitherto unseen or unappreciated facets of human existence.

But the ethical system embodied in Turgenev's works, with its insistence on the hegemony of the ego, demands a different equation of Beauty, Truth, and Goodness. This system requires that Truth, meaning both physical actuality and metaphysical essence, be suppressed or supplanted by the falsehood of fiction, if such falsehood is needed to defend the ego from destruction. In Turgenev's narratives, Truth is often just as hideous, just as horrifying, as it is in Dostoevsky's works. Turgenev is just as aware of the dark side of the human soul as is Dostoevsky; Turgenev knows the cruelty, the greed, the corruption of which human beings are capable just as well as Dostoevsky, who made a career of graphically depicting them. It is Turgenev, after all, who portrays the aristocrat that arbitrarily orders her serf to drown his beloved dog, the guardian who malevolently drives his ward to commit suicide, the femme fatale who deliberately deceives her husband—but these and others like them could as easily have appeared in tales by Dostoevsky. Yet Turgenev refuses to cede such characters pride of place, or to lay bare their perverted psyches for all to examine, as Dostoevsky might have done. Turgenev prefers to keep these figures on the periphery of narratives, subordinating their immoral acts to the representation of the sincere moral struggles of major protagonists. Turgenev does not deny the Truth of evil, but he keeps it distant, aesthetically controlled. And for Turgenev, that is Good.

In Turgenev's fiction, therefore, it is Beauty, not Truth, that equals Goodness—Beauty meaning aesthetic control, harmony, and constraint, and Goodness meaning an expression of moral excellence—for it is the aesthetic transformation of ugly Truth into beautiful appearance that constitutes the highest ethical affirmation of the human spirit. Beauty marks the triumph of that spirit over the adverse forces of disorder, disharmony, and unconstraint that threaten to overwhelm it. Beauty makes manifest the human will to create something better than circumstances might warrant, and thereby to create a better human being—stronger, more secure, more self-sufficient, more enduring. Hence Beauty in Turgenev's works often is not Truth, but it is always Good.

To the extent that Turgenev equates Beauty with Goodness but not with Truth, he sets himself apart from both Tolstoy and Dostoevsky, for each posits distinctive relationships between these three abstractions. To Tolstoy, Truth is absolute Goodness, and the quest for absolute Truth, however difficult, should be the supreme moral goal of all human endeavors. In *What Is Art?*, for instance, Tolstoy contends that the concept of Beauty, at least as understood by "art lovers," is merely an elitist, empty convention, devoid of any connection to Truth whatsoever. Beauty disguises or distorts, and is therefore to be avoided, even condemned. Tolstoy therefore equates Truth with Goodness, but not with Beauty.[47]

By contrast, Dostoevsky identifies Beauty with spiritually transcendent Goodness, and he believes that the two are united through their embodiment in Jesus Christ. Dostoevsky declares his allegiance to Jesus Christ, who personifies Beauty and Goodness, over Truth when he announces that "beauty will save the world" as a form of spiritual redemption, and that "even if somebody proved to me that the truth was outside of Christ, and it really were true that the truth was outside of Christ, I would rather remain with Christ than with the Truth."[48] Yet, as Jackson convincingly demonstrates in *Dostoevsky's Quest for Form*, Dostoevsky never has to make that choice, since he actually finds all three qualities reconciled in Christ.[49] Thus Dostoevsky discovers a way to equate Truth, Beauty, and Goodness that neither Turgenev nor Tolstoy ever did.

Subscription to the ethical vision allying the Beautiful and the Good while periodically removing them both from the True sets Turgenev apart not only from Tolstoy and Dostoevsky, but from the movement of literary Realism as well. Granted, the preeminent Realists, as discussed in Chapter 1, prize both the Beautiful and the True, but like Turgenev, they also subordinate both to the Good. Unlike Turgenev, though, they deploy verisimilitudinous images of Beauty and Truth to summon the reader to become actively engaged with a community, but sacrifice both if necessary to mold an image of community with sufficient moral appeal to persuade readers that such communities should be created in actuality. To do this, Realists employ available linguistic, narrative, and other literary devices that render communal life both vivified and appealing.

Turgenev's ethical ends differ from those of Realism, and so, therefore, do his poetics. Turgenev's ethical ends serve to enable the reader to achieve psychological and moral autonomy independent of any community. Thus Turgenev employs linguistic, narrative, and other literary devices that are drawn only at times from ordinary actuality and that always make communal life suspect. Turgenev seeks to persuade the reader that all forms of society offer merely illusory benefits masking threats to psychological and moral autonomy, and that this autonomy can be achieved only by cultivating a protective distance from social experience. Turgenev's works provide a literary model for establishing this distance, and thus for achieving a kind of equanimous autonomy of which the thoroughgoing Realists would not have approved.

Elucidating these poetics is the subject of Part II, which addresses how Turgenev uses confining images of time and space to limit disruptive action; how he employs language marked by semantic ambiguity to suggest rather than explicitly to portray disordered experience; how he typically invokes shifting narrative points of view to avoid direct expression of disturbing events; and how, in a variety of ways, Turgenev creates characters who either successfully or unsuccessfully embody his ethical ends in attempting to engender and maintain psychologically and morally independent selves. Thus Turgenev was, as the succeeding chapters will show, at once a truly imaginative creator and a consistently demanding moralist who expected the individual to pursue his brand of secular salvation, autonomously and alone.

PART II

The Poetics of
Secular Salvation

3

Parameters of Protection:
Limiting Spaces, Limiting Times

Configurations of space and time establish the dimensions of all fictional worlds. This is nowhere more true than in Turgenev's fiction. But important as these configurations are for Turgenev, little critical attention has been paid to their aesthetic effects, and none to their bearing on Turgenev's ethical principles. This neglect implies that Turgenevan space and time are generally taken to be simply transparent features of Turgenev's purported narrative verisimilitude.[1] But in fact, Turgenev artfully manipulates the spatial and temporal dimensions of his narratives in order to set very deliberate physical, metaphysical, and moral parameters within which the events he portrays can distinctively unfold.

Turgenev's representations of space and time not only impose order on experience, as all representations of space and time do, but they impose a specifically Turgenevan order of limits, constraints, restrictions. In Turgenev's fictional universe, space is not an infinite extension and time is not an endless continuum. Both are portrayed as confined and confining. They proffer not the possibilities of expansion or continuation, but the inevitabilities of containment and conclusion. Limits retarding or even thwarting progress through space and time are repeatedly remarked; images of finiteness and finality are pervasive. An end, whether spatial or temporal, is almost always in sight.

Yet however pervasive, spatial finiteness and temporal finality do not equal fatality in the Turgenevan universe. They do not bespeak philosophical determinism, despite commentators' claims that Turgenev embraced this line of thought.[2] Determinism presupposes an ineluctably fated outcome for every human endeavor, precluding any possibility of free choice and eliminating all moral responsibility. To the contrary, most of Turgenev's characters agonize over choices and are animated by moral sensibilities, never evincing a fatalistic indifference to the causes or consequences of their actions. Thus the limitations of the space and time they inhabit do not militate against choices and morality; indeed, those limitations facilitate them by intensifying the import of characters' actions. Moreover, spatial and temporal limits set by Turgenev create an existential structure on which characters can endeavor to build well-defined identities and well-ordered lives. To be sure, that structure impinges on the characters in different ways, eliciting from them disparate responses, some good, some bad, some impenetrably ambiguous, but all reflecting facets of psychological and moral demands to defend vulnerable selves against inevitable assaults on their autonomy and integrity.

Although images of space and time are closely interwoven in those works, the two dimensions are addressed separately here in order to focus on incidents that particularly illuminate their implications for the quest for self-preservation, the sine qua non of secular salvation.

Space has a palpable presence in Turgenev's narratives. Signs of physical and metaphysical enclosure are everywhere, demarcating specific areas within which actions unfold. Even the domains ruled by nature, particularly woodland regions, are portrayed as either physically bounded or mentally framed.[3] The opening lines of the first of *A Sportsman's Sketches*, "Khor and Kalinych," for instance, carefully establish the specific geographical boundaries that provide the backdrop for this study of rural inhabitants: "Whoever happens to cross over from the Bolkhov region to that of Zhizdra would probably be amazed by the sharp differences between the type of people in the Orel district and the Kaluga type" (3: 7). Although explicitly opening a discussion of personality types, these lines also root the narrative in locations with distinctive characteristics that distinguish them from surrounding regions. In another sketch, "Chertopkhanov and Nedopiuskin," the narrator is reproached for not knowing that he has entered a new territory and is hunting on Chertopkhanov's land (3: 275)—a cautionary note that failure to be aware of established boundaries, even if invisible, can make for trouble.

Throughout these sketches the acknowledgment of specific locations and their specifiable borders adds more than local color or verisimilitude: it conveys the image of nature divided and subdivided, confined and controlled by the imposition of identifiable limits on spaces within nature's uncontrollable vastness. Most of these sketches are set in named, defined places within the forests where the hunter pursues his quarry: Lgov, Bezhin Meadow, the Beautiful Lands, Kolotovka, etc. And when place names are not employed to divide natural space into comprehensible segments, other kinds of divisions are remarked. For example, in the final sketch, "Forest and Steppe," whose title consists of names of contrasting natural environments, most of the sketch is devoted to the narrator's impression of the forest as composed of discrete parts—ravine, village, field of wild rye, little road, separate groves of oak, birch, and aspen trees. The forest is thus presented as an assemblage of distinguishable, easily labeled spatial entities. Even if the narrator cannot see each separate entity, as, for instance, when a thick fog descends "above you, around you—everywhere," he still perceives the perimeter of the forest itself, noting that it "becomes [just] the tall ridge of trees at its border" (3: 358).

The steppe, by contrast, has no such definitive limits or delimited segments—and it receives almost no attention. It is addressed in a solitary paragraph out of the sketch's seven printed pages, and then only in the final line of that paragraph, when it is apostrophized as "the limitless steppe, with no end in sight!" (3: 359). The difference between the steppe and the forest is emphasized by the two adjectives applied to the steppe (*bezgranichnaia* and *neobozrimaia*), since the former literally means "borderless" and the latter "unable-to-be-seen-around." Unlike the forest's visible limits and divisible space, the steppe's expanse cannot be encompassed visually, and therefore cannot be comprehended intellectually or embraced emotionally. Thus nothing more is said of the steppe, despite the title's implicit promise to treat the two natural realms equally. Space that cannot be limited is beyond the pale of Turgenev's narratives.

In addition to the prominence he gives segmented natural space, Turgenev also stresses the segregation of man-made spaces, particularly individual dwellings. Homes that are located in towns or cities are regularly represented as either set apart—the Kalitin house in *A Nest of Gentry*, for example, is situated "on one of the outer streets" of "the town of O"[4] (6: 7)—or separated from its surroundings—the Stakhov house in *On the Eve* sits in the midst of a garden enclosed by a fence. If homes are built on rural estates, they too are described as isolated: the manor houses of Dar'ia Mikhailovna in *Rudin* and of Anna Sergeevna in *Fathers and Sons* stand on hills above other buildings; the Kirsanov residence, Marino, also in *Fathers and Sons*, and Lavretskii's inherited home, Nikolskoe, in *A Nest of Gentry*, are reached only by long drives from other places. Residences referred to in short stories are often noted to be on the periphery of their locales as well.[5]

Not only are these dwellings either positioned on some periphery or circumscribed by some perimeter, but their descriptions often focus on their peripheries or perimeters—doors, thresholds, walls, windows. Turgenev bestows little attention on the appearance of their interiors, in striking contrast to the elaborate care with which he details, for instance, the appearance of human faces. Homes are not seen filled with the objects, or even the many rooms, that would convey the impression of substantive space.[6] More often than not, only forms that divide those interiors within or separate them from exteriors receive notice. The inside of the inn at Kolotovka in "The Singers," for instance, is described with no more detail than the fact of being "divided in two by a partition, beyond which none of the guests has the right to go" (3: 212). Cool and dark, covered with hay, it is a little hut standing "alone, apart from the others," its only distinguishing feature "a single window, like a watchful eye, turned toward the ravine" (3: 208).

And it is typical of Turgenev to observe that peculiar demarcation of space that is the window. Windows appear not only in straightforward descriptions but in the portrayals of moments of deep distress. The title character in "Andrei Kolosov" moves to a window after reporting the death of his closest friend; Liza Kalitina in *A Nest of Gentry* sits by a window when the wife of her beloved Lavretskii comes to call; the self-destructive Susanna in "The Unhappy One" is repeatedly said to be sitting or standing by a window; the suicidal Mar'ia Pavlovna in "A Quiet Place" is last seen through a window. In the Turgenevan universe, windows represent more than spatial partitioning; they symbolize psychological isolation and alienation as well.

While Turgenev's narratives portray the extent of space as limited, they also portray a markedly limited number of spaces. That is, Turgenev's narratives confine themselves to relatively few settings.[7] The short stories, it is true, might not be expected to range over numerous locales, but Turgenev's novels also lack multiple settings. With the exception of a few incidental scenes set in subsidiary locations, almost all of the novels' main events remain chiefly confined to one or two places: *Rudin* takes place mostly on one estate, Dar'ia Mikhailovna's; *A Nest of Gentry* is set primarily at one home, the Kalitins', with a few additional scenes at another, Lavretskii's; *On the Eve* alternates principally between a home and an apartment, the Stakhovs' and Insarov's, in the same town; *Smoke* is fixed in one locale, Baden-Baden; and *Virgin Soil* focuses on one estate, Sipiagin's, and the living quarters of a nearby factory. Only *Fathers and Sons* has more than two main settings, and only one more at that. This narrative mostly takes place on the estates of the Kirsanovs and Anna Sergeevna, along with the village where Bazarov's parents dwell. Granted, past events that have occurred in other, often distant places are also depicted in these novels, but they tend to be related in flashbacks, so that no shift occurs in the primary locale of the narrative. This paucity of physical settings suggests disjunctures in the physical configuration of Turgenev's fictional universe; it is as though unseen barriers disrupt the spatial contiguity of separate sites and preclude easy travel between them. Voyages of any length or duration, if they happen at all, happen offstage; adventures of exploration have no place. Turgenev's protagonists, more often than not, stay put.

The fixed limits of Turgenevan space not only hold protagonists in, as it were, but also keep them out. When characters break through barriers to escape from the place where they have been residing, almost none of them come back. It is as though once the tightly drawn borders of a given space have been transgressed, these borders become ever more impassable, rendering return nearly impossible. Among the novels' chief protagonists, Rudin departs the Lasunskaia estate never to revisit; Liza Kalitina and Elena Stakhova leave forever their childhood homes; Insarov never regains his Bulgarian homeland; Bazarov does go home, but only to die; Nezhdanov never sees Moscow again once he sets forth from it. Likewise, in the shorter narratives, returns are rare: in "The Inn," the innkeeper Akim never visits the region where he had been born and raised; in "The Correspondence," Aleksei Petrovich never shows up again at the home of Mar'ia Aleksandrovna, despite his promise to do so; in "Iakov Pasynkov," the title character is never able to regain Petersburg and the woman he loves once he leaves for service in Siberia; in "The Unhappy One," Susanna's beloved Michel never reappears to elope with her once he has been driven away; in *Spring Torrents*, Sanin never reclaims Gemma for his bride; and so on. Of the few characters who do surmount the obstacles to return—for example, Fedor Lavretskii, Arkadii Kirsanov, and the narrator of "Faust"—most tend to have either significantly aged or changed by virtue of their experiences elsewhere, so that they do not so much return as arrive for the first time as a new persona. Those who return unchanged, such as Varvara Pavlovna in *A Nest of Gentry* and Vladimir Astakhov in "A Quiet Place," do not stay. Turgenevan spaces do not afford a warm welcome to those who have once forsaken their confines.

The limits imposed on space not only restrict movement from place to place, but also restrict the type of movement that can occur within single places. This movement is generally either back-and-forth or circular: the narrator of "Andrei Kolosov" alternates between his quarters and the home of the young woman with whom Kolosov has broken off a relationship; the narrator of "Asya" keeps crossing the Rhine River from his hotel to visit the rented rooms of the title character and her brother; in *A Nest of Gentry*, Lavretskii regularly travels between his estate and Liza Kalitina's home; in *On the Eve*, first Insarov and then Elena are drawn to the other's abode; in *Smoke*, Litvinov cannot stay away from Irina Ratmirova's hotel suite; in *Fathers and Sons*, Arkadii and Bazarov rotate among the three main sites of the novel. Return from distant parts is a rarity; return within a single area is almost an inevitability. Thus the spatial limits that keep Turgenev's protagonists either from going afar or from returning also subject them to repetitive patterns of movement within the spaces they inhabit. Circumscribed by often invisible but nevertheless inviolate boundaries, the spatial confines within Turgenev's narratives install an elemental stability, one that betokens not just the natural order of things but the order envisioned in Turgenev's imagination. For the distinctive delimitation of Turgenevan space illustrates the imposition of creative control over otherwise uncontrolled or uncontrollable expanses.

Turgenev's imagined order of spatial limits accomplishes much more than the establishment of existential stability. Turgenev employs those limits, with varying degrees of intensity, as one means of testing the moral fiber of a number of his protagonists. Their response to spatial constraints, manifested by their choosing either to remain in or to depart from wherever they find themselves, often constitutes a measure of integrity, for in pursuit of self-preservation, the acceptance or rejection of those constraints can bespeak either moral rectitude or moral turpitude. This determination of moral worth depends on both the source of the constraints and the motives prompting the protagonists' decisions to abide by those constraints or to oppose them. Yet such motives are often obscured and hence ambiguous. Their very ambiguity in turn highlights Turgenev's realization that the line between self-affirming and self-destructive behavior is not only fine, but often hard to draw with any certainty. Thus Turgenev illustrates not only the difficulty of attaining secular salvation, but the difficulty of determining whether or not it has been attained at all.

In a few instances, to be sure, a character's decision to remain within spatial boundaries is unambiguously judged to be good or bad. In *A Nest of Gentry*, Fedor Lavretskii's willingness to reside permanently in his ancestral home, instead of attempting to flee painful reminders of his unfulfilled love for Liza Kalitina by moving to some other part of Russia or even Europe, receives unqualified approval. Lavretskii's choice to stay and invest himself in his family's traditional occupation on the estate, so that he "really learns how to till the soil," gives him, the narrator asserts, "the right to be satisfied with himself and his life" (6: 157). Even greater approval is awarded Turgenev's most physically confined character, the paralyzed young peasant Luker'ia in "Living Relics," one of *A Sportsman's Sketches*. Although offered the opportunity to be taken to a distant hospital for treatment, Luker'ia refuses to go, preferring to continue living in her native village, even though she must lie alone in an out-of-the-way hut, since it is there that she finds self-fulfillment in sensory communion with nature. The narrator's emotional conversion from horror and pity at Luker'ia's plight to admiration and even envy of her equanimity only affirms the moral correctness of her decision not to cross spatial boundaries. Both she and Lavretskii root a strong sense of self in a sense of place, in a feeling of belonging to a particular locale.

By contrast, the decision of Irina Ratmirova in *Smoke* not to depart from Baden-Baden to escape her loveless marriage through a revitalized relationship with her former fiancé, Grigorii Litvinov, is exposed as self-destructiveness in the guise of self-indulgence. Despite her promise to leave, Irina discovers at the last minute that she cannot abandon the all-too-comfortable gilded cage within which she has entrapped herself in quest of social status and financial security. Yet in refusing to go, she also concedes that she thereby condemns herself to demoralizing self-reproach and regret. The similar inability—albeit for sexual rather than social reasons—of Sanin in *Spring Torrents* to break away from the physical presence of Mar'ia Nikolaevna Polozova in order to return to his devoted fiancée in Frankfurt is also re-

vealed as cowardly self-degradation, for which he thoroughly re-
viles himself, yet which he is powerless to oppose. Thus the
moral value assigned to the acceptance of spatial boundaries
varies in relation to the degree of self-protection and self-
enhancement achieved.

The moral value attributed to the defiance of spatial boundaries varies as well. For instance, Sofia's determination in "A
Strange History" to break the bonds that ordinarily tie young
women to home and family, in order to live out her spiritual beliefs by accompanying a religious pilgrim on his wanderings, receives moral sanction even as the narrator professes incomprehension of her motives, because she does so to save rather than
to sacrifice herself. She dies not on her pilgrimage, but shortly
after being forcibly brought back to the confines of her familial
home. Sofia's moral convictions thus combine with her emotional compulsions in leading her to reject the constraints that
characters such as Lavretskii accept. Marianna's eager disregard
in *Virgin Soil* for the spatial curbs that have held her in spiritually stifling dependence on antipathetic relatives also merits
moral esteem, as she escapes to find satisfaction in humble service to the peasants of various villages. Turgenev uses these
characters to show that unchosen constraints can cripple or
even crush the spirit if left inviolate.

Yet moral blame is assigned Fustov in "The Unhappy One,"
when he, believing vicious rumors about Susanna, the young
woman he has promised to marry, suddenly ruptures the spatial
boundaries of his family residence to run off rather than fulfill
his promise. The self-loathing he suffers on returning to learn
that the rumors were false and that Susanna has killed herself
in the meantime only underscores the moral bankruptcy that
Fustov has rationalized as self-protectiveness. Rudin likewise
later excoriates himself for having fled the confines of Dar'ia
Mikhailovna's estate instead of standing firm to fight for her
daughter's hand in marriage. His conception of this departure at
the time as an expression of morally mandated resignation to his
hostess's wishes is thus subsequently disclosed to be self-
deluded self-defeat.

By contrast to such relatively clear-cut cases of right and

wrong, more complex instances of submission to or breach of spatial boundaries remain morally ambiguous. By incorporating such instances, Turgenev exposes some of the subtlest complexities inherent in the search for self-preservation, for he implicitly questions how a "self" is defined, and how "preservation" is best achieved. One such morally unclear response to spatial constraints is presented in the third of *A Sportsman's Sketches*, "My Neighbor Radilov." Toward its conclusion, the narrator and Radilov contemplate the inviolability of spatial and other limits as they discuss whether there exists, in the narrator's words, "a horrible position from which it would be impossible to get away" (3: 56). They finally agree that no such situation can exist; boundaries can always somehow be crossed. "It only requires deciding," Radilov declares. But he then stops himself and asks, "What does 'a horrible position' mean?" He gives no direct answer, but implies it is one that threatens an individual's very survival, so that escape, not submission, would be necessary for self-preservation.

Radilov evidently decides that his own situation—living with various family members in the house where his beloved wife had died—is indeed so horrible as to justify his "getting away," for the narrator learns weeks after the conversation that Radilov had "suddenly disappeared, abandoned his mother, and gone off somewhere with his sister-in-law" (3: 57), never to be heard from again. Radilov irrevocably breaks through the spatial barriers that had held him in place, inert and isolated—but is he justified in doing so? Has he merely tried to escape the pain of losing his wife by self-indulgently eloping with a surrogate, leaving his mother ever on the verge of tears at the mention of his name? Or has he concluded that he is being spiritually crushed by continuing to live with the intolerable vision of his wife's corpse haunting him, so that he must depart or die himself? These questions go unanswered, and so Radilov goes finally unjudged, his motives unfathomed and his moral status unconfirmed. Each reader is left to determine whether Radilov was truly in "a horrible position" or not, and whether he acted to increase or to diminish his well-being.

The moral ambiguities are even greater, hence the moral judgments more difficult, in the stories "A Quiet Place" and "The Unhappy One." In each of these narratives a young woman, like Radilov, permanently transcends the spatial limits within which she had lived. But unlike Radilov, each purchases that transcendence with her life—each commits suicide—without proffering any moral justification for taking such drastic action. Unlike Rudin's de facto suicide on the Paris barricades, which is portrayed as a noble exercise of will, and Nezhdanov's suicide in *Virgin Soil*, which amounts to an admission of his lack of will, the moral implications of these women's self-annihilation remain obscure. In "A Quiet Place," Mar'ia Pavlovna, residing on an isolated estate with obtuse, if well-meaning, relatives, is in love with a man incapable of committing himself to marriage, which would take her away from that estate. As the realization of the impossibility of that future dawns on her, she is said to "be found more and more in her room" (4: 441). She tries to enclose herself within even more confining limits, as though they might protect her from the pain of a loveless, stifled existence. When she cannot find that protection in the confines of her room, she leaves the house one night and throws herself into a nearby pond, crying out before she goes under, "Save me . . . save me..." (4: 445). Thus she may have forsaken her suicidal intentions at the last moment, discovering not release but ultimate confinement in death.

After her body is recovered, the narrator observes that "some sort of wounded perplexity appeared on her pale face" and that her lips seemed "set to utter and to ask something," again as though in the end she had not expected or desired death. Yet he concludes, "Who knows what a dead face expresses in those few moments when for the last time it meets the gaze of the living before forever disappearing and moldering in the grave?" (4: 446). Thus the narrator leaves undetermined whether by her suicide Mar'ia Pavlovna has asserted her independence, liberating her soul from a living death within the walls of what has become her prison, or whether she has impulsively surrendered to an illusion of independence that deprived her of any self or soul whatsoever—forever. Turgenev here blurs the distinction between a legitimate if desperate act of spiritual self-assertion (albeit physical death) and a pathetically misguided act of self-destruction.

The assessment of Susanna's suicide in "The Unhappy One" is, if anything, more difficult that that of Mar'ia Pavlovna, for Susanna is bound much more cruelly and involuntarily within her milieu, bound within a circle of not only insensitive but sadistic relations, who take pleasure in her pain. Susanna's desire to free herself of the spatial strictures around her is made more manifest than Mar'ia Pavlovna's: Susanna voices blatant hostility to her confinement, whereas Mar'ia Pavlovna exhibits only depression, and Susanna actually plans several escapes, all of which come to naught. Thus Susanna's suicide is more overtly an act of defiance and rebellion than Mar'ia Pavlovna's—and yet its moral implications are no more clear. It remains equally ambiguous whether Susanna's decision to cast off her restraints for all eternity is a heroic act of self-assertion or a spiteful act of self-abnegation.

The narrator of the tale suggests Susanna's possible motives in pairs of opposites as well: "Who can say what killed her: humiliation or egotism, despair at an inescapable position or, finally, the very memory of that first, handsome, noble being to whom she so joyfully gave herself over in the morning of her days?" (8: 137). A self-affirming refusal to be humiliated further would be moral; a self-annihilating indulgence in egotistical willfulness would not. An idealistic faith in transcendent love would render her suicide an emblem of victory over all limits; a hopeless despair would render it a symbol of defeat by those limits. Yet even if a victory, it is purchased at too high a price for the narrator to exult in, because Susanna's suicide embodies a tragic paradox: the ultimate rejection of spatial constraints is also the ultimate confirmation of their indestructibility.

A final instance of a character manifesting questionable moral standards in reaction to spatial constraints is especially noteworthy, since it is commonly viewed as having little moral ambiguity at all. This is the decision of Liza Kalitina in *A Nest of Gentry* to enter a convent—that is, to immure herself forever within the most severe spatial limits she can find. Liza is traditionally deemed one of Turgenev's virtuously self-sacrificing heroines, giving her life over to a purpose higher than the pursuit of personal happiness.[8] Yet her self-confinement may not be so morally unassailable as this. Liza first appears in the novel standing "on the threshold" (6: 14) of her living room. Liza is thus introduced as one of Turgenev's few characters poised between two spatial enclosures; she can either go forward or back.[9] To go forward into the living room is to enter the space of adulthood and society, with the demands and difficulties of interaction with fallible fellow mortals. To go back is to retreat to her childhood bedroom, where she can give herself over to thought and prayer; the room is even said to resemble a convent cell (6: 150). When she learns that her much-desired marriage to Lavretskii is impossible, Liza immediately retreats to that room, where she decides to enter a convent, to place herself in an actual cell, for the rest of her life.

The decision to devote herself to a life of divine worship might well be expected to secure self-fulfillment that is wholly morally justified—it is earlier said of her that "she loved God alone ecstatically, shyly, tenderly" (6: 113). Yet when Lavretskii visits her convent years later, by which time the ecstasy of devotion should have obliterated any memory of an ephemeral human love, nonetheless "the eyelashes of the eye turned toward him trembled slightly . . . she bowed her emaciated face still lower—and the fingers of her clasped hands, intertwined with a rosary, grasped one another still more tightly" (6: 158). These signs of emotional disturbance, however restrained, suggest her undying attachment to Lavretskii, and render her religious commitment morally ambiguous at best, if not truly suspect. Perhaps her withdrawal into the confining enclosures of the convent represents not self-fulfillment but self-deprivation and self-diminution, betokening moral weakness rather than strength. Perhaps in becoming a nun Liza self-defeatingly attempts to mask the anguish of disappointed love for a man—an ethically questionable act—rather than self-confidently affirm her love of God—an ethically unquestionable act.

Hence to exalt Liza's self-immurement as unequivocally heroic is potentially to misinterpret her moral character. It is also possibly to misperceive Turgenev as explicitly endorsing self-sacrifice, when he may in fact be challenging the conventional morality that deems it unreservedly noble; no diminution of selfhood can be adjudged automatically acceptable in the Turgenevan fictional universe, where selfhood is so hard to win or retain. And it is quite probably to miss the moral questions Turgenev raises by means of spatial configurations, even if the answers to those questions must remain ultimately inconclusive.

In quest of self-preservation, therefore, transgression does not always mean sin, for the transgression of spatial boundaries that contravene self-protection may be an act of moral fortitude, just as failure to transgress those boundaries may betray moral weakness. At the same time, to live within spatial boundaries that serve self-enhancement may be to display well-developed moral sensibilities, just as to cross those boundaries may signify moral malaise. In his differing evaluations of similar responses to the confinements of space, then, Turgenev complicates without compromising his ethical vision, showing it to encompass subtleties of motivation and interpretation that exclude easy adherence or understanding.

The limits Turgenev places on representations of time are even more palpable than those he places on space. To be sure, like all narratives, Turgenev's induce in the reader an awareness of linear temporal progression. Nonetheless, they also subvert, violate, or disengage that awareness by employing what Joseph Frank has labeled "spatial forms," that is, narrative devices that impart an atemporal or antitemporal stasis to fictional works.[10] Turgenev regularly engages his versions of these forms to retard or repel, if not wholly to prevent, the feeling of forward temporal progression. He does so both structurally and thematically, combining narrative patterns of brevity and circularity with images of metaphysical time as similarly abbreviated and cyclical. Thus Turgenev's temporality is marked by a limiting nonlinearity.

Turgenev's most obvious device for restraining the feel of temporal progression in his narratives is to make them relatively short. Many of his stories occupy fewer than twenty pages—on the short side of short stories, and it is noteworthy that Turgenev closed out his literary career with works in the one prose genre still shorter than the short story: the prose poem. Even his novels are short—*Fathers and Sons*, for instance, fills only 180 pages. The very longest of his novels, *Virgin Soil*, runs to fewer than 250 printed pages, appearing distinctly emaciated in comparison to the length of his renowned contemporaries' creations: the more than 500 pages of many of Trollope's works, the 600-plus pages of Balzac's *Lost Illusions* and Eliot's *Middlemarch*, the over 800 pages of Dostoevsky's *The Brothers Karamazov*, and the 1,100 pages of Tolstoy's *War and Peace*. The modest size of Turgenev's novels virtually manufactures temporal delimitation.

That delimitation is readily borne out in several ways. Rather than depicting the evolution of a character over the course of years from youth to adulthood, as in, say, Dickens's *Great Expectations*, or describing a panoramic sequence of events over an expanse of time, as in *Sentimental Education*, *Vanity Fair*, and *War and Peace*, Turgenev's novels treat periods of only weeks or months. Although flashbacks covering the past and epilogues addressing the future are included, the main events of these works are, by novelistic standards, played out over only brief time spans: *Rudin* covers primarily the few weeks of the title character's visit to Dar'ia Mikhailovna's estate; *A Nest of Gentry* treats mostly the few months after Lavretskii's return to Russia from abroad; *On the Eve* portrays essentially the six weeks in which Elena and Insarov's relationship develops; *Fathers and Sons* depicts the period of less than one year after Arkadii and Bazarov return from the university; *Smoke* records the matter of days in which Litvinov becomes reinvolved with his former fiancée; and *Virgin Soil* encompasses little more than the summer that Nezhdanov turns tutor and then revolutionary. Thus does Turgenev sharply curtail time's flow in his novels.

He employs similar tactics in his short stories. Here, he not only keeps the temporal range to a minimum but often places a narrative frame around the story to further circumscribe the reader's sense of temporal advance. A narrative frame, which establishes its own time apart from that of the tale told within, thus confines the time of the tale to that of its telling. The usually brief temporal span portrayed in the framed narrative is therefore placed under further restraint, even to the point, in some instances, where the frame nearly annuls the impression of the passage of time altogether. In the short story "The Dog," for example, the question voiced at its beginning—"But if you accept the possibility of the supernatural, the possibility of its interference in real life, then permit me to ask what role must healthy rationality play after that?" (7: 232)—is repeated almost word for word at its end (7: 246). This repetition renders parenthetical the tale told between the opening and closing utterances, making it seem as though little or no time has elapsed between the two. The encircled depiction of logically inexplicable phenomena is thereby suspended, as it were, removed from the temporal as well as rational course of reality. In this way Turgenev employs structural circularity to convey a psychology and a metaphysics of atemporality.

Turgenev reinforces the antitemporal and atemporal features of his narratives through the construction of their plots, which often might be better termed "antiplots,"[11] for many of Turgenev's narratives have at their core what does *not* happen, rather than what does. Commitments not kept, relationships not continued, loves never consummated, marriages not celebrated, lives unfulfilled—this is the stuff of which much of Turgenev's work is made. The result is not, however, a lack of dramatic complexity or depth; far from it. The portrayal of how and why things do not occur is often more intricate and intriguing than the portrayal of how and why things do occur. But the images of time conveyed as a result of this kind of plot construction are different.[12] The representation of completed events gives an impression of chronological progress; the representation of incomplete or nonoccurring events imparts a sense of chronological stasis.

Events do occur in these narratives, to be sure, but many of them follow the same course over time, based on the temporal pattern Turgenev describes as infinitely repeated in nature: cyclical alternations of growth and decay. As embodied in Turgenev's fictional world, time in nature is not linear but circular. Natural time revolves through a sequence of birth, maturation, deterioration, and death that recurs endlessly and ineluctably, without deviation and without lasting change. Decline will supplant growth, diminution will replace crescendo, death will succeed birth—and then new growth will follow decline, another crescendo will displace diminution, subsequent birth will supersede death. No condition will persist, yet no condition will disappear forever. Hence not forward progress but "eternal return," to use Nietzsche's classic phrase, characterizes temporal movement in Turgenevan nature.

The cyclicity of time in nature is emphasized in "Death," one of *A Sportsman's Sketches*, where a series of human death scenes is depicted and commented on. The first death described, though, is that of a nonhuman—a forest. The narrator prefaces this description by recalling his childhood memories of this forest, composed primarily of oak and ash trees, whose "stately powerful trunks stood in dark splendor against the translucently golden verdure of the hazel and rowan trees," in which vegetation and wildlife flourished, providing such lush shade that even "in the worst heat, at midday—it was as good as night: the quiet, the fragrance, the freshness..." (3: 197). But juxtaposed to this luxuriant and vibrant natural habitat of the past is a portrait of the same locale at present, in starkly contrasting terms. Now some trees, "as if in reproach and despair, raised their lifeless, broken boughs upwards," while others, lacking their usual surfeit of leaves, "brandished fat, dry, dead twigs," and still others "had completely collapsed, and lay decomposing, like corpses, on the ground" (3: 198). The once-vital forest is moribund.

"Who could have foreseen it?," the narrator then asks rhetorically, but nature's cyclical temporality makes the forest's demise inevitable. Where there is life there will be death. At any given moment, every living being occupies some point in the single tracing of the natural cycle it will make. Yet the limiting of each being to a single cycle ensures the opportunity for each being to live through the same cycle, for, as the narrator notes, new foliage is slowly appearing amidst the lifeless timber—the old trees may be dead or dying, but there has also arisen "a young grove, which 'has replaced them, not having reproduced them'" (3: 197–98). The narrator's quotation from Pushkin adroitly summarizes the equipoise imposed on all life forms: each will be replaced, in the sense that new forms will always substitute for old; none will be reproduced, in the sense that old forms will never be renewed.

On the whole, Turgenev's protagonists react more consistently—and more hostilely—to temporal than to spatial limits. Although those who prize spatial constraint might be expected to envision and embrace, both emotionally and ethically, a conception of time as a cycle, not many do. One of the few who does is Andrei Kolosov. He invokes a metaphor, the blooming and withering of apple blossoms over the changing seasons, to describe the evolution of his love for a young woman, Varia, to whom he is no longer attracted: "I remember that in May I sat with her on this little bench... The apple tree was in bloom, from time to time its fresh white little flowers drifted down on us, I held both Varia's hands... We were happy then... Now the apple tree has faded, and the apples on it are bitter" (4: 24). Time's circuit has naturally yet relentlessly brought an end to their relationship, and the narrator lauds Kolosov for comprehending and acceding to this end.[13]

In contrast to Kolosov, most of Turgenev's protagonists find the cycle of life and death, the natural limit imposed on life by time, too demoralizing, too debilitating to embrace. So they deny it. Indeed, damned by the awareness of impending death, they may only be saved by its denial. This denial often takes the form of a conception of time that is both nonlinear and noncyclical. Seeking to inhabit a permanent status quo, the characters create for themselves a temporality of isolated points, "fixed in no time," as one writer puts it. Such an image of time serves to screen the psyche from the prospect, at once terrifying and depressing, of its own inevitable demise.

The reaction of the narrator of "Death" to the desolation he encounters is therefore emblematic. His interrogative response to the forest's devastation, "Who could have foreseen it?," contains no inkling of any recognition, much less acceptance, of the fact that the course of time makes such desolation a certainty—death must come to all living things. Had the narrator been a child, to be sure, this question would betray mere ignorance of time's consequences. But coming from an adult, it suggests an unconscious resistance to them. He has denied to himself the possibility of change in order to deny the passage of time. And he has denied the passage of time in order to deny death.

The narrator of *On the Eve* actually describes such denial as it breaks down, observing, "It happens that a person, on waking up, asks with involuntary fear: Is it possible that I am already thirty... forty... fifty years old? How is it that life has passed so quickly? How is it that death has moved so close?" (6: 299). The sleep from which this person "wakes up," then, is more than a night's rest. It is the sleep that endures as long as time's passing can be concealed from conscious perception. It is the sleep that the narrator of "A Journey to the Forest" desperately seeks when, consumed by self-loathing for the failures of his past and the emptiness of his future, he refuses to answer outright the appalling question he poses to himself: "It is not possible that there is no hope, no return, is it?" Giving himself the commands "Do not look back, do not remember!," he rather allows all his "recent thoughts and regrets to sink into a single sensation of dreaminess and exhaustion, into a single desire to be put back as quickly as possible under the roof of a warm house, to drink tea with thick cream, to be wrapped up in the soft, light hay and to sleep, sleep, sleep..." (5: 140).

This yearning for sleep issues from an ethically justifiable impulse to escape the consciousness of time that brings with it only agonizing regret and hopelessness. The torment begotten by that bleak consciousness can only impair the self's ability to defend against the destructive forces of despair that make efforts at self-preservation seem futile. In contradistinction to the conventional literary psychology according to which, as Hans Mayerhof declares, "awareness of continuity within the self is correlative with the aspect of continuity or duration in time,"[14] in Turgenev's fictional universe, this awareness is often achieved only by denying the continuity of time. Whereas for most individuals memories of the past and expectations for the future may unite to create an impression of a consistent, unbroken identity, for many of Turgenev's characters forgetting the past is more beneficial than remembering it, and resisting the future is more rewarding than anticipating it. For them, memory and anticipation only provide reminders of the progression of time that spells their own annihilation.[15]

Yet if consciousness of time cannot be eluded, some of Turgenev's characters find that a thoroughgoing psychic investment in and moral commitment to the present moment offers an alternative hope of sustaining psychological integration and moral integrity. This sort of investment is advocated, for instance, by the narrator of "Asya." Having repeatedly told himself that he would be happy not today but "tomorrow," he ultimately concludes that he had been deceiving himself, for "happiness has no tomorrow; it has no yesterday; it does not remember the past, it does not think about the future; it has the present—and then not a day, but a moment" (5: 191–92). The elation of well-being prevails in an instant, the narrator insists, which the individual must seize upon and enjoy to the full.[16]

Indeed, the failure of some characters to extract all possible satisfaction from a present instant, in misguided expectation of future gratification, makes them morally culpable. For example, both the narrator of "Andrei Kolosov" and Sanin, in *Spring Torrents*, not only deprive themselves of potentially highly gratifying marriages but deeply wound the women they have committed themselves to when they self-deceptively convince themselves that they will meet their commitments to those women "tomorrow." The former comments on the temporal temptation to which he succumbed in finding excuses not to visit his fiancée: "The word 'tomorrow' was invented for indecisive people and for children; I, like a child, pacified myself with this magical word. 'Tomorrow I will go to her without fail,' I told myself— and ate and slept excellently today" (4: 32). Likewise, Sanin assures himself that he can escape the allure of a seductive married woman by telling himself that "tomorrow all this will disappear without a trace" (8: 358) and that "tomorrow all this will be over forever" and that he will "forever part with this capricious lady—and forget all this nonsense!" (8: 370). The magic of "tomorrow" is black magic, though. The false promise of endless temporal potential enables these protagonists to rationalize the psychological and moral damage they do to themselves and others.

But if a faint-hearted denial of the present in the name of an illusory future is reprehensible in some, so is the opposite extreme in others, the refusal to envision any future at all. One of the correspondents in the epistolary tale "The Correspondence," Aleksei Petrovich, commits this folly, as he confesses in his final letter to his lonely counterpart, Mar'ia Alexandrovna. He writes to explain why he had reneged on a promise to visit her several years earlier: he had fallen hopelessly and unrequitedly in love with a married ballerina and had followed her around Europe for years. He accounts for his past failure by conceding his blindness to the future: "I did not expect that I would have to play such a role. I did not expect that I would hang about at rehearsals. . . . I did not expect that I would carry the shawl of a dancer. . . . I did not expect that I would receive, finally, in one small German village the ingenious sobriquet: Kunst-Barbar" (5: 47). If Aleksei Petrovich had had any truly positive expectations, he never expresses them. Instead, his repetition of the phrase "I did not expect" reflects a mind entrapped in seemingly self-protective but ultimately self-destructive ignorance caused by its own unwillingness to look ahead, to consider the possible future outcome of present behavior. Thus although Aleksei Petrovich merits sympathy for the suffering and remorse he has endured, his failure to contemplate the future leaves him morally at fault.

The passage of time must therefore be acknowledged in some cases and resisted in others, depending on which mental act abets self-preservation. Yet moral ambiguity often prevails in the choices characters make regarding temporal limits, much as it does regarding spatial limits. For example, revision of the past constitutes another expression of the impulse to escape time, but it carries indefinite ethical implications. In *Spring Torrents*, when Sanin acknowledges the unexpectedly overwhelming fullness of his love for an Italian girl, Gemma, whom he has only recently met, the narrator recounts Sanin's reaction to this unprecedented feeling: "One thing surprised him above all: how could he have been different yesterday than he was today? It seemed to him that he had 'always' loved Gemma—and had loved her precisely as much as he loved her today" (8: 317). Sanin revises his own emotional history in order to deny that he has changed and is "different," so that he can enjoy the sense of a coherent, continuous identity and simply assimilate his love into that identity; otherwise he would have to envision and construct a new self entirely. It remains unclear at this juncture, though, whether this inclination to revise his past arises out of mere mental laziness or justifiable self-protectiveness. Hence by allowing a certain ambiguity to color Sanin's sense of time, Turgenev can subtly question Sanin's strength of character as well. Thus temporal sensibilities often serve as delicate moral barometers in the Turgenevan atmosphere.

Nowhere does Turgenev portray the psychological and moral struggles and ambiguities created by the consciousness of time more vividly or movingly than in his most famous novel, *Fathers and Sons*. To be sure, this narrative has often been discussed in terms of temporality—that is, the work is considered timely in its representation of the emergence of a new generation of intellectual rebels in mid-nineteenth-century Russia, or timeless in its depiction of the eternal conflict between different generations. Although both interpretations have validity, neither takes into account the extent to which these themes are overshadowed by the fact that *Fathers and Sons* is very much a novel about time itself. References to time begin and end *Fathers and Sons*; the nature of time is a subject of discussion within the narrative; the central protagonists define their identities in connection with different temporal phases; recurrent changes of tense provide reminders of temporal relativity. Time provides not merely a backdrop but a central focus of this masterpiece.

The inception of the novel marks a precise moment in time, a date: "May 20, 1859" (7: 7), thereby suggesting that the events to be narrated are circumscribed by measurable historical time. But the final words of the text, "eternal reconciliation and life everlasting" (7: 188), convey the opposite message; they take the novel beyond the confines of time itself. Turgenev thus frames his narrative with diametrically opposed conceptions of time, one concrete and limited, the other highly abstract and limitless. This dialectical frame makes possible the inclusion of an entire range of temporal visions within it—and just such a range appears, even as that range too is segmented and confined.

Several narrative digressions in the novel openly address variations in individual perceptions of time. For instance, after describing how "frighteningly quickly" ten years had passed for Pavel Petrovich after an ill-fated love affair, the narrator then remarks, "In no other country does time fly as fast as in Russia; in prison, they say, it flies faster still" (7: 32). This assertion (adumbrating the sanitorium atmosphere of Thomas Mann's *The Magic Mountain*, where time is said to pass most quickly for those who are intellectually and emotionally disengaged from their surroundings, and to slow down for those psychologically engaged with theirs) stresses the subjectivity and relativity of temporal awareness. A second assertion expands on the subject: "Time (it is a well-known fact) sometimes flies like a bird, sometimes crawls like a worm; but it is especially good when a person does not even notice whether it is passing quickly or quietly" (7: 85). Here the narrator unequivocally attributes moral worth to ignorance of time's passage, since such ignorance constitutes a psychic escape from the press of time's chronological progression. Yet whether individuals can truly control their awareness of time and benefit morally as a result remains a subject unaddressed by the narrator.

This question is explored instead through the characterizations of the three main protagonists, Pavel Petrovich, Anna Sergeevna, and Bazarov, for each makes an effort to avoid acknowledging the chronological progression of time, and each finds a moral justification for doing so. Moreover, each does so in the same way, by psychologically entrenching a sense of self in a single temporal stage: one in the past, one in the present, and one in the future. Pavel Petrovich identifies himself wholly with the past. Prizing the values of honor, valor, and civility that he associates with the upper classes of society as organized by earlier generations, he affects the dress, manners, and views of a bygone era. The present and future hold no charms for him; it is with the past that he associates the particular psychological satisfaction of love, albeit unrequited love, and the general exaltation of aristocratic traditions. Hence he does not try to find grounds on which to communicate with the disrespectful and dismissive nihilist Bazarov, who has no use for the past, even after Bazarov's decency during a duel they fight earns Pavel Petrovich's grudging respect. But so invested is Pavel Petrovich in his conviction of the superiority of the past, and so ingrained is his psychic affiliation with past time alone, that he cannot extend himself to someone who does not share that conviction or affiliation. He remains at once defined and isolated by his fixed adherence to the past.

Anna Sergeevna, by contrast, adheres to the present. She evinces no sentimental attachment to the past, when she had to struggle to provide a secure home for herself and her younger sister after their parents' deaths. Having married a wealthy man who left her his estate and fortune upon his demise, Anna Sergeevna is wholly dedicated to the preservation of the status quo. She has no intention of tolerating any divergence from the course of life she currently conducts. Indeed, the prospect of an affair with Bazarov, who for her embodies all that is unknown and unstable ahead, although mildly tempting, mostly fills Anna Sergeevna with horror. She has struggled too hard to mold her immediate circumstances to suit her sense of responsibility to her sister and to satisfy her own need for psychic stability. Despite the relative solitude of her existence, she cannot and will not risk her own present well-being and that of her dependent sister by giving herself over to future uncertainty and upheaval, even if other gratifications come as well.

Finally, Bazarov gives his moral allegiance and psychological energy to the future. As a nihilist, he considers the past filled with outmoded and unconstructive conventions which must be abandoned, and as an idealist—which nihilists so often are—he regards the present as nothing but a workshop in which to labor toward future achievements. This investment in the future makes relationships in the present difficult for Bazarov, since emotional intimacy entails a diversion of strength that could otherwise be devoted to the scientific research that will provide knowledge for the welfare of generations to come. Thus his friendship with Arkadii breaks down, and his romantic desire for Anna Sergeevna is never fulfilled. Only on his deathbed does Bazarov concede having been psychologically and morally misguided; his rigid subscription to his ideas and his fixation on their future realization have deprived him of the satisfactions he might have found in the present.

These three characters are all tragic, therefore, in that none can partake of any intimate relationship with an individual psychically rooted in a phase of time other than the one with which their identity is entwined. And they have ethically valid reasons for this. The cause of self-preservation requires them to resist the incursions into their carefully constructed psychic integrity that such intimacy would inevitably permit: both Pavel Petrovich and Anna Sergeevna are sincerely threatened by Bazarov's obsessive orientation toward the future; Bazarov is rightly ambivalent about Anna Sergeevna's conservative bonds to her present life, and is understandably dismissive of Pavel Petrovich's idealized past. Yet they all pay a high price for their allegiance to their private cause. For they become frozen in time, psychologically removed from the warmth of close human contact, as the novel's complex conclusion demonstrates.

That conclusion shifts to a kind of perpetual present tense, allegedly to satisfy the reader's curiosity about what each character "is doing now, right now" (7: 185). Its effect, though, is to lock Pavel Petrovich into an eternal past, Anna Sergeevna into an eternal present, and Bazarov into an eternal future. Pavel Petrovich returns to the Europe where he had once found happiness: "In Dresden . . . between two and four, at the most fashionable time for strolling, you can meet a man of about fifty, already completely grey and possibly suffering from gout, but still handsome, elegantly dressed, and with that special air which is given only to a person who has spent a long time amidst the highest strata of society. This is Pavel Petrovich" (7: 186). He finally establishes himself in an environment where he can live out the traditional forms of the aristocratic life he so treasures. Nonetheless, tied to a mode of existence characteristic of the past, Pavel Petrovich finds life "hard" (7: 187). He is respected, but not loved by his acquaintances, and he is forced to seek consolation from further past, in the ancient forms of religion: he is often observed to "fall into thought and remain motionless for a long time, bitterly clenching his teeth, then he suddenly recollects himself and begins almost imperceptibly to cross himself."

Anna Sergeevna, the reader is informed, was married "not long ago, not out of love but out of conviction" to "a man still young, good, and cold as ice" (7: 185). Her "conviction," that she requires a husband who will continue to provide the security she insists on, weds her to a loveless marriage of convenience and an endlessly tranquil but probably unfulfilling existence. And Bazarov is consigned to the infinite future of life after death, as suggested by the flowers growing on his grave, which, the narrator concludes, "speak of eternal reconciliation and life everlasting" (7: 188). Thus Bazarov, confined forever to solitary silence, is committed in death as he was in life to the hope of satisfactions of the world to come.

Turgenev brilliantly uses these characters' psychological connections to time in *Fathers and Sons* as a means of illuminating the costly sacrifices that may be required by subscription to his moral program. Pavel Petrovich, Anna Sergeevna, and Bazarov, however forceful their personalities, are sufficiently psychologically fragile to require the support provided by identification with a single temporal phase. Thus they must forgo pleasures that stronger selves can enjoy. The less prominent character Nikolai Kirsanov, for instance, has the constant strength of personality to create for himself an enduring familial circle that surrounds yet does not confine him. He can compose an identity and a way of life that unites past, present, and future. The others, by contrast, do not dare extend their psyches that far, lest they break under the strain.

Throughout his works, then, and in no work more fully and effectively than in *Fathers and Sons*, Turgenev demonstrates the range of moral ends—from those that preserve the self to those that destroy it—to which spatial and temporal limitations lead. In so doing, his treatment of space and time as confined and confining arguably distinguishes his poetics from Realist poetics more thoroughly than any other aspect of his art, for on the whole, Realist poetics portray space as geographically connected and time as chronologically progressive.[17] Adult protagonists travel at will, inspired by faith in the possibility of improving their lives: for instance, Julien Sorel and Eugene Rastignac venture forth from small villages in France to explore their future prospects; Pierre Bezukhov journeys about Russia in order to find existential meaning; even Maggie Tulliver leaves St. Oggs unhindered to seek a satisfactory life farther abroad. Whatever obstacles they may face, at least they suffer no spatial or temporal barriers to success. And Realist ethics would not have them do so, because voyages through space and time reinforce the idea of an elemental coherence in human existence that makes communal affiliation both possible and desirable. Hence the portrayal of spatial contiguity and temporal continuity well suit narratives in the ethical and aesthetic tradition of Realism.

By contrast, the constraints Turgenev imposes on the representation of space and time are more appropriate to Apollonian art, particularly since the exemplary Apollonian art form is sculpture. The very solidity and immobility of sculpture embody a sense of spatial and temporal delimitation, so unlike the exemplary Dionysian art form, music, which exists solely in time and travels freely through space. Indeed, sculpture conveys the impression of space encapsulated and time arrested, of forward progress thwarted—and Turgenev's narratives so often do likewise. But unlike sculpture, whose borders are clearly visible, Turgenev insinuates often unseen and unarticulated but inescapable boundaries of space and time throughout his works. And it is within these boundaries, sometimes even because of them, that Turgenev envisions the solitary struggle for self-preservation being lost or won.

4

Ambiguous Blessings:
A Language of Litotes

In Turgenev's fiction, silence speaks volumes. Frequent telling moments of silence punctuate virtually every serious conversation and reign over many decisive turns of events. Revelations, betrayals, seductions, even suicides take place in Turgenev's fictional world not noticeably and noisily, but wordlessly, soundlessly.

Silence, or a reference to silence, marks the conclusion of every one of Turgenev's novels: in *Rudin* the title character is silenced in mid-shout by a bullet on the barricades in France; the thoughts and feelings of the protagonists at the end of *A Nest of Gentry* belong, as the narrator puts it, to the moments in life at which "it is possible only to point—and to pass by" (6: 158); in *On the Eve* the heroine disappears, never to be heard from again, and a question posed to a minor character in the final line receives no answer, as he "played with his fingers and directed his quizzical glance into the distance" (6: 300); the deceased Bazarov is consigned in *Fathers and Sons* to a grave on which the flowers speak silently, "with their innocent eyes," about "eternal reconciliation and life everlasting" (7: 188); and in *Virgin Soil* Mashurina refuses to answer a series of concluding questions and departs without a word (9: 389).

Silences also obtain at crucial junctures in Turgenev's shorter narratives. In *First Love*, for example, while unwittingly standing outside the bedroom where his father is consummating an illicit affair, the narrator reports that "nowhere was heard the slightest sound" (6: 350). Bouts of silence mark significant con-

versations between Mar'ia Pavlovna and the man she loves, Ve-
retev, in "A Quiet Place"; between Pavel Aleksandrovich and the
woman he loves, Vera Nikolaevna, in "Faust"; between the narrator and the enigmatic Lieutenant Teglev in "Knock... Knock...
Knock!"; and so on. Indeed, the last words of the short story
"Enough" are truly emblematic of this feature of Turgenev's
works: quoting without attribution (but in English) the famous
dying utterance of Hamlet, the narrator asserts that "the rest is
silence" (7: 231).

Silence does assuredly speak volumes in Turgenev's prose fiction—but what exactly does it say? To answer this question is
to note first what silence does *not* say, or signify. Silence in Turgenev does not signify the absence of movement, activity, or
event. To the contrary, many decisions are made, many departures are taken, many deaths occur, signaled by silence. Turgenev's silences are therefore not so much the silences of situations, they are the silences of persons, that is, the absence of
speech. Availing himself of a distinction in Russian that English
speakers seldom make, Turgenev usually conveys silence with
the Russian word *molchanie*, which literally means speechless-
ness, rather than with the word *tishina*, which means general
noiselessness. Ideas, emotions, and actions abound in Turgenev's silence—they are just not given voice.

And more often than not, the silence Turgenev portrays is one
of choice, not necessity. Indeed, some protagonists actively embrace silence as proof of their nobility of character. In "Iakov Pasynkov," for instance, a young woman who has suffered for years
in an unhappy marriage firmly announces that "in our family
we know how to be silent and endure" (5: 84). For her, silence is
both a source and a symbol of pride, a manifestation of her refusal to indulge the self-pitying desire to articulate her misery.
Likewise, Susanna, in "The Unhappy One," does not put into
words the futile fury and wrenching despair she undoubtedly
feels when the man she had hoped would rescue her is driven
away by her hated guardian. Rather, she deliberately shrouds her
feelings in willful wordlessness: despite repeated pleadings by
the narrator to unburden herself and confide in him, she steadfastly "stayed silent" (8: 89), as her mother had once advised her

to do at all costs. Another, less beleaguered young woman, in "Faust," displays the same confidence in the virtues of wordlessness, declaring simply, "I can do only one thing . . . be silent up to the last moment" (5: 125). Numerous other characters who tend to be quite sparing of speech, such as Egor in *A Sportsman's Sketches*, Andrei Kolosov, Iakov Pasynkov himself, Masha in "A Quiet Place," and Dmitrii Insarov in *On the Eve*, are praised and prized for their reticence.

Hence Turgenev weaves a pattern of opposition between silence and speech that could be said to form a commentary on the nature of language itself. Whatever else Turgenev's silences may be construed to say, they must say something about language. And the likely message about language these silences would seem to convey is that it is too limited or too artificial to entrust with the essence of human experience. As George Steiner argues, writers since the seventeenth century have increasingly reached that very conclusion, for they have discovered that "language can only deal meaningfully with a special, restricted segment of reality. The rest, and it is presumably the much larger part, is silence."[1] Steiner adduces Ionesco as an exemplar of this dismissive conception of language, for in his *Journal* Ionesco avers, "There are no words for the deepest experience. . . . Of course, not everything is unsayable in words, only the living truth."[2] Recourse to silence would thus betoken recognition of the utter inadequacy of language to capture and convey that "living truth."

Evidence supporting such an interpretation of Turgenev's silences can in fact be found in several of the narratives. In *On the Eve*, for example, language is said to be unable to capture the depths of the love between the protagonists Elena Stakhova and Dmitrii Insarov. At the moment when they reveal their mutual attraction for the first time, the narrator reports that although Insarov "was silent," nonetheless "Elena could understand that she was loved," and therefore "she had no need of words" (6: 236). In their sudden spiritual communion, these characters find verbal communication superfluous. And when Elena tries later to write a letter elaborating on her love to Insarov, she discovers that "the words came out on paper either dead or false" (6: 243).

For her, words are too artificial and arbitrary to communicate truths of the heart.

Other characters also find fault with language, not for its mere inadequacy in the transmission of truth but for its dangerous distortion or disregard of truth. Lavretskii in *A Nest of Gentry*, for one, breathes a heartfelt "Thank God!" when his newfound love, Liza, unintentionally contrasts herself to Lavretskii's glibly articulate and manipulative wife by confessing, "I have no words of my own" (6: 83). So embittered is he by his wife's easy twisting of words to attain her own self-serving ends that Lavretskii has come to mistrust language itself. The same sentiment appears in the epistolary tale "The Correspondence." There, one of its letter writers, Mar'ia Alexandrovna, complains that when a young woman is attracted to a man "every word of his pierces her spirit: she still does not know how insignificant and empty and false a word can be, how little it costs the one who utters it, and how little it deserves belief!" (5: 30). "Insignificant and empty and false"—should these words be taken as Turgenev's summary condemnation of all of language and as sufficient explanation of Turgenev's silences?

Turgenev's first novel, *Rudin*, might seem decisively to affirm this assumption, since the veritable bankruptcy of language in representing actuality constitutes a main theme of this text. Seeds of doubt about the validity of words are planted early on, when a peripheral character remarks in reference to the local socialite, Dar'ia Mikhailovna Lasunskaia, "I don't believe every word of hers," only to evoke the retort, "She herself hardly believes her own words" (5: 202). An inevitable disparity between words and the reality they purportedly signify is remarked soon thereafter, when Rudin himself is reproached for his rhetorical exaltation of "truth." An irascible new acquaintance scornfully dismisses Rudin's impassioned discourse as rhapsodic nonsense, with the objection that "truth" does not exist in actuality, or, with some refinement, that "such a word exists, but the thing itself does not" (5: 227). Thus, this acquaintance concludes, Rudin merely indulges in the pleasure of admiring his own verbal facility, of speaking for its own sake—no substance informs the speech.

It does appear that Rudin attributes value to experience only as he can attribute value to the word that describes that experience. When, for instance, Dar'ia Mikhailovna's daughter, Natal'ia, tells Rudin that she is very happy living in the country, Rudin responds not by praising the emotion or Natal'ia's fortunate disposition, but by praising the term "happy" itself, telling her, "You are happy... This is a great word" (5: 241). And after Natal'ia evinces an attraction to Rudin, he wants "only a word" (5: 266) as proof of her devotion; he requires no substantive action. Upon her later retraction of this devotion by announcing that, as wonderful as his eloquent words might be, "it is far from word to deed," he is predictably hurt by her "last words" (5: 282). Rudin thus makes his attachment to speech so manifest that he becomes utterly identified with it. Hence when Natal'ia thinks of him, she notes that she can conjure up only an image "not of Rudin himself, but of some word or other spoken by him" (5: 262). And her image is in fact justified by Rudin's constant equation of words with actuality. Actions that confirm or contradict words are of no relevance to Rudin. For him, language has acquired ontological authority.[3]

Unfortunately for Rudin, in this conviction he is revealed to be sadly misguided. Words in this novel are repeatedly shown to be insubstantial at best and deceptive at worst, as suspect as the figure they metonymously come to represent; up to the epilogue he is portrayed as having no more existential significance than the formal shapes of words do. Near the novel's end, even Rudin himself concedes the vacuity of his character and of the words he has mistaken for reality, as he bitterly sums up his existence to have been "words, just words," concluding remorsefully, "There were no deeds!" (5: 319). Rudin's wholly negative assessment of his lifelong investment in words could readily be interpreted as Turgenev's own assessment of language as a collection of empty shells—artificial, conventionalized forms that do not necessarily contain the slightest content.

Yet the novel's final words *about* words are not given to Rudin—and they are not negative. Instead, in striking contrast to the expectations Rudin's portrayal has engendered, the final statement on the subject is given to Rudin's childhood friend

Lezhnev, who, although he has previously criticized Rudin's fac-
ile articulateness, at the end stoutly defends Rudin's devotion
to the expressive use of language, retorting to Rudin's self-
condemnatory claim "There were no deeds!" that "a good word
is also a deed" (5: 319). To another friend, Lezhnev also defends
Rudin in this light, asking, "Who can truly say . . . that his
words have not planted many good seeds in young spirits, to
whom nature has not denied, as it has denied him, the strength
of action, the ability to carry out independent ideas?" (5: 304).
Lezhnev thus faults Rudin's temperament, not Rudin's language, for Rudin's defects, actually giving credit to language
when others have denied it any credit or derided it as destructive, for Lezhnev perceives in words the power to inspire action.
Thus he attributes to them a potentially constructive moral
force.

Lezhnev no more speaks for Turgenev than does any other of
Turgenev's characters. But there are affinities. For notwithstanding the explicit references to language's inadequacy cited
earlier, the actual use to which language is put in his narratives
strongly suggests that Turgenev shares Lezhnev's view, or at
least part of it. To Turgenev, language constitutes a potent inspirational force, albeit a force for evil as well as good. And this
inspirational force works in Turgenev's fiction both to the moral
detriment of individuals and to their moral benefit.

In exploring Turgenev's conception of the moral force of language, this chapter will propound an argument that runs counter to traditional interpretations, which have, for the most part,
emphasized the precision of Turgenev's language. Turgenev's
exquisitely refined, lapidary prose has been taken by most Turgenev scholars to demonstrate his principled commitment, like
that of his friend Flaubert, to le mot juste, the word that will
exactly render the totality of each phenomenon represented.
This exact rendering, such reasoning holds, heightens the reader's awareness of the varieties of human experience, and therefore serves the eminently worthy goal of expanding psychological and moral sensibilities.[4]

Yet careful scrutiny of Turgenev's texts reveals that Turgenev
prized precision only to a point. His descriptions of external ap-

pearances, to be sure, are characterized by expressive exactitude—the variegation and vividness of his depictions of natural
settings are arguably unparalleled. Likewise, his portrayals of
human physiognomy are equally and deservedly renowned for
their meticulous detail. But Turgenev's treatments of human
psychology and morality, particularly his treatments of psychological disturbance and moral distress, evince far less verbal particularity. In fact, those treatments regularly resort to indirect-
ness, to ambiguity, to imprecision—the very obverse of the
qualities with which Turgenev's prose is normally associated.

This seeming contradiction can be reconciled, though, by further consideration of Turgenev's belief in the power of language.
His cultivation of linguistic imprecision—which, as we have
seen, stretches into silence, if needs be—makes sense if he conceived of linguistic precision as possibly dangerous, potentially
psychically and morally damaging. Turgenev suggests that the
ability to transmit distinct details of human suffering empowers
language to do great harm, because it forces immediate confrontations with drastic definitude, when such definitude is better
encountered gradually and indirectly. Only thus can the mind
intellectually conceive and emotionally manage otherwise un-
manageable material, which precise language can make all
too graphically—and hence overwhelmingly—explicit. Without such management, self-protection is jeopardized and the
prospect of self-preservation dims.

In recognition of these dangers, then, Turgenev periodically,
and even predictably, turns to a language of imprecision and ambiguity. In opting for ambiguity, which William Empson defines
as "any verbal nuance, however slight, which gives room for alternative reactions to the same piece of language,"[5] Turgenev
finds an effective weapon in the battle to rescue individuals from
self-destructive directness. He repeatedly demonstrates that
even as ambiguity opens up multiple possible interpretations,
it also closes off the possibility of any single interpretation that
might be devastating to accept as the sole meaning of a complex,
disruptive occurrence. Empson himself, in concluding his discussion, confirms the protective power of ambiguity, granting
that "the object of life, after all, is not to understand things, but

to maintain one's defences and equilibrium and live as well as one can."[6]

Turgenev would undoubtedly agree, since in his fictional world, when understanding can undermine equilibrium and thereby menace psychological and moral well-being, the ambiguity that counters this menace unfailingly appears. He therefore discovers in language itself the moral capacity to ward off its own moral threat, to diffuse and thus defend against the precision harmful to undefended individuals. In one sense, then, this imprecise, ambiguous language can be construed as a metalanguage—it is in part a language about language. For it offers a tribute to the power of language even as it restrains or subverts that power.

The emblematic rhetorical device within this metalanguage is the litotes—the very model of imprecision and ambiguity. A litotes consists of a double negative; it is thus the negation of a negation, as in "not ungrateful," "not without gratitude," "not not rewarding," "not nonrewarding," etc. Belonging to the venerable tradition of oratorical figures of speech originated by the Greeks and developed by the Romans, the litotes is occasionally employed with irony, to imply the direct opposite of the double-negated term; in this way, "not ungrateful" could actually signify "very grateful."[7]

Used without irony, though, the litotes itself signifies nothing precise, but rather conveys a range of *possible* meanings. It therefore embodies a kind of nuanced, semantic unspecificity, its meaning located somewhere between opposed, specific meanings. Hence the nonironic phrase "not ungrateful" may mean merely grudgingly appreciative, somewhat thankful, ambivalently welcoming, or even quite grateful—the relative quantities of gratitude and nongratitude remain unspecified. Reduced to a formula, the litotes can be understood to express at best an imprecise relation between "X" and "not-X." It gives no clue as to how much "X" is included in "not not-X" and how much "not-X" is excluded by "not not-X."

Turgenev studs his works with just such ambiguous litotes. They occur with remarkable frequency in all but the few short

stories where peasant origins are attributed to narrator and protagonists, and thus make sophisticated locutions out of place.
(For the purposes of this chapter, no distinctions will be drawn
between language attributed to narrators and that attributed to
characters; the point here is to elucidate distinctive patterns of
linguistic usage. Chapters 5 and 6 explore Turgenev's creative
patterns in portraying narrators and characters, respectively.)

The litotes Turgenev most often prefers take the form "not
without . . ." (*ne bez . . .*), as can be seen in the following sam-
pling: in "Raspberry Water," one of *A Sportsman's Sketches*, the
narrator observes that a peasant "sneezed and coughed into his
hand not without fear" (3: 33), and in another, "Death," the narrator discloses that he enters one familiar forest "not without a
mournful feeling" (3: 197); the landowner Ipatov, in "A Quiet
Place," decides to accept an invitation to visit his neighbors "not
without a certain boldness" (4: 386); the narrator of "Iakov Pasynkov" offers aid to the bereaved girlfriend of the deceased Pasynkov "not without embarrassment" (5: 87); the correspondent
in the epistolary tale "Faust" reports that a woman with whom
he was once in love was "not without the fanaticism and super-
stition of her sex" (5: 98); the narrator of "Asya" comments that
he spent three days hiking in the mountains "not without pleasure" (5: 166), and upon his return concedes to Asya's brother
"not without a certain bewilderment" (5: 167) that he does find
Asya "a bit strange"; the ingenuous Natal'ia in *Rudin* replies to
questions posed by Rudin "not without shyness" (5: 240); a
friend of the family in *On the Eve* is described as "not without
good nature" (6: 242); the female protagonist of *First Love*, Zinaida, invites her young neighbor to visit her one afternoon by
saying that his companionship would be "not unpleasant" (6:
312); Grigorii Litvinov in *Smoke* uses the same litotes twice to
concede "not without effort" (7: 318, 319) that he had recognized
but not acknowledged a woman he had once loved and that he
might no longer despise her—and that woman is later said by an
acquaintance to be "not without good qualities" (7: 331); an old
friend of Sanin in *Spring Torrents* waits "not without a certain
anxiety" (8: 335) to learn whether he will have to keep their conversation going, and the narrator observes that anyone would

have stayed "not unwillingly" (8: 344) to meet that friend's enchanting wife.

Whatever their specific context, each of these litotes signifies the presence of some emotional or ethical quandary or conflict either within the speaker or within the character to whom the speech refers. In its deliberate semantic vagueness, each litotes betrays an underlying uncertainty, a lack of assurance that equanimity can be preserved if any intended meaning is clarified. At the same time, each litotes bespeaks an attempt, whether conscious or unconscious, to repress or deny confusion or conflict, and thereby to insist that equanimity has not been upset. Turgenev thus uses the litotes to explore the complex interplay between the psychological need and the moral demand for the protective benefits of ambiguity.

Just such interplay is entailed in a seemingly trivial but telling example near the opening of *Fathers and Sons*, when, on returning home from his university studies, Arkadii Kirsanov listens to his father's somewhat rambling if joyful welcome "not without consternation but not without sympathy" either (7: 17). Accompanied by the friend he idolizes, the self-styled nihilist Bazarov, Arkadii is clearly embarrassed, although also touched, by his father's effusions. At once wishing to please Bazarov by disparaging parental authority, but not wanting to hurt his eminently decent father's feelings, these two litotes reveal that Arkadii finds himself awkwardly ambivalent on both emotional and ethical grounds. They signal more than his ambivalence, though. Their semantic shielding of the extent of Arkadii's response mirrors a conscious effort to hide his underlying uncertainty, for Arkadii does not really know how he feels, or how he should feel, toward his father, but he nonetheless thinks he ought to know both. The litotes capture Arkadii's endeavor to appear confident and secure in his behavior and values—to create the self-image he desires. At the same time, they also indirectly convey to the reader the truth behind that image—but only indirectly. This combined concealment and revelation embodies Turgenev's inclination to recast individual difficulty in imprecise and therefore less distressing terms.

Turgenev provides a similar recasting in *A Nest of Gentry*, where he invokes one litotes twice in reference to two different characters. In the first instance, Liza Kalitina, "not without a certain effort" (6: 82) tells Lavretskii, the married man who is falling in love with her as she is with him, that every Christian should honor the religious sanctity of a sacrament like marriage. In the second instance, several years after Liza has abandoned her hope of marriage to Lavretskii and become a nun, Lavretskii asks Liza's sister, also "not without effort" (6: 156), whether Liza is still in a convent. In both instances, the litotes implies that each protagonist harbors a persistent longing for the creation or continuation of a relationship despite all rational and religious obstacles. Yet it also indicates that both have managed, at least to some extent, to suppress their longing, albeit "not without effort."

Moreover, this litotes suggests—in a way that the more explicit, positive formulation "with effort" could not—that both seek to suppress the suppression, that is, they try to speak "without effort," to betray no conflict, as though their emotional needs thoroughly coincided with their ethical standards. And, in part, they do. Both wish to appear to speak effortlessly so as to deny the vulnerability or weakness that an open manifestation of effort would reveal. Thus self-protection provides one reason to disguise any effort. Yet more than self-protection motivates them, since they not only *want* to speak "without effort" but believe that they *should* speak "without effort." Both Liza and Lavretskii consider themselves morally obligated to have no reservations about these utterances and hence obliged to have no hesitation and require no special exertion to voice them. Thus the litotes, which subtly reminds the reader of the possibility of speaking "without effort" even as it rejects the enactment of that possibility, hints at the struggle of these characters to maintain their composure while adhering to their chosen moral precepts. Yet the litotes also envelops that struggle in the protective power of ambiguity—the full extent of their psychic endeavors remains unexposed, unexpressed.

One of Turgenev's most effective uses of a litotes to convey the advantages of ambiguity in at once concealing yet conveying the unexpressed and the inexpressible occurs during an incident at the dramatic core of *Smoke*, where Litvinov breaks off his en-

gagement to his current fiancée, Tat'iana.[8] Litvinov tries to confess that he has succumbed to the pressures of his former fiancée
and his own desires to resurrect their love affair. But when he
cannot bring himself to conclude his confession, Tat'iana generously completes it for him, since in her intelligent, sensitive
love for Litvinov, she comprehends, better than he, his inability
to act otherwise, and she therefore will not force him to acknowledge further his humiliating lack of self-control. Nonetheless, she performs this charitable deed "not without a certain tension" (7: 355). The tension, a physical tautness of voice
and body, that Tat'iana cannot prevent herself from manifesting reflects the psychological strain of undertaking this self-
wounding act so as to spare Litvinov.

That Tat'iana does not aid Litvinov "with tension" but instead
aids him—more ambiguously—"not without a certain tension"
suggests that she has largely, if not completely, succeeded in restraining herself from any display of self-pity, which she abhors,
even though Litvinov has betrayed her love and destroyed her
hopes for the future. Thus the litotes here indicates what
Tat'iana will not do for both Litvinov's sake and her own: express directly self-indulgent, hostile recriminations that would
violate her self-imposed calm. Her psychological and moral impulses are at one in this moment; she is determined to save herself from the otherwise inescapable degradation accompanying
articulated anger and injury. This inherently imprecise rhetorical figure therefore embodies the control Tat'iana insists on
conserving for both emotional and moral reasons, while leaving
unexposed most of the energy she must expend in that conser-
vation. And in this instance the litotes is particularly apropos,
because its form parallels and thus emphasizes its content. The
litotes characterizing Tat'iana's utterance of Litvinov's rejection as "not without a certain tension" is itself "not without" the
tension that enlivens and underscores the ambiguity inherent
in both Tat'iana's behavior and the rhetorical figure that presents it.

The beneficial imprecision and ambiguity of the litotes also
mark a number of other locutions favored by Turgenev. Taken
together, these locutions—grammatical, lexical, and rhetori-

cal—form the base of what might be called a "language of litotes," the metalanguage that Turgenev intertwines with less
ambiguous modes of expression in order to obviate explicit articulation of disordered, disturbing episodes.[9] It is a language
often close to silence, which in turn functions as one of its components by obscuring the fullness of thoughts and feelings too
painful to expose in their entirety. Thus it is a language that fur-
thers the quest for self-preservation by enabling fragile individuals to reconceive their experience in terms both psychically
unthreatening and morally affirming. Yet it is also a language,
Turgenev demonstrates, whose use can be rationalized, made to
seem virtuous when it is actually either unintentionally self-
deceptive and self-defeating or even intentionally vicious. The
language of litotes therefore manifests not only the advantages
but the risks, both psychological and moral, inherent in the admission of ambiguity to Turgenev's vision of secular salvation.

Another component that contributes to the language of litotes is the single negative—negated verbs, adverbs, adjectives,
nouns, and pronouns. Not that every negative turn of phrase in
Turgenev's narratives is semantically, emotionally, or morally
marked as belonging to the language of litotes. Some are simple
and straightforward, belonging to the more referential discourse
Turgenev also employs. But many negative locutions are not so
simple as this. They, too, can foster the semantic ambiguity that
allows psychological and moral confusion and conflict to be reg-
istered without express elaboration. They do so by obviously
precluding or supplanting a positive locution, thereby implying
the existence of some alternative to whatever they reject, yet
leaving unclear precisely what that alternative might be.[10]

For example, in the short story "Asya," when this capricious
girl announces her imminent departure from the town in which
she had recently met and impetuously virtually proposed marriage to the tale's narrator, she adds soberly that "it is not out of
pride that I leave" (5: 193). Having had her proposal rejected by
the narrator, Asya guardedly declines to disclose to him her actual reason for leaving, thereby refusing him the intimacy she
had earlier been so eager to bestow. The negated assertion also
conveys her desire to become independent—she is not going

simply in response to what he has done, but for reasons of her own choosing—and to present herself as a mature, self-controlled young woman who realizes that the correct course of life is to remain a companion to her devoted brother rather than to pursue a hopeless love. In its ambiguity, this line thus embodies the union of self-protection and self-creation, a sense of weakness and a sense of strength, the need for psychological comfort and the desire for moral courage.[11]

Nowhere in Turgenev's narratives do the negatives of the language of litotes figure more prominently than in "The Unhappy One."[12] This text presents its narrator's observations of the last days of the life of a young woman, Susanna, the unhappy creature of the title. She is so called because one man she loved had been driven away by her malicious guardian, and another man who loved her had abandoned her because he believed some lies about her moral character that her guardian had caused to be spread. On learning of her abandonment, believing herself to be without recourse or resource, she commits suicide. This narrative is pervaded by negative terms representing both the narrator's and Susanna's efforts to prevent complete disclosure and the resultant anguished acknowledgment of the totality of her nightmarish existence.

The title itself, clearly, is a negative term that specifies only what Susanna is *not*—happy—and refuses to specify precisely what she *is*. This semantic refusal forms a frame for the entire work as well, since it is repeated twice at the story's end, when the narrator despairingly cries, "Unhappy one! Unhappy one!" (8: 137). Adumbrating Kurtz's appalled pronouncement on the depravity of human nature in Conrad's *Heart of Darkness*— "The horror! The horror!"—this final mournful attestation to the miserable waste of Susanna's life encases the record of her last days in tragic negativity.

Susanna herself couches the first and final statements the narrator records her uttering—as well as the one the narrator senses that she makes even after death—in negative terms, as though all she can do to resist the conditions of a life she so deplores is to reject verbally any connection to those conditions. Thus Susanna makes a series of negative assertions in her initial conversation with the narrator: "Mr. Ratch is not my father," "I did not say that to you," "I do not like it," "No, I did not receive them," "Do not make me perform today! I am in no way so inclined" (8: 71–72). Her final, impassioned speech is likewise loaded with negative phrases, this time proclaimed as exclamations and imperatives: "It is not necessary, nothing is necessary," "Do not restrain me, for God's sake!," "I cannot answer for anything!," "Do not approach, do not touch me!," "Do not follow me . . . do not follow! Do not follow!" (8: 90).

Negatives also abound in Susanna's diary, which she gives the narrator to read before she ends her life, as though negation has become her natural mode of conceptualization and expression. In portraying an encounter with the man who had illegitimately fathered her, she not only relies on but reiterates negative phrases to emphasize her alienation from him: "I will not call him Father! I will not forgive him for my mother or for myself! . . . It cannot be, it cannot be that he would not need it! But there will not be forgiveness for him, there will not be, there will not be!" (8: 101). Indeed, so natural has negative utterance become for Susanna that the narrator even imagines that the reply her corpse would probably give to his mute question "Why did you do this?" would be negatively phrased. He assumes she would fix on the failure of her beloved Michel to appear for their elopement and would therefore respond simply, "He did not come!" (8: 125).

Susanna's negativity is infectious; the narrator, too, comes to report his own encounters with her in negative terms. He accounts for their acquaintance by observing that "not simple trouble led her to me" (8: 87), and that "not just pity alone" filled his soul as he gazed at her corpse. His description of the corpse also deploys negative verbs: "Even death did not take pity on her; it did not give her, I will not go so far as beauty, but even that quietude, the reconciled and reconciling quietude, which so often appears on the features of the deceased." Instead he divines on her face "the sort of expression as though she was about to emit a despairing scream, but had died thus, not uttering a sound" (8: 125). Susanna's moment of death, like so much of her life, is characterized by what did *not* happen, rather than what did. She dies in a silence that carries her rejections of her own experience into the grave.

More than a mere motif, the negative locutions that permeate this narrative combine to provide Susanna and her portrayer with the only means at their disposal at once to express their opposition to her hopeless entrapment and to screen themselves from an excruciating unmitigated confrontation with it.[13] They have discovered the sole form of self-protection possible—the protection of distancing denial. Physical resistance through flight is not practicable; psychological resistance through verbal negation affords the only opportunity to assert some sense of separation from and superiority over Susanna's oppressive circumstances. And although they employ negations to unambiguously affirm that psychic separateness, these sufferers also avail themselves of the ambiguity of negation by implying yet never having to specify positive alternatives to those circumstances. Thus they avoid confronting directly the fact that there are no alternatives—that is, no alternatives in life. In this case the protective ambiguity of the language of litotes may not aid in the attainment of secular salvation, which may be beyond Susanna's reach. But that ambiguity does at least provide some temporary consolation, in redemptive rejections of the destructive forces ranged against an otherwise defenseless victim.

The repetition of a single negative word, "nothing," in *A Nest of Gentry* illustrates a somewhat different type of ambiguity, that engendered not by indistinct meaning but by multiple meanings.[14] Three of the major protagonists utter this word in a deliberate attempt to lie, to consciously misrepresent their thoughts and feelings at the moment of utterance.[15] For two of them, though, this attempt constitutes "honest" lying, since it is motivated in part by moral considerations; for the third, it is motivated solely by the most amoral considerations. But for all of them, the word "nothing" betokens involuntary admission of some truth as well. Although less semantically ambiguous than some other negated terms, this recurrent negation equals the other constituents of Turgenev's language of litotes in its power to both manifest and mask individual efforts at mastering complex and often conflicting urges.

The first to use the word "nothing" in the work is the German music teacher Theodore Lemm, who is secretly and, as he knows, unrequitedly in love with his young and beautiful student, Liza Kalitina. He composes a cantata, as an expression of some of his unvoiced admiration, that is meant for her ears alone, but Liza unthinkingly allows her suavely superficial, publicly declared suitor, Panshin, to hear her perform a segment of this composition. When Panshin is moved to compliment Lemm on his creation, Lemm merely mutters, "It's nothing," and then elaborates self-deprecatingly, "this cantata and I—we are both old fools; I am a bit ashamed, but it is nothing... nothing, nothing" (6: 24).[16] On the face of it, to be sure, Lemm is lying outright. No mere *topos modestos*, this dismissal of his supremely heartfelt creation betokens Lemm's unwillingness to risk revealing his futile enamoration to Panshin's potential ridicule or to Liza's potential pity. His self-protective instincts require Lemm to deny what he knows to be true, that his cantata represents not "nothing" but "something," something so precious—indeed, the single passion of his solitary existence— that he cannot venture to express and hence expose it in words.

At the same time, it must be granted, Lemm's "nothing" quite accurately captures the reality of Lemm's circumstance, for neither he nor his composition can inspire in Liza anything more than the sincere but limited affection of a pupil for a favorite instructor. "Nothing" indeed of a serious adult relationship between the two has materialized, and, whether or not Lemm consciously admits it to himself, he senses that for him, as King Lear declares, "nothing will come of nothing." Thus Lemm's negative response to Panshin's praise correctly evaluates the existential worth of the music and the attraction that inspired it.

Moreover, Lemm consciously realizes that his cantata *should* represent "nothing," because he should not feel such love as he does for his student. He knows he cannot make an appropriate match for Liza—he is indeed "old," if not a "fool," firmly set in a narrow routine, having neither the emotional nor the economic resources to enable a young, sheltered woman to meet the demands of married existence. An embittered and "embarrassed" expatriate without illusions of future professional success, Lemm concedes by his "nothing" that he has no moral right to harbor the dreams he has dreamed. Repeating this negated term, Lemm thus strives not only to protect his most cherished feelings, but to teach himself not to feel them. He seeks to create the emotional condition he considers himself ethically obliged to entertain. In his single word "nothing," therefore, falsehood, truth, and moral fiction coincide. Yet the extent to which Lemm intends to give voice to any or all of these remains obscured.

The same coincidence inheres in Liza's subsequent employment of this negation, although greater intensity and strife accompany it. Having agreed to marry Lavretskii, only to learn that his wife, whom they had believed dead, is still alive, Liza sends him away and falls on her knees in tears. Yet when asked by her beloved aunt, Marfa Timofeevna, why she is so distraught, Liza elliptically answers only "I nothing..." However Liza might have completed this thought—"I want nothing" or "I feel nothing" or "I am doing nothing"—the outspoken Marfa Timofeevna will have none of Liza's "nothing," immediately seizing on the evident contradiction between Liza's appearance and Liza's words, and remonstrating, "Nothing?.... This you say to others, but not to me! Nothing! But who was just on her knees? Whose eyelashes are wet with tears? Nothing! Just look at yourself, what have you done to your face, what has happened to your eyes? Nothing!" (6: 150).

Marfa Timofeevna's knowing, dramatically derisive reiteration of "nothing" underscores the pitiable ineptitude of Liza's attempt to deny the violent distress brought about by her rupture with Lavretskii. And pitiable it is, when Liza cannot even finish the sentence intended to assert that she remains unshaken by the revelation that their planned marriage is an impossibility. The breaking of her phrase mirrors the breaking of her heart, and recovery can only be attained in silent selfministration. Yet, like Lemm, Liza knows that she *should* feel "nothing," she *should* be engaged in "nothing," at least nothing of the self-pitying sorrow her tears suggest. As she herself has argued to Lavretskii, a good Christian ought not to seek personal gratification but rather ought to accede submissively to anything that occurs as a manifestation of the will of God. Her own religious convictions thus compel her to create a spirit of acceptance and to express that spirit in her words.

Also like Lemm, Liza actually speaks the truth even as she once falsifies and fabricates her emotional state. "Nothing" of the course of life she had envisioned has been left to her; she has abruptly and irrevocably been deprived of the fulfillment she had anticipated from love, marriage, motherhood, friendship, a future filled with intimacy and affection. Indeed, her association of the pronoun "I" with the word "nothing" is particularly apt, since the very identity she had mentally fashioned for herself as Lavretskii's wife has been effectively annihilated. To avoid both the psychic agony and the moral error—the active pursuit of personal happiness—incurred by having imagined that identity, Liza thus sees no other choice than to give herself over to religious seclusion dedicated to transcending and thereby obliterating individual identity. She, that is, her sense of self, has become as "nothing," and she seeks to ensure that it remains as "nothing." Thus this single negative term embodies the union of instinctive denial, ethical desire, and intellectual discipline that command Liza's response to a devastating turn of events. Yet again, as for Lemm, the relative magnitude of each of these components cannot be discerned.

The moral energies at least partly inducing Liza's use of the word "nothing" appear particularly impressive when contrasted to the thoroughly cynical use of the same term by Lavretskii's wife, Varvara Pavlovna, upon her return to Russia from the life of dissipation and debauchery in Paris that had driven Lavretskii away. Having arrived to refute the erroneous report of her death, only hours after Lavretskii had openly declared his love for Liza, this self-indulgent and self-centered woman responds to her husband's question about what she wants from him now by assuring him that she desires "nothing, nothing . . . I know, I have the right to demand nothing" (6: 115). Yet Varvara Pavlovna's very presence at Lavretskii's estate suggests that she most certainly does want something—readmission to his home, to his financial support, to the social legitimacy a husband and married life bestow. She dares not explicitly request this readmission, for fear of further antagonizing her disenchanted spouse, so she deliberately camouflages her goals in protestations of humility and the absence of any desires. The insincerity of Varvara Pavlovna's repentant pose only highlights the integrity of Liza's intentions. Unlike Liza's, Varvara Pavlovna's "nothing" truly means nothing.

Except that those words, her repeated "nothings," do literally mean "nothing" as well, because even for the duplicitous Varvara Pavlovna, falsehood and truth are more closely intertwined than she may know. Despite her self-serving misrepresentation of her motives, she too is correct in selecting the term "nothing," for that is precisely what she wants—no substance, no real recommitment, only the superficial appearance of such. She aspires only to a semblance of marital stability and harmony, not to real reconciliation and resumption of marital relations, as her subsequent rapid seduction of Liza's erstwhile suitor, Panshin, proves. Ironically, then, Varvara Pavlovna's efforts to conceal her intentions and create a new persona in her husband's eyes also expose the hypocrisy of her behavior. Hence the multiple messages conveyed by this negation exemplify the devious purposes to which ambiguity can be put by an individual in quest not of self-protection and moral self-enhancement but of self-indulgence and amoral self-aggrandizement.

Another component of the language of litotes is simply a short suffix attached to other words. This suffix, a hyphen followed by the Russian particle *-to*, has no independent semantic content but may be added to semantically independent words to alter their meaning. Regularly affixed to interrogative adjectives, adverbs, and pronouns, it imparts what might be called a "semi-definite" quality.[17] By "semi-definite" I mean a semantic range between the completely indefinite or imprecise (often rendered in English by the word or prefix "any," in Russian by the suffix *-nibud'*), and the completely definite or precise, whether positive or negative (the positive form lacking any particular affix in either English or Russian, the negative form generally indicated by the prefixes "no" in English and *ni-* in Russian).

In English, this semi-definite range is often indicated by the term "some," either as a prefix or separate adjective. Its presence assigns to a term a meaning between precision and generality, as in somewhere, somehow, someone. Similarly in Russian, the words for somewhere, somehow, someone, etc., are formed by suffixing the particle *-to* to other, related terms—e.g., the Russian word for "sometime," *kogda-to*, is formed by adding *-to* to the Russian word for "when." Both English and Russian, therefore, provide a means to instill semantic imprecision in many locutions, and Turgenev takes full advantage of this in Russian. To be sure, semi-definite terms are by no means unique to Turgenev. But his placement of these terms, along with their prevalence in his narratives, is distinctive.[18] For they occur again and again at points where underlying psychological or moral disturbance could erupt but is not allowed to do so, instead remaining suppressed, or at least contained, by the intrinsic ambiguity of semi-definiteness. Yet this containment may facilitate harmful self-delusion rather than salutary self-defense—an innate danger of Turgenev's ethical program.

Semi-definite terms often appear in the description of a protagonist's physical and psychological makeup, rendering unclear the relative significance of the various qualities mentioned. A few examples: in the eyes of the reclusive Mar'ia Pavlovna in "A Quiet Place," the narrator discerns "something wild, beautiful, and mindless" (4: 390); the narrator of "Faust" perceives in the eyes of a young girl "something strange, some sort of warmth and tenderness" (5: 99); the narrator of "Asya" detects "something soft, feminine" (5: 177) to sweep across the face of the impetuous girl at one point, and "something touchingly helpless" (5: 186) at another; in *On the Eve*, Insarov's voice after a fight with a rude German officer conveys "something unkind, something dangerous" (6: 222); in *Fathers and Sons*, Bazarov's voice, as he converses with his philosophical adversary, Pavel Petrovich, manifests "something coarse, almost crude" (7: 27); the narrator of "The Unhappy One" finds that "the very openness" of Susanna's guardian conceals "something bad" (8: 105).

In each example, the presence of the semi-definite term— here always the word "something"—attenuates the subsequent adjective, rendering it equivocal. Also equivocal is the cause of the equivocality. Does the character so described deliberately attempt to cloak or stifle some aspect of temperament or behavior that might be deemed inappropriate or even immoral? Or does the observer consciously or unconsciously choose to avoid a closer, more definitive analysis for fear of bringing to light inclinations all too threatening to some already established order or to a character's self-image? Ambiguous in both import and intention, these semi-definite descriptions prevent, or at any rate mitigate, such threats, even as they camouflage the moral implications of their intervention.

This ambiguity is particularly marked in "Faust," where the word "something" is stressed in the first of the nine letters that constitute the epistolary narrative. Writing to a friend, the protagonist, Pavel Aleksandrovich, broadly paraphrases Hamlet's renowned remark to Horatio about there being "more things in heaven and earth than are dreamt of in your philosophy," turning the general observation into a personal confession: "Despite all my life experience, there is still something on earth, friend Horatio, that I have not encountered, and this 'something' is nigh unto the most important" (5: 94). Pavel Aleksandrovich thus transforms "more things" into "something," and reduces what all of "philosophy" has not contemplated to what he alone has not "encountered." While overtly claiming experiential deprivation, Pavel Aleksandrovich hints that he may simply be reluctant rather than unable to name that unknown explicitly. Explicit articulation of what he has not yet undergone, if it is as important as he suggests, might obligate Pavel Aleksandrovich to seek it out. As long as he cannot name it, though, he need not pursue it. In this case, a semi-definite term appears to make it possible for self-defeating weakness to masquerade as self-affirming strength.[19]

By contrast, the semi-definite term "something" in *Smoke* does provide self-affirming, or at least self-sustaining, strength, by providing a temporary obstruction of painful memories, for it enables the novel's main protagonist, Grigorii Litvinov, to retain some psychic stability, which might otherwise have been lost. Awaiting the arrival of his current fiancée in Baden-Baden, Litvinov discovers in his hotel room a gift bouquet of heliotrope from an anonymous benefactor. Upon noticing the flowers, the narrator records, Litvinov "touched them and sniffed," at which point "something seemed to stir in his memory, something extremely distant... but precisely what he could not imagine" (7: 278). Although Litvinov tries to turn his attention to business affairs, he finds that the heliotrope's "inescapable, persistent, sweet, heavy fragrance gave him no peace, but ever more strongly spread in the darkness, and ever more insistently reminded him of something that he could in no way seize hold of" (7: 279).

Eventually Litvinov does "seize hold of" the elusive yet intrusive memory that explains the significance of the flowers. He had given a corsage consisting of heliotrope to his former fiancée, Irina, during their youthful love affair, just before she broke off their relationship to marry a far wealthier, socially prominent soldier. The flowers' fragrance triggers conflicting desires to recover and to repress the recollection of past loss and despair. Litvinov can cope with this conflict, though, because the semi-definite "something" provides a kind of linguistic shield that fends off the otherwise possibly overwhelming onrush of his memories. Litvinov thus subconsciously gives himself an opportunity to retrieve them while remaining calm and controlled. Hence this use of the language of litotes establishes a psychic environment into which disordered incidents can be cautiously drawn and carefully dealt with.

Almost every page of *Fathers and Sons* contains at least one semi-definite term, as a result of which an aura of ambiguity comes to overlie the narrative. To mention some instances: when Arkadii announces that he has initiated a relationship with his father's peasant mistress, he has "an expression of some sort of tender and good triumph on his face" (7: 23–24); "something unusual" (7: 31) shone in Pavel Petrovich's face when he fell in love as a youth; "some sort of tender and soft strength" (7: 68) wafts from the face of Anna Sergeevna when Arkadii and Bazarov first meet her, and when they first visit her home, "everywhere it smelled of some sort of decorous odor" (7: 76); Anna Sergeevna's sister, Katia, gazes "somehow comically-seriously" (7: 77) as she speaks to the guests and "somehow innocently cried" (7: 167) after Arkadii proposes marriage to her; Arkadii's father, Nikolai Petrovich, greets his son and Bazarov with conversation marked by "some sort of neither childish nor nervous laughter" (7: 130); Bazarov, dying, agrees to make a final confession, while across his face creeps an expression of "something strange" (7: 180).

At each of these moments, whether referring to action or to ambiance, a semi-definite term at once veils and signals mental discomposure. Moreover, the vagueness of the term itself also leaves vague whether the individual is unable or unwilling—for either psychologically comforting or morally compelling reasons—to provide the precision so markedly missing. Semi-definiteness in this novel marks precisely only the effort to sustain at least some measure of composure.

Such is the case in the portrayal of the deterioration of the friendship between Arkadii Kirsanov and Bazarov. When both characters develop a romantic attraction to Anna Sergeevna, while in residence as her houseguests, a psychological distance sets in between them, with the result that "for a certain time they kept up some sort of pseudo-light bantering" (7: 101), which, it is said, "always serves as a sign of secret dissatisfaction or unspoken suspicions." The semi-definite term itself serves to suggest secrecy, that is, the deliberate avoidance of admission that each is erecting a false emotional facade. More signs of this avoidance are furnished by the semi-definite observations that Arkadii "for some reason rejoiced" (7: 101) to learn that Bazarov intended to depart from Anna Sergeevna's home, and that on Bazarov's return Arkadii felt "somehow ashamed" (7: 160). Neither explicitly accuses the other of deception or disloyalty for placing self-interest above friendship in seeking a private, selfish conquest of Anna Sergeevna, although each suspects that the other harbors the desire to do so. Thus, as the semi-definite terms betray, the two characters allow their feelings about one another and about Anna Sergeevna to remain unarticulated in order to spare both themselves and one another direct confrontation with self-serving desires and uncharitable opinions. A veneer of companionship thereby remains intact.

Semi-definite terms in *Fathers and Sons* are particularly effective in the representation of the nascent relationship between Bazarov and Anna Sergeevna. Such terms are extremely well-suited to its portrayal, since neither character has ever undergone, expected, desired, or sought an intense attraction such as the one that begins to develop between them. Thus the imprecision of the statements describing their interactions aptly reflects the uncertainty and ambivalence of their reactions. So it is that Anna Sergeevna, who admittedly has "wanted something, she herself not knowing precisely what" (7: 84), discovers in Bazarov "something new" (7: 83) that she either cannot or does not try to identify, but that does cause her to want to know him better. Consequently she announces to Bazarov only that "something nonetheless tells me that we have not met in vain" (7: 97). Bazarov likewise cannot or will not pinpoint the precise nature of his response on meeting her: having always considered love "something on the order of a weakness or an illness" (7: 87), he nonetheless discovers that his heart pounds each time he thinks about her, and that "something else settled in him that he in no way expected" (7: 87). As Bazarov yields to this "something else" and fully falls in love with Anna Sergeevna, she reacts with "some sort of horror still not comprehended by her" (7: 98). These indeterminate locutions mirror the resistance the two mount in defining and thereby coping with their newfound reciprocal fascination, so unanticipated and unwelcome. Perceived by both as a palpable threat to carefully tended, self-defensive autonomy, they struggle to delay as long as possible the unambiguous acknowledgment of their emerging emotional interdependence.

Much the opposite effect is achieved by a semi-definite term at the conclusion of *Rudin*, where imprecision bespeaks self-affirmation. The term refers to words spoken by the title character, who had formerly constructed his very identity on the elegance and precision of his verbal expressivity. In the novel's epilogue, though, Rudin has abandoned his earlier, passive pursuit of the intellectual joys of eloquence and has joined in the Paris uprisings of 1848. Making a last heroic stand, he leaps to the futile defense of his barricade with a red banner in one hand and a curved, dull saber in the other. At that moment, the previously articulate Rudin is reported simply to have "shouted something in a tense, thin voice, climbing aloft and waving both the banner and the saber" (5: 322), only to be felled immediately by a bullet through the heart. Thus the champion of eloquent expression dies not with a brilliant epigram but with an indistinct shout coming from his lips. Yet the incomprehensibility of his final words, as much as his final glorious gesture itself, constitutes a triumph for Rudin. Both symbolize recognition of his reliance on rhetoric as a crutch for evading engagement in actual experience. The semi-definite term here thus perfectly encapsulates Rudin's newborn indifference to the refined forms of language; he has discovered ultimate meaning in the contents of action. This instance of ambiguity signals Rudin's unambiguous moral victory.

Another contributor to the language of litotes is diction. Although any word or group of words that cultivates indirection, imprecision, and ambiguity belongs to this language, a few select words, by virtue of their specific semantic content, most readily further these aims—and it is these to which Turgenev repeatedly turns. Most prominent among them are "slightly" (*slegka*) and "strange" or "strangely" (*strannyi/stranno*).

"Slightly" is Turgenev's favorite adverb; he liberally distributes it throughout his narratives. This word is admirably suited to the language of litotes, for Turgenev can engage it to portray at once the upsurge of an irresistable impulse and the conscious constraint of that impulse; thus an action occurs or an emotion appears only "slightly." Mention of a few of the myriad instances in which this adverb is adduced will illustrate its effects; but to give some idea of its pervasiveness, it should be noted that "slightly" appears a dozen times in the novella *Spring Torrents*, and no fewer than thirteen times in the story "The Unhappy One" alone.[20]

In *Rudin*, for example, Volyntsev, the young admirer of Natal'ia, speaks with a "slightly changed voice" (5: 274) when he tries to but cannot completely hide his disappointment and hurt after learning that she has declared her love for Rudin. He thinks he should take this rebuff manfully, without any display of the upset that would betray vulnerability. But in fact that upset is too great to master and repress without a trace, and Volyntsev's vocal apparatus discloses—albeit only "slightly"—his pain. In this instance and many like it, Turgenev employs the term "slightly" to flag the conjunction of the psychological need for concealment and the moral demand for restraint and self-control in behavior that might otherwise lapse into self-wounding revelation of frailty.

In other instances, though, "slightly" may suggest the disjunction of psychological need and moral imperative. Such disjunction is signified, for example, in "Iakov Pasynkov," when Sof'ia Nikolaevna, accused by an admirer of pretense and prevarication, winces "slightly" while her hands tremble "slightly" (5: 56). She in fact deserves these reproaches, since she has feigned indifference in conversation toward a man for whom she has boldly declared her love in writing, because she is unwilling to expose that private love to public scrutiny. Yet she loathes the thought of stooping to deception and false denial. Her "slight" external physical responses therefore bespeak great internal divisions, as her pride and fear compel her to conceal what her honesty and commitment impel her to reveal: the truth. The very "slightness" of Sof'ia's movements betray the depth of both her conflict and her determination to repress it, thereby preventing it from doing her irrevocable damage.

An opposite conflict occurs in *Smoke*, when Irina Ratmirova blushes "slightly" (7: 297) upon meeting her former fiancé, since she can only be attempting to repress her guilt at having abruptly broken their engagement without a satisfactory explanation years earlier. Here she endeavors to stifle her ethical sensibilities, which remind her of her failure to treat decently someone who had deeply loved her, as she seeks only to maintain her visible decorum. The use of "slightly" thereby betokens an effort to conceal moral, rather than psychological, vulnerability.

At times, ethical and emotional uncertainty, rather than conflict, is intimated by the adverb "slightly." In "Faust," for instance, Vera Nikolaevna "slightly turned and tilted back her head" to look at a former suitor as he seeks to renew their acquaintance after a lengthy separation, and she "slightly moved

away" after he kisses her hand (5: 103,113). Unsure of his intentions, she cannot react too explicitly, lest she insult him by appearing to interpret them as more than friendly gestures if they
are only that. Yet she cannot ignore them, either, since she suspects that they are indeed more than simple friendly gestures.
Thus Vera Nikolaevna reacts "slightly," conflating civility with
self-protection as she seeks to decipher his behavior.

In *Fathers and Sons*, "slightly" is repeated so often as to become a virtual leitmotif of the work. And almost every instance
suggests that a character is trying to disguise deep-seated, disturbing thoughts or feelings that for both psychological and
moral reasons the character prefers not to exhibit to the fullest
extent. At the beginning of the novel, for instance, Pavel Petrovich, staunch defender of the aristocracy, "bowed slightly" and
"smiled slightly" (7: 19) on meeting the uncouth and unkempt
nihilist Bazarov. The "slightness" of bow and smile demonstrate, as much as a concomitant unwillingness to shake hands,
that Pavel Petrovich has immediately recognized an enemy in
Bazarov, but does not wish to depart from standards of socially
approved behavior by openly displaying any enmity.

Pavel Petrovich continues to veil his antipathy for Bazarov by
moving or gesturing "slightly" during their subsequent encounters—most notably, when he discovers Bazarov kissing the peasant mistress of Pavel Petrovich's brother, and he remarks the discovery simply by proceeding to "bow slightly" (7: 139). Exhibiting the sheerest disregard for the sensibilities of his host,
Bazarov violates Pavel Petrovich's most prized principles of hon-
orability with cavalier behavior that can only engender deep disgust in the other. Yet Pavel Petrovich's commitment to those
principles runs equally deep. Therefore, in bowing "slightly,"
Pavel Petrovich can uphold the conventional formalities required by those principles while still signaling his disgust at Bazarov's audacity. He can thereby combine the emotional gratification of restraint with a moral justification for that restraint.

It is Anna Sergeevna, though, the widow with whom Bazarov
truly falls in love and who is in turn attracted to him, who most
often performs actions "slightly," studiously laboring to maintain hard-won control over herself even when tempted by pas-

sionate self-abandon. She "slightly" turns her head (7: 90) when Bazarov speaks of leaving her home after having been her guest, "slightly" shrugs her shoulders (7: 90) as she admits she will be bored without him, and "slightly" pales (7: 95) at the prospect of never seeing Bazarov again. These physical alterations imply that Anna Sergeevna reacts viscerally to the prospect of losing contact with Bazarov, but she refuses to express this reaction overtly. Instead, she fights to retain the self-command that she has determinedly developed in the conduct of her personal affairs. Thus this adverb, as a constituent element in the language of litotes, masks the fullness of her feelings, giving assurance in its very ambiguity that Anna Sergeevna will not sacrifice herself to instinctive urges for intimacy that could compromise her psychic integrity.

No matter what its specific context, the adverb "slightly" thus generally conveys someone's conscious effort to impose control on impulsive responses and their attendant physical manifestations, thereby leaving unspecified the actual degree of intensity of those responses. The adverb "strangely," and its adjectival counterpart "strange," work to somewhat different effect, tending to suggest an unconscious urge to repress uncomfortable or disturbing sensations. This urge induces the impression of "strangeness" as a comforting rationalization, one that attributes any such sensations to an encounter with something unfamiliar, alien. Often, in fact, this urge is caused by recognition of something actually familiar but upsetting, even threatening, were the familiarity to be acknowledged. Thus the application of the attributive term "strange" distances and diffuses any threat by denying the possibility of such familiarity before that possibility can be consciously examined and morally evaluated.

So it is, for instance, in "Faust." Whereas Vera Nikolaevna seeks to comprehend the character and motives of her suitor, Pavel Aleksandrovich, he remains content to categorize unreflectively much that he perceives as "strange." Thus he records as a "strange fact" that the odor of his former home stimulates his imagination (5: 92); he twice labels the mother of Vera Nikolaevna "a strange woman" (5: 98, 101); he notes that Vera Ni-

kolaevna used to have the "strange habit" of thinking out loud
(5: 99); he finds himself in a "strange state of mind" after spend-
ing time with her (5: 111); he declares that "something strange"
happened after he kissed her hand in the garden (5: 113); and he
announces that the two of them had an "extremely strange conversation" one evening (5: 116). By labeling these interchanges
and emotions as simply "strange," Pavel Aleksandrovich can
deny and hence escape consciously facing the painful implications of being forcefully attracted, as he immediately is on renewing her acquaintance, to a married woman. Only when Pavel
Aleksandrovich finally admits that he has fallen in love once
again with Vera Nikolaevna, and she with him, does he cease to
employ this self-defensive term.

In similar fashion, Elena's admirer Bersenev in *On The Eve*
experiences "a strange feeling" after first talking to Elena about
Insarov (6: 201), as though Bersenev senses a potential rival; she,
in turn, professes incomprehension when she notices that her
father "somehow strangely looked at" her and Insarov together,
refusing to concede that their relationship might be more than
friendly and therefore deserving of unusual parental observation (6: 228). In *Spring Torrents*, Sanin and Mar'ia Nikolaevna
even exchange words on the subject of "strangeness," when she
declares it "strange" that someone calmly announces an intention to get married, but not to commit suicide, for, she asks,
"What is the difference between them?" to which Sanin replies:
"It is impossible to imagine anything stranger than *your* marriage" (8: 364; emphasis Turgenev's). Her profoundly ironic use
of the term "strange"—she understands perfectly well that there
is nothing whatsoever odd about the habit of not equating marriage with suicide—only highlights Sanin's ingenuousness,
since he cannot yet allow himself to face the fundamental per-
versity of Mar'ia Nikolaevna's marriage of convenience, which
allows her the freedom to seduce whomever she chooses, including Sanin himself.

The difficulty of discerning whether it is inability or unwillingness to acknowledge vulnerability that leads to the use of various forms of "strange" is displayed in the aptly titled short story
"A Strange History," in which the entire narrative trades on the

narrator's self-proclaimed inability to penetrate and interpret the surface appearances of the characters and events he beholds. Hence he maintains he can describe an old friend's daughter, Sofie, only as making an "enigmatic" impression on him and as having, for him, a nature with a "special" but "opaque" quality (8: 139), as well as a "strange" gaze (8: 140). After she preaches "self-denial," "humiliation," and destruction of the will as precursors to true religious belief, he finally summarizes his incomprehension of her by exclaiming, "What a strange being!" (8: 149). When Sofie then follows her own precepts by abandoning her wealthy family in order to accompany an impoverished religious fanatic on his peregrinations, the narrator emphatically reiterates, "I did not understand anything, I did not understand," (8: 158) and he expresses only sorrow at the subsequent news of the demise of this "poor, enigmatic being" (8: 159). By stressing the unfathomability of Sofie's personality and performances, the narrator thus has no need to examine her spirituality too closely, nor to consider too carefully his own lack of comprehension of a character far more morally noble than his own. Without risking self-critical comparisons, he can simply classify her as "strange" and therefore not amenable to his superficial modes of analysis and judgment.

In *Smoke*, the tenor of much of Grigorii Litvinov's stay in Baden-Baden is said to be "strange," an apt appellation for the disorienting, disturbing environment Litvinov senses this resort town to be, although he cannot quite put his sensations into precise words. For example, Litvinov remarks that a new acquaintance and fellow Russian, Sozont Potugin, is a "strange person" (7: 277); he thinks that a seemingly chance meeting with Irina, his fiancée of long ago, is "amazing, strange" (7: 305); he finds the fact that Potugin turns out to be well acquainted with Irina "somewhat strange" (7: 309); and he notes that Irina's eyes glisten with "a strange gleam" (7: 319) as she reproaches Litvinov for failing to pay a promised visit to her hotel. The iteration of this adjective perfectly captures Litvinov's estrangement, malaise, and uncertainty in a geographically, socially, and psychologically foreign locale.

Further on in the novel the word "strange" conveys not only Litvinov's sense of alienation from his surroundings but from himself as well, as Irina's machinations irresistibly lure him away from the commitment to his current fiancée. After a number of "strange" interactions with "strange" people in Baden-Baden, Litvinov begins to find his own thoughts and behavior "strange," too: he perceives in himself a "strange change" (7: 352) that causes him to become, in his own eyes, a different man; during a dinner conversation with his current fiancée and her aunt, before breaking his engagement, Litvinov feels that he "somehow strangely became animated" (7: 359); and, once he has made the break in order to run off with Irina, he discovers that "his personal intentions presented themselves to him in a strange light" (7: 379). So estranged has Litvinov become from his own consciousness that he cannot clearly elucidate his own motivations, even to himself. Moreover, Litvinov's use of "strange" obscures the moral import of his estrangement: does it arise from the self-protective instinct to deny his own susceptibility to the wiles of a powerful woman, or does it derive from the unsettling, unreal atmosphere of the resort town, in which all motive and meaning is conveniently concealed? The recurrence of the adjective "strange" in this narrative serves as an emblem of the confusing moral climate that cloaks all conclusions in a smokescreen of ambiguity.

Although Turgenev periodically signals his awareness that the language of litotes can be put to questionable purposes, his final deployment of it affirms its ethical power. For Turgenev presents a testimonial to the psychological and moral value of ambiguity in his last literary statement about language. This is also the last literary creation Turgenev released for publication during his lifetime: the oft-anthologized prose poem "The Russian Language." The three sentences that compose this briefest of the offerings in Turgenev's collected *Poems in Prose*, the fifty-one sketches Turgenev wrote and permitted to be published between 1878 and 1882, are generally seen as a somewhat overblown, sentimentalized tribute to his mother tongue. In this prose poem, Turgenev affirms to himself, to his country, and to the world the dignity and strength of his language and of the nation that gave rise to it:

> In the days of doubts, in the days of grave reflections on the fortunes of my country, you alone are encouragement and support to me, o great, powerful, righteous, and free Russian language! Were it not for you, how could one not fall into despair in the face of all that is occurring at home? But one cannot believe that such a language was not given to a great nation! (10: 172)

The first sentence, at a glance, may seem little more than an overwrought exaltation of his subject, but the claims staked for the Russian language—that it is great, powerful, righteous, and free—are borne out in the subsequent sentences. In the second sentence, Turgenev shifts from the direct to the indirect affirmation of this language, in the form of two negative phrases: "Were it *not* for you . . ." and "how could one *not* fall into despair in the face of all that is occurring at home?" These queries betray the fact that Turgenev has indeed contemplated despair. Yet they reveal that he has found protection against despair in language itself—not in the buoyant and unambiguous assertions of the first sentence, but in the subtleties of imprecision and ambiguity displayed in the second, since the negative interrogatives in the conditional mood make it possible to avoid the explicit articulation of their implication: without the Russian language, despair is inescapable.

The third and last sentence of the prose poem carries this indirect affirmation still further. It offsets the weight of the first line's "doubts" and "grave reflections" with a counterweight of comforting ambiguity. It achieves this through a double negative—essentially, if not technically, a litotes—that conveys a range of possible meanings. For the conclusion that "one can*not* believe that such a language was *not* given to a great nation" actually fails to specify, and therefore leaves ambiguous, what it is that one *can* believe about that nation. The "doubts" have done their work; they have restrained the unequivocal assertion of unalloyed belief. Yet the Russian language combats the doubts, as it shrouds them in an ambiguous denial of disbelief. Moreover, the Russian term in the third sentence, *nel'zia*, translated above as "cannot," the declaration of impossibility, may also be interpreted to mean "must not," the declaration of moral necessity.[21] Thus the final line of "The Russian Language" may also be understood to read "But one *must* not believe that such a language was not given to a great nation!"

Hence psychological capability becomes conflated with moral obligation, as it so often does when Turgenev employs the language of litotes. Read this way, the line actually admits the possibility, though without explicitly articulating it, that one *might* believe "such a language was not given to a great nation," and therefore that Russia is not "a great nation" at all. But it also urges against doing so, because such a thought not only jeopardizes psychic calm but transgresses morally mandated bounds. For such a thought inevitably gives rise to the very doubts and despair that undermine the integrity of a country as well as of an individual.

In sum, then, a country that has a language supple enough and strong enough to guard its speakers from direct confrontation with emotionally disturbing and ethically debilitating experiences and ideas must endure. Paradoxical as it may seem, the most indirect and ambiguous use of the Russian language thus provides the best proof that this language is indeed great, powerful, righteous, and above all, free. It is free in having the autonomous flexibility not merely to articulate a patriotic paean to the Russian motherland but to engender a means of self-protection for its inhabitants, the speakers of this language, as they strive to safeguard themselves from the foes, material and spiritual, that all too often beset them. Thus to Turgenev, the Russian language, encompassing both silence and the language of litotes, bestows the saving grace of ambiguity on experience too awful to otherwise endure.

Thus, contrary to traditional critical thought, it is the presence of indistinction and imprecision, as much as the prevalence of distinctness and precision, that distinguishes Turgenev's literary style. It comes as no surprise, though, that the latter has been singled out for critical attention, because the cultivation of linguistic precision is traditionally associated with Realism, and those who deem Turgenev an adherent of Realism expect to find him upholding its linguistic standards. As Fanger puts it, Realists seek in their language "to present the object with maximum clarity and a minimum of emotional or stylistic deformation,"[22] or in other words, "the rendering of objects in their essential quiddity."[23] Thus Realists give the impression of rendering, so Watt says, "no more than a transcription of real life" by "exhaustive presentation rather than by elegant concentration" of a language that is "much more largely referential" than that of earlier, conventionalized literary styles.[24] And although qualifying the referentiality of the language of Realism, Levine finds that this language not only accepts the possibility of correspondence between word and object, but energizes what he terms Realism's "quest for the world beyond words" by inducing the reader's expectation "that the world be there, and that it be meaningful and good."[25] Levine therefore adds support for the idea that Realists intend to attract the reader toward integration into extraliterary reality.

And indeed, as noted earlier, proponents of Turgenev's association with Realism regularly point to passages in his prose laden with the fastidious particularity and transparency that augur his admiration for that reality. Those passages are there, to be sure, and they are admirable. However handsomely honed, though, they are not as distinctive of Turgenev's artistic and ethical vision as are those passages imbued with ambiguity—those passages that hold the reader at a psychological distance from extraliterary reality by refusing to specify the precise nature of that reality, much less to make it inviting. For Turgenev, engagement with that reality is often too hazardous for fragile individuals to venture into, even when mediated by its fictional reformulation. Thus in order directly to protect the reader and indirectly to provide the reader with models of self-protection, Turgenev explores the most crucial yet psychologically and morally treacherous ground his characters tread without portraying the breadth of its frightening expanses in explicit terms.

These quintessentially Turgenevan instances of ambiguity thus bring to mind Wittgenstein's famous dictum "Whereof one cannot speak, thereof one must remain silent," since Turgenev shrouds in the silence surrounding ambiguity the reasons, some ethically valid and some not, for individuals' inabilities to express their innermost conflicts. At the same time, these instances inspire a paraphrase of Wittgenstein: "Whereof one must not speak, thereof one can remain silent." This altered version better encapsulates the proximity Turgenev's narratives expose between moral and psychological mandates for the imprecision that confers redemptive power upon that unique product of human creativity, language.

5

Deliverance at a Distance: Model Narrative Voices

Turgenev's language of litotes models for the reader one mode of self-protection. Leaving experiences that threaten the self only indirectly expressed or altogether unexpressed is shown to prevent the infliction of unbearable pain on vulnerable psyches striving to maintain equilibrium and integrity. This language is complemented by other means of self-protection that Turgenev reveals to his audience. For instance, his orchestrations of narrative voice offer exemplary demonstrations of self-defensive tactics available to the individual at risk of psychological and moral assault. And like the language of litotes, the ethical import of Turgenev's narrative voices has gone largely unnoticed. Even the most perceptive and admiring of Turgenev's critics have generally failed to recognize the subtlety and sophistication governing Turgenev's deployment of such voices. When the subject is raised at all, Turgenev is usually said to use only first-person narrators who blatantly represent Turgenev's own thoughts and experiences, or omniscient third-person narrators who allow Turgenev's authorial identity to be completely obscured.

Percy Lubbock, for instance, typifies the first of these views in claiming that "Turgenev was never shy of appearing in his pages as the reflective storyteller. . . . With perfect candor he will show his hand; he will draw the reader aside and pour into his ear a flow of information about the man or woman, information that openly comes straight from Turgenev himself."[1] By contrast, Freeborn exemplifies the second of these views, remarking in particular of *Fathers and Sons* that "the novel possesses an organic unity, in which there are no narrative devices that obtrude into the fiction to distort, however slightly, the final impression of naturalness," and that Turgenev therefore leaves "the impression that the novel is 'telling itself,' as it were, almost without the author's agency or participation."[2]

Such opinions even hold for a critic who takes Turgenev's narrative practices as her central topic. In her essay "One of Turgenev's Compositional Devices," M. A. Rybnikova typologically reduces Turgenev's narratorial technique to the introduction of (1) first- or third-person observers and (2) first-person participants. According to Rybnikova, the observer-narrators directly present Turgenev's own views; the participant-narrators present views of their own that may diverge from Turgenev's.[3] Although she does admit the possibility that Turgenev is capable of presenting points of view other than his own, Rybnikova adduces nothing to controvert the assumption that the narrative perspective within each of Turgenev's texts is formally, dramatically, and ideologically constant, implemented by Turgenev solely for the purpose of portraying an unvaried vision of characters and events.

Only S. E. Shatalov has raised his voice firmly against these critical presumptions, declaring that the time has come to "dispense with the mistaken opinion" that Turgenev's works are characterized by a "self-evident simplicity" deriving from the ubiquitous assertion of the author's consciousness.[4] Shatalov is right, although he stakes his claim on limited ground.[5] The narrative point of view in Turgenev's prose fiction never provides a merely "monological" or monolithic perspective on characters and events. It is a radical underestimation of Turgenev's artistry—and a signal unacknowledgment of Turgenev's ethics—to assume that his works rely on an unvarying narrative voice, whether a voice transparently the author's own or impersonally the author's invention, because in fact Turgenev regularly alters the narrative stance during the course of individual works. He employs a highly fluid narratorial technique in both the novels and short stories, shifting smoothly from one point of view to another; indeed, the very smoothness of those shifts no doubt accounts at least in part for their having gone largely undetected. They should be comprehended as the embodiment of Turgenev's moral mandate to reenvision experience that threatens psychic well-being.

In some texts Turgenev overtly shifts the role of narrator from one persona to another, as in "Andrei Kolosov," where the narratorial responsibility switches from an impersonal narrator to an identified narrator, or between two personified narrators, as in "The Unhappy One." But much more common are alterations within a single voice in what may be called the narrative mode, that is, the combination of formal and functional features that convey the status of relations among narrator, text, and reader. The narrative mode expresses both the type and the degree of the narrator's commitment to the substance of the narrative, to the act of narrating, and to the audience. In so doing, narrative modes always contribute to the moral resonance of a work, because they impart impressions of the value attributed to these relations and to this commitment.[6] This is particularly so with Turgenev, since all three of his preferred modes inculcate some form of protective psychological separation between the reader and the text.

Three types of narrative modes are most prominent in Turgenev's works: (1) an apperceptive or discursive mode, in which the narrator is positioned at the greatest psychological distance from both the text and the reader, conveying information about external appearances seemingly objectively, without significant intrusions by the narrator's personality or opinions; (2) an assimilative mode, in which the narrator is positioned somewhat closer to the reader and psychologically most closely to the text, seemingly reproducing a character's thoughts and emotions through the narrator's voice, so that the reader is drawn into that character's subjective experience, again without significant intrusions by the narrator's personality or opinions; and (3) an autonomous mode, in which the narrator endeavors to come closest to the reader by seemingly turning away from the text to express opinions directly, thereby exhibiting a distinctive personality.

Each mode suggests a different type of narratorial obligation.

That of apperception assumes the task of representation, the ordering and recasting of appearances to achieve a desired form and effect. Not mere reportorial accuracy but aesthetic and ethical influence is sought in the shaping of information to provide models of safe psychic response for the audience. In *A Nest of Gentry*, Lavretskii's first sight of the woman who would become his wife, Varvara Pavlovna, is couched in the apperceptive mode, and constitutes a subtle warning against her allure. She is portrayed as appearing "so calm and self-assuredly gentle that everyone in her presence at once felt at home; and from all of her captivating body, from her smiling eyes, from her innocent sloping shoulders and pale-pink arms, from her light and at the same time seemingly tired walk, from the very sound of her voice, slow and sweet, wafted, like a delicate odor, ineffable, ingratiating charm" (6: 47).[7]

What the narrator does not explicitly articulate this sultry description nonetheless captures—the insidious irresistibility of a physically attractive woman who will employ her charm to ensnare male victims in her web of desires. The apperceptive mode of this passage deliberately draws on the poetic powers of rhythm, sound, and syntax to adumbrate the subversive danger to Lavretskii's integrity posed by Varvara Pavlovna. In the Russian, rhythmic stress alternations (*plenítel'nogo téla . . . nevínno-pokátykh plechéi . . . blédno-rózovykh rúk*); paronomastic play with the letters "p," "r," and "l," (*plenitel'nogo tela; pokatykh plechei; rozovykh ruk*) which unite in the climactic word for charm (*prelest'iu*); and the five repetitions of the preposition "from" (*ot*) replicate the cloyingly sweet spell this woman casts, encircling and enticing anyone susceptible to her wiles. The mode of apperception gives not only witness to but warning against those wiles by effectively exposing them to the reader. Thus this narrative mode molds its material not simply to offer reportage, but to offer moral guidance as well.

The mode of assimilation dons the responsibility of recreation, in the sense of reproducing the mental condition of a character not as the narrator might observe it objectively, but as the character experiences it subjectively. This mode, sometimes referred to as *style indirect libre* (it should be noted that all three modes have been described and variously labeled by students of narratorial devices),[8] enables the reader to perceive more intimately than if rendered in the mode of apperception the uncertainties, the conflicts, the dilemmas with which a protagonist internally struggles. Not merely the narrator's observations of the workings of that protagonist's mind—observations distinctly articulated in the narrator's voice, alleging what "he felt" or "she thought"—the assimilative mode adopts and transmits the language, the phrasing, the style of the protagonist's psychic processes through the narrator's voice. Hence the narrator's identity becomes blurred, as temporal, spatial, and psychological perspectives shift from those of the narrator to those of the protagonist. At the same time, this mode deliberately obstructs the complete identification of the reader with the protagonist, an identification that could result in the reader's excessive emotional participation in the protagonist's suffering, because the mode of assimilation insistently maintains the mediating presence of the narrator's persona—even as the narrator's voice becomes obscured—instead of allowing the protagonist to assume all narratorial control. The reader is thus consistently confronted by evidence that experience can be consciously reenvisioned in order to sustain a protective psychological reserve.

The assimilative mode takes over the narration in "The Song of Triumphant Love," a short story set in sixteenth-century Italy presented by an impersonal third-person narrator, when one protagonist, Fabius, returns home believing he has just murdered another, his friend Mucius. The narration remains technically in the third person, but the jaggedness, the urgency of the language mirrors the distraught mind of Fabius, not the dispassionate mentality of the narrator. The mode changes from the apperceptive to the assimilative after the narrator observes that Fabius has begun to contemplate the enormity of his actions:

How should he proceed now? What to undertake? If he had killed Mucius—and having recalled how deeply the blade of the dagger had penetrated, he could not doubt it—if he had killed Mucius, then it was absolutely impossible to conceal it! It was necessary to bring it to the attention of the duke, the courts... But how to explain, how to account for such an incomprehensible act? He, Fabius, had killed, in his own home, his relative, his best friend! They will begin to ask: why? for what purpose? But if Mucius were not dead?

At this point the narrator returns to the apperceptive mode, stating that "Fabius did not have the strength to remain in uncertainty any longer" and returned to the scene of the supposed crime (10: 62).

The assimilative mode thus illustrates not only *what* Fabius contemplated, but *how* he contemplated it. His horror and disbelief are encapsulated in the disjointed fragments of questions and exclamations that differ markedly from the flowing narration that precedes and follows. This mode thus offers an emotional paraphrase of an individual's conflicts, portraying them more graphically and thereby drawing the reader closer to them than would be possible in the apperceptive mode. Nonetheless, the indirect presentation of these internal battles, formally retaining the stance of third-person discourse instead of invoking direct quotations cast in the first person, leaves ambiguous the degree of closeness the reader can achieve. Some distance inevitably inheres, since the consciousness of the narrator always lurks behind that of the character being re-created; the narrator can reassert his own voice at any moment. The reader is therefore forced to be on guard, not wholly drawn in to the protagonist's point of view. As a result, the assimilative mode teaches tentativeness even as it heightens empathy.

Finally, the mode of autonomy accepts the obligation of reevaluation, by enabling the narrator to emerge from the frame of the story to speak expressly to the reader, as it were, often to offer general analyses or assessments that broadly interpret the specific events portrayed in the modes of apperception and assimilation. The autonomous mode thus frequently unites the immediacy of the narrator's personal point of view and the abstractness of philosophical disquisition. In order to emphasize the independence of narration in the autonomous mode from that in the other modes, its utterances are set forth in what may be called the "eternal" present tense, a time frame outside the one in which the narrative takes place. That is to say, in this mode the narrator appears to address, explicitly or inexplicitly, the reader's present, rather than that of the narrative. Hence the reader is both drawn into the text, by being addressed, and distanced from it, by being made self-consciously aware of the actuality beyond it.

Narrators resort to this mode repeatedly throughout Turgenev's novels and short stories. It comprises interjected observations, such as these in *Rudin*: "With the intellect alone, however strong it may be, it is difficult for a man even to know what is going on within himself" and "No one gets as easily carried away as passionless people" (5: 278). And this from *Smoke*: "It is impossible to sustain the same thoughts for long: they constantly change, like the little lenses of a kaleidoscope... You look, and suddenly there are completely different images before your eyes" (7: 379).

Sometimes the narrator will simply speak to the reader in this mode, without offering any grand observations, but still establishing a broad context in which the narrated events take place. At the beginning of the story "Brigadier," for instance, the narrator asks: "Reader, are you familiar with those small settlements in which our great Russian Ukraine abounded twenty-five or thirty years ago?" (8: 39). Or the narrator will even speak for the reader, as near the conclusion of *A Nest of Gentry*, where the narrator almost becomes a surrogate for the reader, posing questions on his behalf: "'And the end?' asks, perhaps, the unsatisfied reader. 'But what ever happened to Lavretskii? to Liza?'" (6: 158). The narrator then proceeds to deny any certain knowledge of the "whereabouts" of the protagonists. Hence the narrator virtually steps outside the narrative to become allied with the reader's point of view.

In this mode, then, Turgenev's narrators rise above the particulars of setting, characters, and events—the very concerns of the modes of apperception and assimilation—to establish a separate perspective from which to comment on those particulars, sometimes in a familiar, chatty tone, sometimes in an abstracted, meditative manner. This separate perspective in turn reminds the reader of separate perspectives outside the text as well. Addressed as an autonomous entity, the reader is forced to become conscious of playing the role of interpreter, even if directed in that role by the narrator. This mode too, therefore, keeps the reader at an emotional distance from the text even as it intentionally recognizes the reader's existence.

These three narrative modes are frequently interwoven in a single work, or even in a single page or paragraph, to instill manifold patterns of narration in Turgenev's prose fiction. To be sure, Turgenev cannot by any means be adjudged unique for relying on multiple modes of narration—other authors often employ the same or similar modes, as well as others, and shift among them as readily as Turgenev does.[9] His distinction rests instead on the use of those shifts in ways that promote self-preservation both explicitly and implicitly. Turgenev explicitly advances this moral goal by regularly altering narrative perspective so as to create a sense of distance, sheltering the reader from psychically disruptive encounters with destructive events.[10] And he inexplicitly advances this goal by furnishing the reader with proof of the availability of alternative visions of experience, visions designed to avoid or attenuate confrontations with the awful exigencies of human existence. Thus, as illustrated in the following analyses of the evolution and deployment of narrative modes, Turgenev discovers in them a means of bestowing on his reader models of conscious mechanisms ideally designed for self-defense.

Turgenev's first major prose work, *A Sportsman's Sketches*, provides valuable historical insight into the development of Turgenev's narrative techniques.[11] These "sketches," a series of brief narratives ranging from character studies to full-fledged short stories, gave Turgenev an excellent vehicle for experimenting with narrative modes. They function as études in which we can readily transform the role of the sportsman/narrator from that of interlocutor of peasants, as in "Death," to effusive friend of the reader, as in "Tat'iana Borisovna and Her Nephew," to passive observer of youthful storytelling, as in "Bezhin Meadow," to mere recorder of another's story, as in "Chertopkhanov's Conclusion." And in so doing, the sportsman emerges as a character not merely hunting for game, or even simply hunting for new experiences, but as an individual hunting for a manner of *narrating*, that is, for a way to comprehend

and communicate those experiences. The sportsman, of all Turgenev's narrators, is the one most overtly searching for ways of
ordering and understanding what he perceives; thus he tacitly
attempts to devise a model of consciousness. In this search, the
sportsman labors particularly to find an appropriate style and
tone for the modes of apperception and autonomy but relatively
rarely explores the mode of assimilation. Nonetheless, all of
Turgenev's subsequent narrators clearly benefit from the sportsman's efforts.

As he assumes the role of narrator, the sportsman introduces
the first sketch, "Khor and Kalinych," with an uneasy alterna-
tion between the modes of apperception and autonomy, insert-
ing allusions to himself as an observer into passages of otherwise impersonal observations. He also begins this sketch with
implicit self-deprecation, evincing little narratorial confidence
or privilege, as though he were no different from any other person recording observations after traveling through the area he
describes: "Whoever happens to cross over from the Bolkhov region into that of Zhizdra would probably be amazed by the sharp
differences between the type of people in the Orel district and
the Kaluga type" (3:7). The term "whoever" suggests that the
"differences" discerned do not proceed from the workings of a
single consciousness expressing its individuality, but from an
objective assessment of incontrovertible facts that anyone could
garner.

Yet the narrator soon starts to probe the potential of the autonomous mode for distinctive self-expression, albeit tenta-
tively. He does this first through learned comments on the local
language. As he offers a few remarks on the regional differences
he has witnessed—always assuming a familiarity on the reader's part with Russian geography, since he never indicates the
precise location of these regions—he adds a bit of quasischolar-
ly commentary on a dialectal vagary of one region in a footnote:
"The Orel dialect is distinguished in general by a multitude of
idiosyncratic, sometimes remarkably apt, sometimes rather
meaningless words and expressions" (3:7). Later, he parenthetically interjects a personal note when he uses the word *zhivalyi*,
a colloquial term for an inhabitant of the Orel region, adding,

"as they say among us in Orel" (3: 16). Thus the sportsman advertises himself a bit as a knowledgeable and therefore reliable commentator.

He nevertheless makes a point of reproducing portions of his dialogues with the peasants he describes meeting, refusing to accept the responsibility of paraphrasing their exchanges. "Here is a little sample of our conversation for you" (3: 12), he announces to the reader before presenting an interchange between himself and Khor. And he respectfully quotes folk sayings and expressions, stating, for instance, "Khor spoke with me about much that you could not pry out of another person, or, as the peasants put it, that you could not grind out with a millstone" (3: 16–17). Thus although displaying his personal sensitivity to the peculiarity of language that identify individual speakers, the narrator shows little confidence in his own, autonomous voice. Indeed, he accords the peasants a verbal expressivity and authority that he does not wholly grant himself. At this point, he does not avail himself of the autonomous mode's capacity to present a narrator's unique point of view.

In subsequent sketches, though, the sportsman evinces greater self-assurance and explores the potential of the mode of autonomy in greater depth. As early as the second sketch, "Ermolai and the Miller's Wife," he commences by reporting in the mode of apperception that he and "the hunter Ermolai set out for 'cover,'" but promptly turns to the mode of autonomy to demonstrate his civilized solicitude for the reader, politely pausing to concede that "perhaps not all my readers know what cover is. Listen, ladies and gentlemen" (3: 19).[12] After elaborating on this particular form of duck hunting, he resumes his presentation of the events of the hunt by reiterating "Then Ermolai and I set out for cover," only to interrupt his narrative again with an autonomous apology: "Excuse me, ladies and gentlemen, I must first acquaint you with Ermolai" (3: 20). An assured, authoritative tone has now entered his narration. He is evidently developing confidence in the mode of autonomy as a means of controlling the tenor and pace of narration in the guise of supplementing the reader's understanding of that narration.

The sportsman also gradually starts to represent his own emotional relation to an incident as part of his expanding use of the mode of autonomy. In the first few sketches, he volunteers little or no commentary on his encounters with the peasants or on the stories he hears from them, even when he portrays his exposure to psychologically and morally troubling incidents or ideas.[13] But in the fifth sketch, "My Neighbor Radilov," the narrator's reactions to his visit to an isolated rural landowner's home acquire a force and value equal to those of the other characters he delineates. He uses for the first time phrases such as "I thought" and "it seemed to me," as well as "I could in no way imagine" (3: 54) and "I no longer remember" (3: 55), to assert his authority as a mediating consciousness in the transmission of the events portrayed. And when Radilov confesses to having beheld an intimate and shocking sight—a fly walking across the eyeball of his wife's corpse—the sportsman puts forth his own response as testimony to the horror caused by this graphic demonstration of nature's indifference to human beings. He remarks his indelible image of the reaction of the deceased woman's sister as she listens to Radilov's confession. The narrator simply states: "In eternity I will not forget the expression on her face" (3: 56). Yet he never limns this expression in detail; he conveys the impact of that instant in the mode of autonomy by reporting the ineradicable impression it made on his memory, rather than by offering the exact representation of the sister's face that would have been rendered in the mode of apperception. He takes it on himself, therefore, to serve as the reader's measure of that instant's awful intensity—and at the same time, he refrains from painting too graphic a portrait of psychic torment.

In addition to including forthwith in his narratives his own responses to events, the sportsman slowly learns to expand the compass of the mode of autonomy to include the communication of existential wisdom. He comes ever more assuredly to incorporate obiter dicta and philosophical meditations into the mode's repertoire. In "Ermolai and the Miller's Wife," for instance, he generalizes as a hunter and an animal lover: "It is well known that dogs are able to smile, and even smile very sweetly" (3: 20). In subsequent sketches he offers general observations from the perspective of a man of the world. Thus in "Raspberry

Water," he proclaims that "every man has some sort of position in society, some kind of connections; to every serf is given, if not a salary, then at least a so-called allowance" (3: 32). By the fourth sketch, "The Rural Doctor," the sportsman is comfortable digressing from the main narrative in a lengthy commentary on the oddities of human relations that commences with the generalization, "Strange things occur in the world" (3: 41). No longer the average observer or even the above-average teller of hunting tales, the sportsman has enlarged his narrative role through the capacity of the autonomous mode to transmit his views on the nature of human existence and experience, the capacity Turgenev's later narrators will make much good use of.

Just as Turgenev investigates the power of the mode of autonomy to broaden the sportsman's narratorial authority and the substantive realm of discussion in *A Sportsman's Sketches*, so he pursues the power of the mode of apperception to increase the narrator's effectiveness in signaling extensive complexities beneath simple surface appearances. In some of the early sketches, when the hunter employs the apperceptive mode to present dramatic moments, he tends to revert at the climax to the autonomous mode in order to stifle immediately any embarrassing emotionality that might otherwise intrude into his resolutely cheerful narration. Thus, for example, in "Lgov," the sportsman describes a bizarre, almost grotesque scene in which he and two of his companions, shooting ducks from a boat in the middle of a small lake, suddenly capsize the boat and find themselves standing up to their necks in water, completely "surrounded by the floating carcasses of dead ducks." Yet the macabre impact of this scene, potentially a haunting indictment of senseless slaughter, is at once attenuated by the narrator's adding that "now I cannot recall without laughter the frightened and pale faces of my companions" (3: 83). By emphasizing the foolish rather than the ghastly aspect of this adventure, the sportsman stimulates a particular reaction to his reader—to laugh as well. Thus he attempts to exercise control over the reader's encounters with such incidents through the application of the mode of autonomy.

Once he has affirmed his control in that mode, though, the

narrator loosens his hold on the narration and permits the mode of apperception—and thereby the reader—a greater independence, not invoking the mode of autonomy to explain or qualify the images portrayed. Nowhere in *A Sportsman's Sketches* is this mode more independent than at the conclusion of "The Singers." After completing the main narrative, the depiction of a singing contest featuring transcendently beautiful songs performed by rough laborers in an inn at Kolotovka, a tiny village perched on the brink of a desolate ravine, the narrator portrays an exchange he overhears as he departs the competition. This exchange of words is shouted by two boys, one summoning the other, Antropka, to return home. The narrator initiates the conclusion of this sketch with the remark, in the mode of apperception, that Antropka, upon hearing that he is being hailed

"because daddy wa-a-a-nts to beat you," . . . no longer called out, and the boy again began to summon Antropka. His calls, more and more infrequent and weak, still reached my ears, when it had already become completely dark, and I was going around the edge of the forest surrounding my little village and lying four versts from Kolotovka...
   "Antropka-a-a!" still resounded in the air, full of the shadows of the night. (3: 225)

Thus concludes "The Singers." Rather than assessing this final moment in the mode of autonomy, the narrator leaves the calls echoing in the night air. He finds in the mode of apperception a narrative technique for suggesting the incident's implications that is at once simpler and more vivid—albeit more enigmatic—than an explicit summary comment. So the sportsman does not declare, as he might have, that Antropka's flight from his father's anger parallels the freedom from mundane actuality that the singers find in their music. Nor does the sportsman expressly observe that their freedom is transitory: the singers must eventually stop singing and return to their ordinary lives; Antropka must eventually return home to face his father. The narrator instead allows the reader either to draw these conclusions or simply to admire the scene's eerie beauty. For he has discovered that the ambiguity of such unexplicated images sustains and even heightens his narratorial control. By purveying imagery without further clarification, the sportsman manifests a newfound conviction that his apperceptive powers are sufficient to grant the reader some interpretive independence while still making the reader aware of an intervening artistic consciousness that reformulates events to suit its own purposes.

In comparison to the extended explorations of the narrative potential of autonomy and apperception, there is relatively little investigation of assimilation in *A Sportsman's Sketches*. To be sure, it might be said that the sportsman, in often adopting a chatty, even colloquial, manner reminiscent of the *skaz* technique popularized by Gogol, has at least partially assimilated the verbal style of some of the uneducated but loquacious characters he presents. But the mode of assimilation requires a narrator first to establish a temporal or spatial distance from the characters he represents, and then to bridge that distance, not to imply from the outset that little distance exists. Moreover, the educational, psychological, and even philosophical differences between the sportsman and the peasants he encounters far outweigh any minor stylistic similarities.[14]

Granted, in several of the sketches, the narrator does employ what might be considered an early version of assimilation, as he attempts to create a kind of identification between himself and his reader. At several points, instead of employing the pronoun "I" or "one" to refer to the person undergoing the experience, he switches to the personal pronoun "you," as if to suggest that "you the reader" undergo the experience as well.[15] In "Burmistr," for example, the sportsman portrays a young landowner of his acquaintance as an affable gentleman and yet confesses, "I, in any event, do not visit him too eagerly" (3: 125). But he then ceases to describe the reluctance "he" feels in encountering this man and instead relates those "you" feel: "A certain strange disquiet takes you over in his home; even comfort does not please you, and each time, in the evening, when the curly-haired valet appears before you in light-blue livery . . . you feel that if instead of his pale and lean figure suddenly a stout young man with amazingly wide cheekbones and an unbelievably flat nose stood before you . . . you would have wordlessly rejoiced" (3: 125). Or in "Kas'ian from the Beautiful Land," the narrator avers, in the mode of autonomy, that "it is an amazingly pleasant occupation to be on one's back in the forest and look upwards!" He then shifts to the pronoun "you," though, to describe further the sensations enjoyed: "It seems to you that you are looking at a bottomless sea, that it spreads *beneath* you. . . . You don't move—you look: and it is impossible to express how joyous and quiet and sweet it becomes in your heart" (3: 115; emphasis Turgenev's).[16]

In such instances the narrator, by changing pronouns, imparts immediacy and intimacy to his presentation, subtly drawing the reader into the narrative as he steps aside, as it were, for a moment. For whatever reason—whether having decided that such a narrative maneuver draws the reader too close or moves the narrator too far aside—Turgenev abandons this technique in most works subsequent to *A Sportsman's Sketches*. Yet he has availed himself of the opportunity to survey the fundamental narrative properties possessed by these three modes, properties he can put to use in the representation of the models of consciousness his ethical vision endorses.

Prior to consideration of works in which Turgenev interweaves all three narrative modes to promote that vision, let us look further at the specific properties of the mode of assimilation. As noted above, Turgenev does not completely exploit these properties until after he has benefited from the narrative experiments of *A Sportsman's Sketches* and is comfortable exposing the reader more directly to the intellectual and emotional flux entertained by individual characters. Turgenev now knows that he can control that exposure, reverting to the modes of apperception or autonomy if the flux becomes too turbulent in the mode of assimilation. And he can control it using both first- and third-person narrators.

In "Asya," for example, a first-person narrator assimilates his own state of mind from an earlier time as he relates his past encounter with a young man and that man's half sister, Asya. That is, this narrator at times abandons his stance of temporal and spatial distance from the events he traces—and of his mature comprehension of them—to mingle past and present consciousness. Thus when depicting his return to his rooms after having begun his new acquaintance, he recalls, "I felt myself happy. But why was I happy? I didn't want anything, I wasn't thinking of anything... I was happy" (5: 156). Yet the narrator's "older self" knows why he was happy at that moment—he had just met and been attracted to the alluring and unconventional Asya—but he also knows that his "younger self" lacked sufficient security and self-awareness to recognize it. Since the narrator allows the question "Why was I happy?" to remain unanswered, though, he chooses to reflect the state of mind of the younger self. Still, the use of the past tense indicates that the question is voiced by the older self, because the younger would have said "Why *am* I happy?" In this instance the narrator has recast unaltered the naive sequence of his youthful musings, and he refrains from expounding on them in order to convey graphically the self-ignorance and self-deception to which he was formerly subject. By proffering this mental paraphrase, however, rather than reportorially reproducing the exact wording of his thoughts at that time, the narrator continues to remind the reader of his superior adult self-comprehension. He thereby implicitly invalidates his former oblivion and retains his distanced hold on the narrative point of view, reverting in the following paragraph to the mode of apperception to register that he then "immediately fell asleep, like a child in a cradle" (5: 156). Hence he employs the two narrative modes both to emphasize his previous emotional immaturity and to prevent the reader from giving too much credit to his impressions at that time.

The potentialities of assimilation are more thoroughly explored in the novella *Spring Torrents*, where Turgenev employs that narrative mode in several forms. Throughout the text, an impersonal narrator, who formally relates a series of experiences undergone by the main protagonist, Dmitrii Sanin, frequently invokes the mode of assimilation to convey dramatically Sanin's sense of those experiences. This narrator, after first placing Sanin before the reader in a pensive pose, uses the mode of apperception to narrate the memories passing through Sanin's mind, making the claim, "Here is what he remembered" (8: 256). Those memories are then formally presented not in Sanin's voice but in the narrator's, as attested to by the use of the

third person: "Sanin had turned twenty-two, and he found himself in Frankfurt on a return trip from Italy to Russia" (8: 257).
The ensuing tale of Sanin's accidental acquaintance with, rapid
engagement to, and guilty abandonment of a young Italian girl,
Gemma, whom he encounters in Frankfurt, remains phrased in
the third person.

Yet the narrator's consciousness is periodically suppressed
and Sanin's is allowed to come forth and dominate the narration.
As a result, this tale can be read as an exercise in assimilation.[17]
Notwithstanding a few scattered general observations interjected by the impersonal narrator—for example, "Weak people
never finish anything themselves; they always await the end" (8:
363)—the psychological rapproachment that arises between
narrator and character intrinsically guides the course of the entire narration, as the perceptions and conclusions offered issue
from a participant's, not an observer's, mind. The narrator
evinces too much fervency, resorts to too many exclamations in
describing incidents for an individual uninvolved in them. Thus
it must be concluded that the impersonal narrator uses the
mode of assimilation to duplicate Sanin's reactions as they occurred. Yet this impersonal figure nowhere wholly forsakes his
narratorial responsibilities; he constantly if subtly modulates
Sanin's mental upheaval during the process of attachment to
and rupture from Gemma by maintaining the third-person
stance throughout. Thus Turgenev circumvents any inordinate
emotionality that Sanin's self-pitying or self-loathing first-person narrative might have engendered in the reader.

The implicit assimilation of Sanin's consciousness by the narrator's becomes explicit at points where the narrative past (conveyed by the past tense representing action completed prior to
the time of the events portrayed) is interrupted by statements in
the narrative present (conveyed either by the present tense or by
the past tense representing actions ongoing at the time of the
events portrayed); these are interruptions that can only come
from Sanin's consciousness at the time of the events. One such
interruption transpires, for instance, when Sanin has first been
invited to Gemma's home and sits watching her attending her
mother. Abandoning the apperceptive mode, the narrative flow

lapses into abrupt questions: "What is this? A dream? A fairy tale? And for what purpose is *he* here?" (8: 276; emphasis Turgenev's). To embody Sanin's joyous mystification at his good fortune, the narrator thus sacrifices the narrative mode and past tense of his impersonal stance to recreate Sanin's thoughts in their own tense and mode. Yet by continuing the use of the third person—instead of asking, "And for what purpose am *I* here?"—the narrator nonetheless keeps Sanin's bemused uncertainty somewhat at bay.

The narrator likewise communicates Sanin's ecstasy after realizing "for what purpose" he was "here"—to become Gemma's husband—by turning again to the assimilative mode. As announced by the narrator in the mode of apperception, Sanin, after declaring his love for her, "felt that he even looked differently at Gemma" (8: 323). But then the narrator permits the mode of assimilation almost to insinuate itself, as Sanin "fleetingly noticed several distinctive features in her walk, in her movements—and my God! how infinitely sweet and dear they were to him!" The exclamatory emphasis of these expressions and the ones that follow, as Sanin's enamoration unfolds, echo the exclamations he makes in direct discourse as he vows his eternal devotion to his beloved.[18]

But the narrator quickly departs from that mode to shift first into the apperceptive mode and immediately thereafter into the autonomous mode, so that Sanin's ardent uplift does not endure and overwhelm the reader:

Sanin and she—they had fallen in love for the first time; all the marvels of first love were performed around them. First love is a veritable revolution: the monotonously correct order of a well-composed life is broken up and destroyed in one moment, youth stands on the barricades, waving its bright banner on high, and to whatever waits for it in the future—death or a new life—it sends its rapturous welcome. (8: 323–24)

By reverting to these modes in succession, the narrator can paint a more balanced portrait of love than Sanin's initial experience could entertain. Thus the reader's own emotional balance is not jeopardized by protracted exposure to Sanin's temporarily extreme point of view.

The mode of assimilation subsequently also characterizes the narrator's report of Sanin's confused reaction to an acquaintance's wife, Mar'ia Nikolaevna Polozova, who has the financial resources to buy Sanin's Russian estate and thereby free Sanin to marry Gemma. The record of this reaction forgoes the past tense of the apperceptive mode, which has preceded it, to proffer a series of rhetorical questions, commencing with the acknowledgement: "This lady is evidently making a fool of him and in this way gets round him. . . . Why is this? What does she need? It cannot be that this is only the caprice of a spoiled, rich, and practically amoral woman? And that husband?! What kind of being is he? What are his relations to her?" This string of queries concludes with the assertion that "tomorrow all this will disappear without a trace" (8: 358). These questions and their conclusion, which the narrator even couches in the future tense, can only come from Sanin's bewildered brain. They thus disclose the conflation of narrative past and present, narrator and character, observer and participant. Yet having allowed Sanin's consciousness to take over momentarily, the narrator promptly adopts the apperceptive mode anew to reestablish temporal and psychological distance from Sanin's ordeal.

This narrator recurrently engages the mode of assimilation not only to incarnate Sanin's psyche, but to represent other characters' psychological states as well. The impersonal narrator re-creates the disposition, for example, of Gemma's younger brother when he visits Sanin the day after Sanin had heroically revived him from unconsciousness. The narrator notes that the brother "suddenly felt an extraordinary attraction to Sanin—and not in the least because Sanin had saved his life the night before, but because Sanin was such a nice man!" (8: 272). The tone, the phrasing, the emphasis all belong not to the impersonal narrator, not to Sanin, but to the brother, although the brother does not utter the words in direct discourse. The narrator similarly captures the vapid conceit of Gemma's former fiancé and the self-satisfaction of her family's servant with ejaculatory phrases that reflect their obtrusive personalities. Yet he never allows their voices to monopolize the narration and procure unwarranted admiration or sympathy.

Thus distinctions of time, role, and identity become repeatedly obscured as the narrator departs from the distance of apperception and the directness of autonomy to achieve the intimacy and immediacy of assimilation while still mitigating those qualities with his controlling consciousness. Yet even as the mode of assimilation draws the reader more closely into the psychological states of characters, it also disrupts the reader's common expectations of temporal and psychological consistency in narrative point of view. And these disruptions not only suggest a distinctive narrative sensibility at work, but also introduce a self-consciousness into the act of reading, for the reader must repeatedly question his cognitive relation to the world of the text. In encountering this narrative mode, the reader cannot help but wonder, What is going on here? When is this happening? To whom do these thoughts belong? As a result, the reader is inevitably alienated from the narrative even while being drawn into it by the mode of assimilation, while the narrator's control over the revelation of a character's emotionality remains secure.

Turgenev effectively interweaves these three narrative modes, while varying the extent to which he uses each one, in all his mature works. But to particularly facilitate frequent shifts in narrative mode, Turgenev often turns to one literary device— the narrative frame. Before exploring the use Turgenev makes of this device, a few remarks on narrative frames in general are necessary. By the term "narrative frame" I mean the structural device of a narrative presented in a novel or short story that provides a context in which another narrative of that novel or short story unfolds. The narrative that provides this context usually introduces and concludes a text and thus physically surrounds it, somewhat as a traditional frame surrounds a painting. But unlike the frame of a painting, which most often serves a purely formal, often decorative function, a narrative frame has a substantive function as well. A narrative frame not only physically surrounds another narrative but also contains its own narrative, thereby portraying characters and events belonging, as Boris Uspensky points out, to "a special world, with its own space and time, its own ideological system, and its own standards of behavior,"[19] all of which are normally separate from the characters and events, space and time, systems and standards presented within the narrative it frames (hereafter referred to as the *framed* narrative). Most often, in the course of the narrative that constitutes the frame (hereafter the *framing* narrative), the source for the framed narrative—a personified narrator or the discoverer of a set of letters or a lost or abandoned manuscript—is introduced.[20]

Prior to the nineteenth century, novelists made extensive use of narrative frames, primarily to stress the verisimilitude of the framed narrative and to suggest a communal consciousness ready to receive the story to come. One has only to think of such novels as Cervantes's *Don Quixote*, Sterne's *Tristram Shandy*, Rousseau's *The New Heloise*, or Goethe's *The Sorrows of Young Werther* to recognize how well accepted this structural device was. Each of these works makes use of a frame in which a narrator directly addresses the reader, appearing to acknowledge the reader's existence and the reality the reader inhabits.[21] Although some recent critics, such as Robert Alter, have suggested that the use of such framing narratives is not a sincere attempt to increase verisimilitude but an exercise of self-conscious aesthetic play or irony,[22] up to the nineteenth century readers on the whole accepted those framing narratives' assurances of the reality of what was presented by the framing narrator. For instance, as the historian Robert Darnton demonstrates in his study of the popular reception of *The New Heloise*, many of this epistolary novel's readers so believed in the existence of the correspondents that they besieged Rousseau for further information about Saint-Preux, Julie, and the others. Indeed, Darnton reports, so many of Rousseau's readers pursued him in quest of more letters that "he needed a trap door to escape those who sought him out in his retreat on the Ile Saint Pierre."[23] For Rousseau, the framing narrative of *The New Heloise* evidently did its work too well.

By contrast to their predecessors, most nineteenth-century novelists, especially the Realists among them, did not widely use narrative frames, for they did not see them as a means of increasing verisimilitude or encouraging communal integration. Rather, they saw them as a structural device that had been unmasked as a mere literary convention. And once they—and their readers—perceived the framing narrative as literary convention, its artifice became transparent and the frame lost its ability to introduce art as a part of reality. These authors therefore abandoned narrative frames and invited their readers to encounter the narrative directly, as though the art were already a part of reality to which no transition was needed.

Yet despite this trend, Turgenev clearly favored narrative frames. Throughout his career, he repeatedly created framing narratives, some quite elaborate, others quite simple. For example, complex framing narratives surround the short stories "The Correspondence," "The Dog," and "Brigadier," as well as the novella *Spring Torrents*, describing in some detail the circumstances and the motives for the presentation of the framed narrative. The framing narratives around the short stories "The Watch," "The Unhappy One," and "Knock... Knock... Knock!," by contrast, consist of only an introductory sentence or even a single phrase establishing merely in passing the identity of a narrator and the presence of an audience for the framed narrative. And yet other stories, such as "Asya," begin with the briefest possible frame, barely remarking a narrator and an audience, only to conclude with an extended discussion of the implications of the framed narrative.

Narrative frames also appear in Turgenev's novels, although none of these novels is formally framed as a whole. For example, the course of Rudin's self-discovery in *Rudin*, the upbringing of Lavretskii and Liza in *A Nest of Gentry*, the fate of Elena after Insarov's death in *On the Eve*, the unrequited love affair of Pavel Petrovich in *Fathers and Sons*, and Litvinov's youthful infatuation with Irina in *Smoke* are all presented in clearly framed narratives. In each case, a narrator, whether a character in the novel or an omniscient voice, shifts the reader's attention from the narration of the main plot to another, framed narrative.

This extensive reliance on narrative frames suggests that Turgenev shared the pre-nineteenth-century predilection for that structural device. But such a predilection must not be dismissed

as an idiosyncratic preference for an anachronistic aesthetic maneuver. As the social theorist Erving Goffman maintains, recognizable frames are deployed in literary works—and in social
interactions as well—because "participants in an activity are
meant to know and to openly acknowledge that a systematic alteration is involved, one that will radically reconstitute what it
is for them that is going on." Goffman claims therefore that a
reader of a literary work often actively seeks out frames that provide clues not only to "what . . . is going on but to the author's
conception of the "proper perspective" from which to comprehend "what . . . is going on."[24] Thus he concludes that the employment of a narrative frame enables an author to guide the
reader's determination of what is "proper," that is, of what are
appropriate emotional and ethical responses to the events portrayed.

Like his contemporaries, Turgenev was undoubtedly well
aware of the conventionality of such frames, but they served his
ethical purposes too well to resist. Turgenev's frames do indeed
convey to his readers the proper perspective from which to comprehend what is going on. But in Turgenev's case there is no one
single, proper perspective. What is proper is to adjust from one
perspective to another as needed in order to preserve emotional
equanimity and moral integrity. And a narrative frame affords
Turgenev a particularly effective vehicle for offering a model of
shifting perspectives by enabling easy alterations of narrative
modes.

As early as in his first published prose work, the short story
"Andrei Kolosov," Turgenev creates a narrative frame that illustrates the advantages of careful alterations in point of view. This
tale of a young man's attempt to supplant his most admired acquaintance, Kolosov, in the affections of a sheltered young
woman opens by epitomizing emotional restraint and distance,
as the first sentences introduce, in the mode of apperception, an
objectively observed, ordinary social scene:

In a small, tidily clean room, before a fireplace, sat several young
people. The winter evening had only just begun: the samovar was boil-
ing on the table, the conversation warmed up and ranged from one subject to another. They began to discuss unusual people and what distin-

guishes them from ordinary people. Each set forth his opinion as best he could; the voices rose and resounded. (4: 7)

All these statements seem to originate from an uninvolved, impersonal, omniscient narrator speaking in the third person. Only at the conclusion of the fifth sentence is the narrator of the frame revealed to be among the group of young people in attendance, when he parenthetically announces that "I, too, was among the discussants" (4: 7). Thus Turgenev replaces the point of view of a third-person narrator with that of a first-person narrator, all the while employing the apperceptive mode.

Turgenev complicates this replacement, though, by employing not a first-person singular but a first-person plural narrative voice, as when the narrator observes that "a small little fellow . . . suddenly stood and addressed *us all*" (4: 7; emphases here and below are mine). After this little fellow's suggestion that discussions such as those they have embarked on have no purpose, the narrator reports that "*we all* fell silent." Next the narrator notes that "one of *us*" asked how to proceed in that case, and that "*we all* became thoughtful" when challenged by the little fellow to tell the story of an encounter with an unusual person. When challenged in return, the little fellow is told, "If your story does not please *us, we* will hiss" (4: 8). And after the little fellow agrees to such terms, the narrator then states that "*we all* sat down around him and grew quiet," in response to which "the little fellow looked at *us all*, glanced at the ceiling, and began" (4: 8). His first-person account of his relationship of long ago with Andrei Kolosov and Varia, the girl to whom Kolosov introduced him, constitutes the substance of the framed narrative within the work.

Thus each point of view presented at the outset of "Andrei Kolosov" is positioned at a temporal and spatial distance from the events of the framed narrative to come. This distance in turn reflects the emotional distance of the little fellow's audience—and presumably of the reader—from these events. And this distance is preserved as the narrative perspective gradually narrows in this opening segment of the frame, only slowly moving from the completely impersonal to the somewhat more personal collective to the most personal, individual point of view. Such a cautious narrowing of the perspective in the framing narrative deters the strong identification between reader and narrator that could be generated if the narrator's personal point of view were solely presented from the start.

The framed narrative then rotates among the modes of apperception, assimilation, and autonomy, as the little fellow at times records, at times re-creates, and at times comments on his youthful self-delusive thoughts and feelings.[25] After completing this narrative, the little fellow, in the framing narrative's closing segment, shifts between the modes of apperception and autonomy to underscore the model of moral behavior that the frame embodies formally and advocates substantively: the conscious imposition or acceptance of limitations on experience. It is precisely this value that the little fellow discerns informing Kolosov's behavior and praises to his audience in a series of rhetorical questions, reverting to the temporal and spatial setting of the framing narrative to ask:

Who among us could divorce ourselves from our past at the right time? Who, tell me, who does not fear reproaches, I do not mean the reproaches of women, but the reproaches of any fool? Who among us has not given himself over to the desire at times to brag about our generosity, at other times egotistically to toy with another person's devoted heart? Finally, who among us has the strength to oppose petty egoism— petty good feelings: pity and repentance? (4: 32)

With this series of questions the little fellow relentlessly exposes the immorality in the self-indulgent unrestraint, artificiality, and conformity that he perceives in the conduct of most human relations. That conduct, he reveals, is made morally bankrupt through the deception of self and others that excessive self-consciousness rationalizes.

By contrast, what the little fellow finds remarkable is Kolosov's knowing, self-aware integrity, manifested by the capacity to establish an independent, honest relationship without debilitating attachments to past experience, traditional opinions, or social expectations, and by the capacity to conclude that relationship when it has run its course. The little fellow then summarizes this admiration for Kolosov's unswerving integrity in a final, autonomous assessment of Kolosov's character: "At a certain age, to be natural is to be unusual" (4: 33). The little fellow means this not simply in the sense of Kolosov's being authentic, that is, true to inborn temperament, but in the sense that Kolosov, unlike "usual" men, apprehends natural limits, and willingly espouses those limits as moral imperatives. In essence, the narrator suggests, Kolosov can be said to frame his own experience.

In the concluding lines of the framing narrative, Turgenev indicates just how difficult it is to limit or frame socially expected and accepted emotional responses. For even after hearing the little fellow's peroration, as the narrator records in the mode of apperception, an audience member asks, "What happened to Varia?" (4: 33), the girl whom both Kolosov and the little fellow courted and then abandoned without even a farewell. This question obviously anticipates a reply characterized by the very qualities the little fellow has just debunked as veiled self-aggrandizement, pity and repentance. The questioner has not fully learned Kolosov's lesson on the folly of socially sanctioned sentiments.

But the little fellow himself has learned this lesson well, as his simple, three-word answer to the question proves: "I don't know" (4: 33). At first, this abrupt, stark, nearly stunning reply sounds utterly self-indulgent and heartless, as though he had cavalierly neglected to make even a mere inquiry as to Varia's fate. Yet this reply reveals how thoroughly the little fellow has faced the truth about his own self-serving motives in engaging the affections of a girl in love with the man he most admires. He has finally realized that to pursue any relationship with Varia would have been basely self-gratifying for him and blatantly deceptive and destructive of her, or, in a word, immoral. Furthermore, in his complete indifference to the tender sensibilities of his audience, whom he must suspect he shocks with his evident unrepentance, the little fellow displays an independence from social expectations that he lacked when he knew Varia. Once so exquisitely self-conscious, he no longer fears the reproaches of any fool.

But Turgenev does not leave the little fellow's audience wallowing in outraged sympathy for Varia. Instead, Turgenev suggests the possibility that each member of the audience—and thus, by implication, each reader of his story—may acquire the integrity and self-sufficiency achieved by Kolosov and the little fellow, by closing the frame with an apperceptive statement as dispassionate and abrupt as the little fellow's preceding one. The frame's narrator momentarily reasserts the collective point of view as he observes, "We all got up and went our separate ways" (4:33). Yet this collective point of view immediately breaks down as each member of the audience departs silently and singly into the night. Apart, at a physical distance, each one—and the reader likewise—may now contemplate the self-protective benefits of the psychological distance engendered by altering perspectives on painful events, as enacted by the narrator and as illustrated by the work's narrative frame.

First Love, one of Turgenev's finest narratives, is so precisely because it most completely makes use of alterations in narrative mode. And it employs not one but two narrative frames to do so. The first, outer frame is not formally complete—no closing segment is included. Instead, that frame gives way to another, inner frame, which is interwoven into the framed narrative itself. In shifting between the framing and framed narratives, Turgenev readily makes use of all three narrative modes and thereby embodies the very theme of *First Love* in its intricate structure: the psychological and moral need to instill a balance between the restraint and excess inherent in human relations. Intensity of emotion and subjective response to experience are portrayed only in conjunction with constraint of emotion and objective commentary on experience. This conjunction in turn elucidates how necessary such a balance is to self-preservation.

The outer narrative frame begins in the mode of apperception, as an omniscient, impersonal narrator sets the scene, almost as though it were continued from the conclusion of "Andrei Kolosov": "The guests had long ago departed. The clock struck 12:30. Only the host, along with Sergei Nikolaevich and Vladimir Petrovich, remained in the room" (6:303). A few close friends have stayed together to recollect a certain intimate rite of passage, that of first love. The apperceptive mode is sustained throughout the opening segment, as though the events to be portrayed in the framed narrative to follow are so emotionally charged that they require a constant, unemotional counterweight from the start to offset them, although this segment actually discloses only that one of the friends, Vladimir Petrovich, has had a first love that, as he diffidently admits, "actually belongs to the ranks of the not altogether usual" (6: 303).

Yet Vladimir Petrovich, who will assume the role of narrator for the subsequent enclosed account of his first love, refuses to recite that account aloud and at once. In response to his friends' demand that he relate his story immediately, he declares: "No. I will not begin to relate it" (6: 303). Instead, he announces to his friends, "If you will permit, I will write down everything I remember in a little notebook and I will read it to you" (6: 304). Two weeks later, Vladimir Petrovich does just that, reading aloud the narrative he has written about the love he developed for an impoverished aristocratic neighbor, Zinaida, and his discovery of her love affair with his own father.

Why does Vladimir Petrovich insist on reading his story rather than telling it, even to close friends? He explains by claiming, "I am not a master of narration. Either everything comes out drily and briefly or verbosely and falsely" (6: 303). This explanation displays his belief that an impromptu presentation is more liable than a written one to failures of either omission or commission that will violate the truth of his narrative. But beyond that, Vladimir Petrovich's insistence on writing down his experience of first love instead of orally presenting it implies a desire to transform that experience aesthetically, thereby controlling his own reaction, that of his auditors, and that of any future readers. That control is greatly enlarged by the opportunity to change narrative modes, a verbal technique that can be difficult to apply smoothly in an extemporaneous oral presentation but that can be easily integrated into a carefully considered written account. Thus Vladimir Petrovich signals his sensitivity to the highly personal and revealing, potentially disturbing nature of the account of his first love, as well as his intention to curb any such disturbance.

He further ensures his control over the reaction to his story, and further betrays his recognition of the need for such control, by creating a frame for the written narrative that facilitates alterations of narrative mode. He selects first the mode of apperception to indicate firmly that the events of his recorded narrative took place well in the past, making this point explicitly in his opening line: "I was sixteen years old at that time. The matter occurred in 1833" (6: 304). By noting his age, the date, and by employing the adverbial phrase "at that time," Vladimir Petrovich clearly marks the events he will describe as belonging to an earlier, long-gone time. And he goes on to describe those events with the apperceptive mode in the past tense.

Yet periodically he introduces an alteration from the apperceptive to the assimilative, as he allows the consciousness of the sixteen-year-old Vladimir Petrovich to take over narratorial responsibility from that of the adult Vladimir Petrovich. This alteration is always accompanied by an increase in emotional intensity, as, for instance, when he depicts his first glimpse of Zinaida. He recreates so eloquently the quickening of his feelings and their subsequent subsidence into wordless admiration that the adolescent's point of view prevails: "I forgot everything. I devoured with my gaze that lovely figure and little neck, those beautiful hands and that slightly disheveled blond hair beneath a white kerchief and that half-closed intelligent eye and those lashes and the tender cheek beneath them..." (6: 307).

Lest this highly charged point of view come to monopolize the narrative, though, Vladimir Petrovich rapidly returns to the mode of apperception, and he regularly resorts to the mode of autonomy to reassert his adult point of view—that is, he reverts to the point of view of the written account's framing narrative. Terms or phrases such as "I shall never forget" and "I remember" autonomously root the adolescent's emotions firmly in the past, modulated and mitigated by the distance of time and space. And the more intense the attraction the adolescent experiences, the more deliberate the assertion of the adult's voice in the mode of autonomy, as, for example, in the pivotal seventh chapter, when Vladimir Petrovich movingly recalls the epiphanic moment when "I became cold at the thought that I was in love, that here it was, here was love" (6: 332). He romantically recollects watching a late night summer storm at this moment that mirrored the oscillations of turbulence and calm within him. But the narrative then promptly switches to the mode of autonomy and adopts the present tense, as the adult voice of Vladimir Petrovich offsets the power of this epiphany by emphasizing that it belongs only to the past: "O sweet feelings, soft sounds, goodness and peace of a moved spirit, the melting joy of the first tender emotions of love—where are you, where are you?" (6: 323). This adoption of the autonomous mode in a reversion to the frame lyrically yet firmly separates past from present, youth from adulthood, emotion from recollection.

Vladimir Petrovich incorporates a final change of modes and tenses by turning from the framed narrative back to the framing one in the concluding chapter of *First Love*. In this chapter he presents himself not at age sixteen, but at age twenty, and he confesses that at that time he had gone from one emotive extreme to another. Whereas at sixteen Vladimir Petrovich had been deeply sensitive and passionate, at twenty he has become insensitive and dispassionate, as his response to the news of Zinaida's death demonstrates. To summarize this response, in the mode of autonomy he quotes two lines from a poem by Pushkin: "From indifferent lips I heard the news of death,/And indifferently I heeded it" (6: 363). At what might have been the climax of his narrative, Vladimir Petrovich presents instead an epitome of emotionlessness, not even using his own words but quoting those of another author and thus rendering his own response more distant still.

He then commences the longest portion of the written narrative frame, in which he first observes the foolishness of youth, in its ignorant and arrogant self-absorption, again using the autonomous mode. Yet he also perceives a redeeming strength in youth's very arrogance, exclaiming, "Oh youth! Youth! . . . Perhaps the entire secret of your charm lies not in the ability to do everything but in the ability to think that you can do everything" (6: 363). He next proceeds to glorify the recollections of his own self-absorbed youth: "And now, when evening shadows are beginning to fall over my life, what has remained to me that is more fresh, more dear, than the memories of that quickly fleeting, morning spring storm?" (6: 363).

But why should Vladimir Petrovich conclude his frame by engaging the mode of autonomy to praise the tumult of his early, stormy love, which he appears to have worked so hard to avoid in his narrative? The answer to this question is revealed, albeit indirectly, further on—for although Vladimir Petrovich concludes the frame of the written narrative with his rhetorical question, he does not conclude his entire narrative with it. Instead he adds one final paragraph, couched in the mode of apperception, that illustrates the reason for his attachment to the seeming excesses of his youth. In this final paragraph, he portrays the horrible terminal moments of an old woman, which he witnessed several days after learning of Zinaida's death. Though he had felt no particular pang at the report of her demise, he is clearly disturbed when confronted in person by a desperate, pathetic, and utterly hopeless struggle against the inevitable end. In the final line of the work, he confesses that "there, at the deathbed of this poor old woman, I became afraid for Zinaida, and I wanted to pray for her, for my father, and for myself" (6: 364).

By concluding his narrative with the word "self" in the accusative case [*sebia*], Vladimir Petrovich ends with the image of himself as an object—a mortal object. At that moment he sees death all too clearly and confronts his own mortality all too directly, for however accurate, such a vision of death, in constant sight, would destroy the ability to see anything else. Such knowledge, always in force, would destroy the will to live at all—hence his desire to pray for his profoundly threatened "self." The affectionate evocation of youth that is the essence of the framed narrative offers an antidote to the psychological poison of the ceaseless awareness of ineluctable death. Likewise, the complex narrative structure with its intertwined narrative modes exemplifies adjustments in perception and comprehension of experience, including the experience of death, that can enable the individual to maintain psychological health through a sanity- and life-preserving balance between ignorance and knowledge, subjectivity and objectivity, excess and limitation.

Turgenev presents the most complicated interweaving of these three narrative modes in his novels, taking advantage of the genre's greater length to introduce subtle variations in the point of view within each mode as well as between modes. Thus Turgenev can fully exploit nuanced shifts in perspective on the events portrayed in order to instill maximum control over the reader's response to those events. Moreover, the shifts within modes can compile a more elaborate model of consciousness than can the undifferentiated usages of each mode. It should be noted that this model does not appear in *Rudin*, where Turgenev relies most heavily on dialogue and almost completely ignores the mode of autonomy, but it distinctly manifests itself in his mature novels, *A Nest of Gentry*, *On the Eve*, *Smoke*, and above all *Fathers and Sons*, whose narrative intricacies exemplify best the model of consciousness Turgenev most favors.

The narration of *Fathers and Sons* commences *in medias res* in the apperceptive mode, as an unnamed narrator reports a brief and almost comically repetitive exchange between a landowner, Nikolai Petrovich Kirsanov, and his servant about whether or not the servant has caught sight of a carriage bringing Nikolai Petrovich's son, Arkadii, home from university. But the narrator quickly shifts to the mode of autonomy, stopping the narration, which consists of action in the past tense, to introduce Nikolai Petrovich to the reader in the present tense. The narrator in effect freezes Nikolai Petrovich in place, commenting, "Let us acquaint the reader with him, while he sits with his legs tucked under him and pensively looks around." The narrator then imparts fairly detailed information about Nikolai Petrovich and his parents: "His name is Nikolai Petrovich Kirsanov. He has a nice farm of 200 souls, 15 versts from an inn. . . . His father, a general of the War of 1812, a half-educated, coarse, but not evil, Russian man, toiled all his life. . . . His mother . . . belonged to the ranks of 'mother-commanders,' wore luxuriant caps and rustling silk dresses" (7: 7).

The narrator conveys this information in an informal, conversational manner. He observes, for instance, that as a child, Arkadii "grew 'n' grew" (7: 10), and he humorously notes at one point that Nikolai Petrovich's parents were disappointed in him for falling in love with a clerk's daughter, whose chief fault lay in her habit of reading "serious articles in the 'Sciences' section of magazines" (7: 8). Thus the narrator establishes an identity as a knowledgeable, chatty, occasionally tongue-in-cheek friend of the family—and friend of the reader as well, for the narrator deploys not the first-person singular pronouns that would distinguish him as an individual with a unique point of view but the first-person plural pronouns that mark him as a representative of a broader outlook.

This use of the plural—"Let *us* introduce him" (emphasis mine)—instills its own distinctive point of view in *Fathers and Sons*, one that allies narrator and reader as a first-person singular narration could not. Although the use of "we" may seem editorial at the beginning of the narrator's first statement in the mode of autonomy, it quickly takes on a collective implication as the narration progresses, embracing the reader's consciousness into its own. After concluding his history of the Kirsanov family, the narrator says, "And here we see him [Nikolai Petrovich] in May of 1859" (7: 10). And later the narrator refers to "our Nikolai Petrovich" (7: 10) and "our acquaintances" (7: 57, 76), and describes Arkadii and his young love, Katia, by noting that "their faces have changed since we saw them the last time" (7: 78).

Invoking the first-person plural rather than the first-person singular to address and engage the reader, the narrator actually disguises his own personality: the consciousness, the sense of character and event are "ours," not his alone, so precisely are his perceptions implied to mirror those of the reader. He thus deflects attention from himself as a solitary perceiving consciousness, a deflection that enables these autonomous assertions to assume an authenticity and an authority that they might lack if offered as the perceptions of a single individual. In turn, this authority expands the narrator's control over the reception of the events described, since they are not rendered as the whimsical product of a possibly subjective or idiosyncratic interpreter but as the shared and hence more objective understanding of an assemblage of minds whose assessments can therefore be relied on.

Having asserted this claim to collective credibility, the narrator can then go on to report in the mode of apperception thoughts or feelings not voiced by the characters. For example, the narrator observes that in response to seeing the fields and workers of his home, "Arkadii thought, 'This poor region, it nurtures neither satisfaction nor diligence; it is impossible, impossible to let it remain thus'" (7: 16). Later the narrator conveys Bazarov's reaction on surveying the Kirsanov home: "'Aha,' he thought, having looked around, 'this little place is not much to look at'" (7: 21). And immediately after Bazarov has confessed his love for Anna Sergeevna, the narrator records that "however Odintsova [Anna Sergeevna] controlled herself, however she rose above all prejudices, she was nonetheless uncomfortable when she appeared in the dining room for dinner" (7: 99).

As further proof of his authority, the narrator at times uses the apperceptive mode to reveal knowledge superior to that of some characters. For instance, when an ailing Pavel Petrovich feverishly mutters incoherent imprecations against Bazarov for his audacious kiss of Nikolai Petrovich's adored Fenechka, the narrator notes that "Nikolai Petrovich only sighed; he in no way suspected to whom these words referred" (7: 149). Later, the narrator steps even further outside the narrative frame to comment that "that self-assured Bazarov did not even suspect that in [some peasants'] eyes, he was nonetheless something of a buffoonish joke" (7: 173). And near the conclusion of *Fathers and Sons*, the narrator interjects another such insight, noting of Pavel Petrovich that "life for him is hard... harder than he himself suspects" (7: 187). The validity of these omniscient insertions appears unquestionable; their objectivity has been tacitly endorsed by the omnipresence of a plural point of view.

Yet in other instances the narrator employs modes of both apperception and autonomy seemingly to undercut his own established authority by declaring a lack of omniscience, as reports on the nature of characters' experiences are qualified or limited by the narrator's denials of total knowledge or comprehension. For example, when Fenechka, Nikolai Petrovich's peasant mistress, appears before Arkadii and Bazarov for the first time, the narrator announces, "It seemed that she felt guilty for appearing and at the same time she seemed to feel that she had the right to appear" (7: 26). Here the narrator does not report Fenechka's precise thoughts or feelings, offering only an impression of them. Any discomfort at her ambiguous moral and social status within the Kirsanov family is only intimated, not explicitly stated. Similarly, when Arkadii announces to Anna Sergeevna, after she has rejected Bazarov's romantic overtures, that he and Bazarov will depart, the narrator remarks simply that Anna Sergeevna "seemed distracted and tired" (7: 102). Any psychic discomfort inducing this condition goes unarticulated.

At still other moments, the narrator not only fails to express a character's thoughts and feelings, or even what that character seems to be thinking or feeling, but denies all possibility of expressing them. For instance, after Pavel Petrovich visits Fenechka and her child, a visit that evidently distresses him, he returns to his study where, as reported by the narrator in the apperceptive mode, "he threw himself on the couch, put his hands behind his head, and remained motionless, staring at the ceiling almost with despair." Then the narrator modulates the apperceptive mode to register ignorance of Pavel Petrovich's motivations, asserting, "Whether he wanted to hide what was expressed on his face from the very walls, or for some other reason, he got up, unfastened the window's heavy curtains, and again threw himself on the couch" (7: 21).

At this juncture the narrator implies he cannot represent Pavel Petrovich's silent thoughts or private motives. Nor can he evidently do so after Bazarov's arrival at the Kirsanov estate, when the narrator alleges an inability to disclose Pavel Petrovich's subsequent reflections, merely observing, "God knows where his thoughts wandered, but they did not wander only in the past: the expression on his face was fixed and gloomy, which does not happen when a man is occupied with memories alone" (7: 21). Only external behavior, not internal mental activity, is depicted; the reader is left to intuit the antipathy toward Bazarov impelling Pavel Petrovich's cheerless musings.

The narrator takes the same evasive tack when discussing the woman with whom Pavel Petrovich had fallen in love years earlier, averring: "What nestled in that heart—God knows! It seemed that she found herself in the power of some sort of secret forces unknown even to her" (7: 31). Unknown as well, it would appear, to the narrator; God may know, but the narrator avows that he does not. Another such manifestation of the narrator's lack of special privilege appears on Bazarov's return to Anna Sergeevna's estate for a second visit, at which point the narrator declares only that she greeted Bazarov and Arkadii, Bazarov's then traveling companion, "with her usual politeness, but she was surprised by their quick return and, as much as was possible to judge from the slowness of her movements and utterances, it did not overly please her" (7: 129). Within a single, apperceptive sentence, the narrator switches from the revelation of internal experience—surprise—to the description of external gestures— "as much as was possible to judge from the slowness of her movements and utterances"—while offering no definitive interpretation of those gestures. Nowhere in the novel is the reversion to a condition of outside observer from that of inside informer more abrupt.

And after recording in the mode of apperception that Bazarov and Anna Sergeevna finally agree to be "good friends, as before" and concur that love is "an unnatural feeling," the narrator concludes: "Thus spoke Anna Sergeevna and thus spoke Bazarov: they both thought that they spoke the truth." But then follows a remark in the mode of autonomy: "Was there truth, complete truth, in their words? They themselves did not know, and neither does the author" (7: 162). Whether representing himself as the author or simply as the author's intermediary, the narrator rejects the possibility of revealing the characters' self-deception, while nonetheless hinting, by introducing the idea, that they are indeed self-deceived regarding both love in general and their own love for one another in particular.

Such narrative alterations between assertions of knowledge

and ignorance, intimacy and distance, and the modes of apperception and autonomy might seem to mark technical lapses or changes of mere convenience on Turgenev's part, inconsistent with a sustained narrative consciousness and point of view.[26] Yet there is in fact a most consistent pattern to these changes. What the narrator avoids revealing, sometimes with a show of unwillingness, more often with a claim of inability, pertains to incidents evoking singular intensity in a character—torment, anguish, or dismay. The narrator does report directly the mental processes that reveal simple characterological quirks or biases—such as Arkadii's mild political pretentiousness in his notions of reforming his father's estate or Bazarov's condescension toward that estate—but will only adumbrate serious psychological disturbance, insecurity, or ambivalence. Thus the discomfiture of Fenechka, the loneliness and hostility of Pavel Petrovich, the covetousness of Pavel Petrovich's femme fatale, the conflicts of Anna Sergeevna—all are evoked obliquely, indirectly; the very depth of feeling aroused in those characters is indicated by this act of oblique rendition. If their emotional states were not intense or lasting, the narrator might well have presented them explicitly—he had established his narratorial right to do so. Moreover, the very obliqueness of their evocation reflects the characters' psychic efforts to deny, repress, or deflect their powerful presence so as to control their traumatic force. Thus Turgenev invokes alterations in narrative mode both to convey the unwillingness of various characters to confront their most difficult dilemmas and to exemplify for the reader his moral model of the self-protective, distancing consciousness that will not dwell on those dilemmas so extensively that they prove self-destructive.

Arguably, Turgenev's most daring and dazzling narrative achievement of all is the short story "Enough," in which he almost fuses the modes of apperception and autonomy to create an overall effect of assimilation. The failure to recognize the narratorial sophistication of this work, though, has led to some misunderstanding of its nature and import. It has often been interpreted as Turgenev's personal lamentation over the unfavored status of human beings in the universe.[27] But such an interpretation does not take into account the extent to which Turgenev creates a narrator with a distinct personality who is trapped within the circularity of obsessive thoughts from which he cannot escape.

This "excerpt from the notes of an artist who has died," as the subtitle sets the text forth, starts in the mode of apperception, as the artist reports his repeated intonation of the word "enough": "'Enough,' I said to myself as my legs, not wanting to step along the steep slope of the mountain, carried me below, toward the quiet little river; 'enough,' I repeated . . . 'enough,' I said yet again. . . . 'Enough!'" He then continues with another set of iterations, but these combine apperception with autonomy:

Stop hurrying, stop striving, it is time to withdraw: it is time to take your head in both hands and force the heart to be silent. Stop comforting yourself . . . stop running . . . stop grasping. . . . Everything has been experienced—everything has been felt many times. . . . Everything has occurred, occurred, repeated, repeated a thousand times— and if you recall that everything will continue thus for all eternity, as though by command, by law, you even become irritated! Yes . . . irritated! (7: 220)

Ostensibly addressed only to himself, these half-apperceptive, half-autonomous generalizations nonetheless are also meant for a reader's edification, for in a subsequent section of his "notes," the artist continues in this fused narrative mode to disclose that he is directing his narrative to a reader outside the text: "I write this to you, to you, my only and never-to-be-forgotten friend, to you, my dear girl, whom I have abandoned forever" (7: 221). Most of his other statements, many of which are equally repetitive, blend apperceptive reports of his own actions past and present with autonomous comments allegedly aimed at this fictional reader. Yet they are actually couched as universal observations intended for any reader. For instance, he asserts at one point, "There is no hope and no return—there is no bitterness in me, and no pity" (7: 221), and then argues that Shakespeare likewise beheld the unvarying hideousness of reality that has generated the artist's existential alienation. He obsessively insists that Shakespeare also perceived everywhere "the same mixed and in essence uncomplicated picture. . . . The same credulity and the same cruelty, the same demands . . . the same base satisfactions, the same senseless sufferings . . . the same coarse enticements . . . the same seizures of power, the same habits of slavery, the same natural inequality—in a word, the same noisy leaps of a squirrel in the same old, unrenovated cage" (7: 227–28). And then at the conclusion he simply repeats two words he has repeated before: "No... no... Enough... enough... enough!" (7: 231).

Although able to conflate artfully the representations of apperception with the reevaluations of autonomy, this narrator nevertheless evinces no ability to depart from his solitary, embittered point of view. These fatalistic, despair-filled utterances proceed from a mind that has imprisoned itself, a mind that cannot elude the hopelessness engendered by its own inability to instill novelty or variety in life and thereby impose meaning on life. And by giving that mind full play throughout the narrative, Turgenev thus actually fabricates a tour de force of assimilation, in which he allows the re-created consciousness of a character to control completely the course of the narration in order to expose, subtly yet unrelentingly, its inadequacy. Indeed, so inadequate is this artist's imaginative capacity that he must even have recourse to the words of another artist, albeit the one with whom he identifies, Shakespeare, in order to conclude his narrative, declaiming, "The rest is silence" (7: 231).

The inability to author his own conclusion only confirms what the narrator's repetition of words in the conjoined modes of apperception and autonomy has already demonstrated. These final words make clear that Turgenev has depicted an artist who has indeed died because, unlike Turgenev, he cannot creatively alter his point of view. He cannot replace one perspective with an alternative that will provide some protective psychological distance from what is otherwise a destructive closeness to the immutable horrors of human existence—for him, everything is always "the same." Therefore, although this is a character with whom Turgenev can sympathize, this is definitely not one to be taken for Turgenev himself. The true Turgenev is able, as the dying artist is not, to espouse and to illustrate with both positive and negative examples the necessity of redemptive shifts in perspective, not only in art but in life.

Turgenev's characteristic use of multiple narrative modes does not in itself necessarily differentiate Turgenev's narrative style from that of Realists—but the relation among those modes does. Disputing the commonplace that a single, consistently unobtrusive, depersonalized voice holding sway throughout a narrative constitutes a hallmark of Realism,[28] Elizabeth Ermarth has convincingly argued that the narrative perspective typifying Realism is distinguished not by a single point of view at all, but by the conjunction of several points of view in what she terms "a consensus." Suggesting that "realism is an aesthetic form of consensus, its touchstone being the agreement between the various viewpoints made available by a text,"[29] she demonstrates that these viewpoints reinforce one another so as to create the impression of a coherent, comprehensible, "common world."[30] Such consensus in narrative perspectives is perfectly suited to the ethical ends of Realism, since it conveys to the reader the comforting assurance that reliable, communal comprehension and evaluation of events can and should occur.

By contrast, Turgenev's various narrative perspectives, although often complementary, are not consensual. Each is positioned at a different remove from the substance they narrate and from the reader, whereas the various perspectives of consensus are ranged relatively equally from both substance and audience. And each of Turgenev's modes embodies a distinct point of view that implicitly revises or at least questions the perspectives of the others, instead of confirming their validity, as does each viewpoint contributing to a consensus. Turgenev's narrative modes therefore remind the reader not about the merits of communal integration but about the value of a detached point of view that can readily be replaced, if need be, by another one more distant and therefore more conducive to the solitary quest for secular salvation.

6

Strategies of Self-Creation:
Apollonian Individuation

In *The Birth of Tragedy*, Nietzsche stresses the importance of delimitation to the Apollonian tendency in art. Delimitation "tranquillizes the individual by drawing boundary lines"[1] around experience, producing a calming sense of order, proportion, and harmony. And these "boundary lines" produce such tranquillity because they guard individual consciousness from the Dionysian "world of torment,"[2] in which primordial chaos reigns. Acceptance of these boundaries therefore allows the individual to conceive and conserve an identity apart from the elemental mass of vital energy that destroys all differentiation between living things.

Borrowing from Schopenhauer, Nietzsche dubs this differentiating force of limitation and individuality the *principium individuationis*, or principle of individuation. By this term Nietzsche means not simply the discernment of distinct entities among the circumstances surrounding them, but the combined intellectual, psychological, and moral dedication to the specific vision of what he calls an "individuated world."[3] This vision deliberately blinds itself to the deformation and dissolution that inevitably characterize the assimilation of every distinct entity into one inchoate whole. It looks instead to the imagination for the construction of manifold discrete entities whose integrity and autonomy are respected at all costs. Adherence to this vision thereby converts, as he puts it, "fits of nausea into imaginings with which it is possible to live."[4] Thus Nietzsche's principle of individuation is a principle of creation as well—the creation of forms that are adaptive if artificial, life-affirming if truth-denying, redemptive if unreal.

Human beings adopt the principle of individuation when they insist on everywhere affirming their integrity—meaning at least their psychic integration, if not their social probity. And they manifest this affirmation by consciously defining themselves in terms of temperamental and circumstantial limits—limits of knowledge, strength, ability, etc. Having set these limits, they then become free to create for themselves an authentic, coherent, consistent identity. Thus the human incarnation of the principle of individuation displays a dynamic interplay between self-limitation and self-expression, between self-control and self-creation.

Turgenev's characterizations have not traditionally been seen to partake of such dynamism. Rather, most critics have viewed them as fixed representations of one of two fundamental personality types: the Hamletic—generally, male protagonists who seem to have no will and therefore cannot act, often categorized as "superfluous men"; and the Quixotic—frequently, heroic females capable of sacrificing themselves for some noble ideal. The assumption that these two types dominate Turgenev's conceptualization of characters derives from a nonfictional essay he wrote entitled "Hamlet and Don Quixote," in which he compares these two literary figures as exemplars of contrasting psychological styles. Don Quixote, he maintains, represents an idealistic and selfless devotion to the pursuit of exalted goals, whereas Hamlet stands for the cynical rationalizing and paralyzing self-consciousness that precludes the pursuit of any goal at all.[5]

Kagan-Kans goes perhaps farthest in tying Turgenev's aesthetic practice to this theoretical meditation, arguing that "in 'Hamlet and Don Quixote' Turgenev attempts to create a universal yardstick of human types"[6] against which he would measure all his protagonists. She concludes that Turgenev considers each type absolutely at odds with the other—at the opposite ends of the yardstick—because, in Turgenev's view, "thought and will are irrevocably severed."[7] Turgenev is therefore given to an "ambivalent vision" of human nature that results in the creation of two types of characters.

It is fair to assume that Turgenev partook of the nineteenth-century cultural curiosity about individual or social "types" represented in literature to provide, as René Wellek documents, "realistic pictures, as sources of information about social stratification."[8] Nevertheless, the essay on Hamlet and Don Quixote is better understood as a critical and philosophical commentary on the distinctive creations of Shakespeare and Cervantes than as an attempt to set forth a theory of literary types that his own works embody. Turgenev's conceptions and renditions of his protagonists are far more subtle, various, and tension filled than any typological scheme can do justice to. Indeed, these renditions raise not so much a problem of types as a type of problem, a type of problem to which Turgenev offers as many different solutions as the number of characters he portrays. And this problem can be summarized as the search for the strategies of self-protection most effective in ensuring individuation—as Turgenev conceives it.

In truth, Turgenev carries the concept of individuation farther than Nietzsche does. Both accept as its basis the rational imposition of psychic boundaries around the self that defend against destructive forces beyond rational control. But Turgenev envisions those forces less mythically, more particularly than Nietzsche, perceiving them as the indifference of nature, the arbitrariness of society, and the impulsiveness of irrationality. The mental barriers erected therefore do not merely arm the self against opposing but morally equivalent energies, such as the transcendent joys of Dionysian self-abandon. The energies attacking the Turgenevan self have no morally redeeming value; they are enemies pure and simple. Thus in Turgenev's narratives the principle of individuation enables not only psychological security but ethical triumph as well, for optimal individuation means the continuation of not just an autonomous self, but the best possible self. This is the self the individual purposefully envisions and remains committed to as the most appropriate, the most fulfilling—and the most defensible. This is the self the individual consciously creates through complete knowledge of temperamental capacities and incapacities, the self that constantly unites thought and feeling, intention and action, without undergoing debilitating conflict or degrading deception. Hence this is the self characterized by the greatest integrity.

To uphold the principle of individuation according to Turgenev's standards requires ceaseless self-awareness. The limits of the self must be guarded vigilantly; individual uniqueness is thereby confirmed even as individual fallibility is acknowledged. To be sure, the constellation of Turgenev's protagonists demonstrates Turgenev's recognition of the danger of active self-awareness: it is all too easily transformed into paralyzing self-consciousness. Like his Romanticist predecessors—along with artists, philosophers, and critics down to the present day—Turgenev understood the emotional and even physical disablement that can set in when unchecked self-consciousness prevails. The need to interpret every thought, every feeling, every experience, intensifies until no spontaneous action or reaction is possible.

Critics have long remarked Turgenev's sensitivity to the existential affliction wrought by overweening self-consciousness. The remedy for such affliction most often associated with Turgenev is the one prescribed by Schopenhauer: self-transcendence, a psychic rejection of individuality through a sense of merging with a universal spirit oblivious to specific human sufferings.[9] Numerous commentators have argued that Turgenev's noblest protagonists are those most unself-conscious, most self-sacrificing, most able to forsake any concern for their private interests in pursuit of some ideal or cause they value more highly.[10] Thus, traditionally, Turgenev's antidote to the disease of self-consciousness is taken to be self-denial.

Yet this conclusion is at once too narrow and too far-reaching, implying that Turgenev's value system demands that all sense of self be eliminated in order to achieve true virtue. It disregards evidence of significantly differing degrees of self-consciousness among his characters, and also fails to account for admirable efforts on the part of some characters to become more self-conscious rather than less so. In essence, this conclusion ignores the subtle and sophisticated psychology informing Turgenev's characterizations, a psychology that comprehends remarkably various manifestations of self-consciousness. And it therefore overlooks the morality that accepts the risks of self-conscious excesses as the potential price of conscientious self-protection.

Turgenev's characterizations may best be understood, therefore, not as representatives of fixed character types but as individuals ranged along a psychological continuum of individuation from utter absence to plenitude; no two characters occupy precisely the same position. Few characters are to be found toward either end of this continuum, and many shift their position during the course of a narrative as they face social and psychological dilemmas that cause them to confront and cope with hitherto unacknowledged limits in themselves or their circumstances. Thus virtually every protagonist, in one way or another, illuminates some aspect of individuation—its possession, its lack, its acquisition, its loss, its benefits, its costs.

The very high costs of lacking individuation are revealed by the few characters who evince little or none of it. Among them are Liza Kalitina's mother, Mar'ia Dmitrievna, in *A Nest of Gentry*; Elena Stakhova's father, Nikolai Artemevich, in *On the Eve*; the elderly princess Zasekina in *First Love*; and an acquaintance of Anna Sergeevna Odintsova, Avdot'ia Kukshina, in *Fathers and Sons*. All play minor roles, since they are not given sufficient strength of character to become a focus of events for more than a brief span of time. They exhibit none of the self-awareness betokening genuine individuation. Rather, they are horribly unself-aware, often babbling away in ignorance of their own impotence as they ineffectually attempt to manipulate others. Their pathetic attempts at self-aggrandizement are inevitably doomed to failure: Mar'ia Dmitrievna cannot effect a reconciliation between Lavretskii and his wife; Nikolai Artemevich cannot prevent Elena's elopement; the princess cannot in any way control her daughter, Zinaida; and Kukshina cannot endear herself to anyone.

Indeed, these characters represent the very antithesis of individuation. Though they might be viewed as wholly selfish, they are better understood as wholly "selfless." They have no authentic ideas and emotions to integrate into individuated selves; they merely imitate behaviors they imagine will convey the impression of individuation, and in so doing, they irritate or alienate virtually everyone they come in contact with, particularly those they seek most to influence. Devoid of all original thought or sincere feeling, these figures have only enough of a semblance of self to foster a false belief in their own wit and wisdom, while actually possessing neither. Thus the self-congratulatory air each exudes while engaged in fruitless machinations is especially ironic, since none has a legitimate self to congratulate.

In truth, such figures generally constitute caricatures more than characters, their appearances, gestures, and actions often humorously exaggerated in comparison to those of other figures. Were their numbers greater in Turgenev's works, they might reasonably be construed as a character type. Given their relative rarity, though, they serve more as cautionary, if comic, figures, for the consequences of their lack of individuation are serious. No matter how hard they try, they can neither comprehend nor control the course of events around them; indeed, they cannot truly control themselves. They are subject to every passing whim that chances to cross their minds. Enslaved by impulse, enamored of ever-elusive self-aggrandizement, these portraits of unself-consciousness illustrate the utterly unconstrained pseudo-selves that the absence of individuation causes.

At the opposite end of Turgenev's characterological continuum can be found figures who embody thorough individuation, albeit in markedly divergent ways. One is Dmitrii Insarov, hero of *On the Eve*. Although some commentators point to the Bulgarian patriot as an exemplary model of selflessness,[11] Insarov actually reveals an affirming self-awareness. Introduced to Elena Stakhova, a young, sheltered Russian girl, as a man having but "one thought, the liberation of his native land" (6: 199), Insarov directs all his energies into efforts to win political independence for Bulgaria from the occupying Turks. In Russia, where he has been forced to flee, Insarov thus works for a cause intended to benefit the lives of many others. Yet he conveys no impression of self-denial or self-sacrifice in these efforts. Rather, he displays only self-gratification and self-growth as he labors not for his fellow countrymen alone, but also for himself. He has drawn the limits defining his identity so as to incorporate the welfare of his country within them.

Insarov guards those limits, fixed both physically and emotionally, with care. He lives in an apartment which is "not easy" to reach (6: 186)—one has to pass through narrow, twisting lanes and ascend dark, rickety staircases to arrive there. And access to his inner life is no more readily attainable. One acquaintance declares to another that the Bulgarian is by nature "the silent type" (6: 200) and that "you will never use the familiar form of *'you'* with him, for no one has ever used the familiar form of *'you'* with him" (6: 207; emphasis Turgenev's). Insarov's reticence, coupled with his insistence on formal modes of discourse when he does converse, symbolizes the distance he keeps between himself and anyone desirous of intimacy. He erects a linguistic boundary around himself that precludes possibly distracting, even draining, close relationships that might sap the psychic strength sustaining his autonomous quest to fulfill the identity he has delineated for himself.

Nonetheless, this acquaintance concedes that in Insarov "there is something childlike, sincere, for all his concentration and even secrecy," but that his sincerity is "not our worthless sincerity, the sincerity of people who decidedly have nothing to hide" (6: 200–201). This distinctive sincerity bespeaks the integrity of an individuated being who knows precisely what of himself can honestly be revealed and what must equally honestly be concealed. Insarov is carefully attuned to the limits on self-expression he must accept in order to preserve that self. Yet he is said to be by no means shy, since "only egotistical people are shy" (6: 201). And indeed, Insarov is the antithesis of the egotist, whose inflated sense of self is so vulnerable to punctures that it cannot risk exposure and withdraws into shyness that it masks as superiority. Insarov has such a strong self that he need not secretively retreat from social interactions, enjoying the confidence that he will decide correctly what to say and what to do.

Just as Insarov is not egotistical, neither is he heroic, at least as Elena conceives of this quality before she meets him. He does not blatantly parade his virtues in dramatic performances, nor adopt enigmatic postures of preparation for self-sacrifice. Having "expected something more 'fatal,'" she discovers on making his acquaintance that "she did not want to bow before him, but to give him a friendly handshake" (6: 206). He behaves simply, naturally, normally. Insarov is not given to the brooding self-absorption of a "man of destiny" who tacitly indicates his social and moral preeminence by shunning ordinary encounters with mere mortals. Nor does he fit the more cynical image of a hero, held by a friend of Elena, who avows that "a hero does not have to speak; a hero bellows like a bull; he moves his horns—walls collapse. And he himself does not have to know why he moves, he just moves" (6: 207–8). Insarov does not act purely according to blind instinct, as this observer concedes when he admits that Insarov is possessed of "a healthy and lively mind, substance and strength, and even the gift of words" (6: 207) when speaking of Bulgaria. Fully self-aware but in no way self-dramatizing, Insarov does not conform to stereotypes. He shapes his behavior to suit what he knows to be his own nature in order to live out his independently determined destiny.

Elena reflects this assessment when Insarov asks her how she interpreted his departure for several days with what she had been told were "some disreputable people." Having decided that "one must always speak the truth" to Insarov, she replies straightforwardly, "I thought that you always know what you are doing, and that you are not capable of doing anything bad" (6: 211). Elena discerns the integrity that enables Insarov to retain complete control over his actions; his self-awareness guarantees self-restraint. And she connects self-awareness to morality— she implies that the capacity for doing "anything bad" is found only in those who are not self-aware and therefore cannot control themselves. Moreover, she discovers that his self-control enables him to control her actions as well, for she cannot lie to someone for whom lying is so foreign. Insarov's strength of character imparts strength to hers.

Insarov makes clear to her that he consciously conserves that strength, refusing to waste energy pursuing self-indulgent, purely personal satisfaction that would only distract him from the single-minded course focusing and fostering his sense of self. When Elena asks Insarov whether he had avenged the murder of his parents by a Turk, for instance, he replies that he had not, albeit, he notes, "not because I didn't consider myself justified in killing him—I could have killed him very calmly—but because there is no place for private revenge when national, general vengeance... or no, that word won't do... when the liberation of a people is at stake. One would interfere with the other" (6: 213). To give himself over to seemingly self-satisfying acts would actually prove self-denigrating, since the identity he has created for himself derives from a psychological investment in the public cause of rebellion rather than the private cause of vengeance.

This investment entails not psychic loss but gain. As he explains to Elena, his love for his native land is "beyond all doubts," uniting "the last peasant, the last beggar in Bulgaria, and I" in "one goal" (6: 214). His identity does not get lost, as if merged and fused with those of his compatriots in the common revolutionary endeavor. It becomes broadened and reinforced because, in his words, "when your country needs you . . . how this gives conviction and strength!" (6: 214). He perceives Bulgaria's entreaty as an affirmation of his personal capacity to contribute to its rescue. Awareness of his own autonomy is concentrated and intensified by his country's very lack thereof.

It is only when Insarov develops and succumbs to a passionate attraction to Elena that his self-image is shaken and his autonomy is compromised. The first sign of these changes occurs when Insarov refuses to shake Elena's hand in farewell after announcing his intention to move elsewhere. When Elena confronts him with the unfriendliness of his refusal, this man of supreme conviction and constant self-control finds himself fumbling for words, revealing that, by contrast to his previous serene openness, he now is concealing something. What he conceals— his love for Elena—has already begun to undermine his will, rendering him self-conscious, constrained, and uncomfortable. He senses that even the contemplation of private satisfaction constitutes a temptation in which possible self-assertion disguises actual self-erosion.

And Insarov is right: as noble as this love may be on both sides, it subsequently destroys not merely his psychological but his physical well-being, as he falls dangerously ill after exposing himself to inclement weather in seeking to obtain the papers necessary to take Elena away with him. While still weakened, his physical desire for Elena overwhelms his will as no other desire ever has, extracting the admissions from him that "this is beyond my strength!" "I am not in control of myself," and "I cannot bear these bursts of passion" (6: 268). Instinctive impulses toward intimacy that Insarov has so long kept in check as he pursues a public cause suddenly assert themselves when Insarov is most vulnerable, and they prove to be his undoing; he never fully regains his health, and he dies in transit back to Bulgaria. The strength of his individuation has been predicated on the sublimation of those impulses, and their release, however lovingly enacted, destroys the integrity of the firm bounds demarcating his vital self-definition and ensuring his individuation.

The female protagonist of Turgenev's epistolary tale "The Correspondence," Mar'ia Aleksandrovna, displays a different aspect of individuation. By contrast to Insarov, who wears the mantle of individuation so easily, at least until it falls away, she reveals that, for some, individuation is not readily achieved and requires constant energetic nurturing to uphold, since it is constantly threatened. Living in a sheltered rural environment, Mar'ia Aleksandrovna has encountered entrenched familial and social opposition to her allegedly unfeminine delight in solitary, intellectual pursuits rather than in convivial, domestic ones. She has insisted on her right to independence of mind, if not of action, but criticism of that independence has caused her to become cautious, even suspicious, of any cordial overtures, fearing that they mask some intention of assaulting her hard-won autonomy.

Thus she queries her would-be correspondent, Aleksei Petrovich, when he proposes that they exchange letters, as to his motives—"*Why?* What are you to me; what am I to you?"—and she declares that she eschews any such potentially intimate relationship: "I do not feel the slightest desire to become closer to anyone" (5: 22). She has learned through bitter experience with her relatives and neighbors that any attempt at intimacy means the exposure of vulnerability, and hence provides ammunition with which to assault the psychic defenses she has erected around her self-identification as a reclusive intellectual. Still, her curiosity piqued and her desire for solitude not as absolute as she first implies, she agrees to the correspondence, discerning in it a forum in which to deliver her ideas about independence, which she cannot express in person at home.

Warming to this opportunity, Mar'ia sends to Aleksei Petrovich her evaluation of the basic nature and "fate" of "the Russian woman." She laments her conviction that, unlike a Russian man, a Russian woman "cannot cast off her past, cannot cut herself off from her roots," and therefore remains physically and emotionally tied to the place of her birth, "gradually losing hope and faith in herself" (5: 31). Rather than instilling confidence in a secure identity, Mar'ia's communal experience has led her to perceive a general entrapment and demoralization of females. Thus trapped and demoralized, Russian women find the present and the future offering no alternative to the past, and therefore have no reason to hope for any change or improvement in the conditions of life; they can envisage no possibility of self-expansion through increased control over those conditions.

Despite being couched in general terms, even the expression of these observations evidently encroaches on the limits of Mar'ia's self-defenses, by revealing her heartfelt fears not only for Russian women as a whole but for herself in particular. As a result, she feels compelled to reassert those limits in a subsequent letter, promising that "today I am much more cold-blooded and in much greater control of myself" (5: 34). The heat of emotion generated by simply articulating her views poses a threat to the self-restraint she so prizes as a means of maintaining her distance from those who would deny or subvert her independence.

Mar'ia goes on to explain her need for self-restraint by describing how keenly and repeatedly that independence is challenged by the people around her. She reports a neighbor's derisive dismissal of her as a "lady philosopher" and an extravagant romantic who "secretly wear[s] men's clothes and instead of 'Hello' say[s]: 'George Sand!'" (5: 34).[12] The implicit criticism of Mar'ia for transgressing traditional gender boundaries and thus betraying her appropriate identity is made explicit in reproaches from her family over her rejection of the conventional female path of marriage and motherhood. She summarizes their message as this: "What do you think, to what end have all this philosophizing and books and acquaintances with scholars led you?" (5: 35). To her relatives, the lack of any substantive social attachment renders Mar'ia's intellectual endeavors merely vain exercises in futile willfulness. They see not fruitful self-fulfillment but barren self-indulgence as the result. And at times she even entertains the same thoughts, confessing that she occasionally envies her sister, a mother and wife with a doting husband who can say to Mar'ia, "I am like everybody else . . . and you?" (5: 35). Mar'ia is thus by no means blind to the comforts that conformity and dependence can bring. And she grants that her chosen identity offers few comforts, going so far as to wonder dispiritedly, "What have I to wait for? to hope for?" (5: 35), knowing that the answer to both questions may be "nothing at all."

Mar'ia nonetheless proudly proclaims her right to determine the form her self-fulfillment takes, no matter what the social consequences:

Let them call me a lady philosopher, a crank, whatever they please—I will remain true to the end... to what? an ideal, perhaps? Yes, an ideal. Yes, I will remain true to the end to that which caused my heart to beat for the first time, that which I acknowledged and acknowledge to be the true, the good... If only my powers do not betray me, if only my idol does not turn out to be a soulless and mute false god. (5: 35)

In this outpouring she articulates, perhaps for the first time, her idealistic commitment to abstract, absolute values that animate her solitary existence and inform her identity. At the same time, she concedes the possibility that the very intensity of this commitment may cause her to deceive herself, to draw inspiration from a flawed image feigning perfection while actually fostering degeneration.

She adheres to her ideals, despite the realization that she may be misguided in doing so, by refusing to marry a young, educated, well-to-do neighbor, thereby ending her social ostracism. She tells Aleksei Petrovich that she refused the neighbor because "he is so dull and petty, all his desires are so limited that I cannot fail to recognize my superiority over him. . . . I cannot respect him, although his heart is excellent!" (5: 38). Notwithstanding her recognition of the security, acceptance, and companionship that marriage can provide, Mar'ia retains her independence for the sake of the self-definition whose borders she has carved out and conserved amidst such adversity.

Yet the contours of this self-definition become somewhat clouded: like Insarov, she is not wholly immune to the charms of someone she deems capable of equal individuation. Her eager anticipation of a promised visit by Aleksei Petrovich suggests that she may be holding out hope for a more-than-friendly relationship with him. In implicitly endowing him with the attributes of her ideals, though, she has indeed turned to a god both "soulless and mute," for he abruptly ceases to correspond with her, confessing only two years later that, despite his admiration for Mar'ia, he had become enthralled by another woman and had wholly given himself over to that thralldom. Mar'ia is thus forced to confront her error, regretting "that I allowed myself to be bestirred in vain, that I stretched out my hand to someone else and left, albeit only for a minute, my solitary little corner" (5: 44). Hurt and embittered, she painfully realizes the dangers of lowering her psychic guard even slightly against the allure of emotional intimacy and ease. Hence her parting shot at Aleksei Petrovich: "In the future I will be smarter..." (5: 44). She will rely solely on her intellect to determine which relationships will reinforce her individuation and which will diminish it. Having been so brutally disillusioned, Mar'ia must ensure that she never again falls prey to her own irrational desires, much less those of anyone else she meets. Now girded against the illusory appeal of dependence, she will be ever stronger in her self-protective isolation.[13] She has confronted the high cost of individuation, has paid dearly for it, and will forever hereafter know its worth, as those to whom it comes more readily may not.

In comparison to the individuation manifested by Insarov and Mar'ia Aleksandrovna, that shown by Tat'iana Petrovna in the novel *Smoke* exhibits a greater consistency, one born of complete continence. Though truly in love, Tat'iana does not jeopardize her self-definition, and can therefore retain it even when love disappoints. Threatened by the humiliation of her fiancé Litvinov's emotional defection, Tat'iana retains the self-mastery needed to maintain her identity and integrity. Prior to Litvinov's betrayal, she radiates self-assurance and calm, so much so that even though Litvinov feels guilt ridden at his intention to break off their engagement shortly, he finds in simply looking at Tat'iana that "an involuntary quietude entered his heart: the undisturbed expression of her honest, open face filled him with a better feeling" (7: 353). Tat'iana's spiritual tranquillity is contagious; her own self-confidence enables her to transmit a semblance of confidence to him.

As soon as she suspects that Litvinov intends to desert her for another woman, though, her openness and serenity are transformed into self-constrained withdrawal. She immediately retracts the offer of intimacy implicit in her engagement so as to escape irrevocable damage to her self-respect, to the self-definition she has selected—that of an independent woman who has no need for a man's support in any form. As Litvinov leaves her in her hotel room for a rendezvous with the other woman, "Tat'iana walked to the corner and sat down on a chair, tightly crossing her arms on her chest" (7: 360). Thus she physically evinces her self-protective instincts to retreat and shield herself against Litvinov's betrayal. And she draws on her shield to hide any overt signs of distress that would betray vulnerability in front of Litvinov. During another of his visits, it is observed that "no change in her was noticeable; she behaved just as calmly" as ever (7: 368). The term translated as "behaved" (*derzhalas'*) literally means "held herself," subtly conveying Tat'iana's palpable self-constraint. She knows that to concede visibly or verbally her unhappiness would only diminish her self-control and defy her self-definition.

Actually, in one way her behavior does change in order to preserve a poised facade: before Litvinov's change of heart, Tat'iana had always looked straight into his eyes; now she avoids exchanging glances with him and instead, during their conversations, "her gaze did not once rest on Litvinov, but somewhat condescendingly and nervously glided across him" (7: 368). Tat'iana comprehends the threat that Litvinov poses to her composure and hence to the self she has composed—a self refusing to depend on others for satisfaction or sympathy—so she will not dare even the intimacy of eye contact with Litvinov, who still possesses the power to upset her.

So successfully does she maintain her composure, though, that she seems to Litvinov to have transcended mortal substance and achieved immortal stasis: "Tat'iana appeared taller, stronger, to him; her face, shining with unusual beauty, seemingly had frozen like a statue . . . and her gaze, even and cold, was also the gaze of a statue" (7: 382). In her near-sculptural self-containment, Tat'iana assumes an aura of a goddess, superhuman in her psychological and moral supremacy. Indeed, so rigidly self-controlled is she that she can inflict the final psychological blow on herself when Litvinov cannot do so, announcing for him, "You have fallen out of love with me and do not know how to tell me." Moreover, she makes this announcement, whose import destroys the basis of all her hope for future happiness, "in an even voice" (7: 371). Her determination to preserve her identity and autonomy enables her to exercise absolute authority over her own actions.

Tat'iana's dispassionate insistence on the open declaration of Litvinov's change of heart proceeds as much from ethical conviction as from emotional inclination. For she informs Litvinov that "the most bitter truth is better than what went on yesterday" (7: 373), that is, Litvinov's guilty and hypocritical pretence of unaltered affection, as well as her painful uncertainty about the sincerity of those affections. Tat'iana believes, as she later tells her aunt-companion, in "truth above all—and freedom" (7: 380). But to Tat'iana, freedom means not freedom of action or freedom from all constraint. Freedom means complete understanding, both of herself and of others, so that her psychic integrity can be preserved within self-erected barriers against the incursions of deception and betrayal.

Tat'iana is free, then, in that she understands herself well enough to realize that the pain caused by the "truth" in these circumstances (which drives her to a sickbed after her final interview with Litvinov) is only temporary. At the same time, she forgoes social integrity, deliberately telling a lie in order to protect her psychic integrity from further unwanted intrusions, however well-intended: she responds to her aunt's question about whether she is crying one night with the simple statement "I have a cold" (7: 369). She is undoubtedly crying, and hence lying. But she also later tells her aunt that "this will soon pass" (7: 400), and she thus transforms her lie into truth. She knows that her misery will abate eventually, since she has kept her autonomous identity intact.[14] Thus her character illuminates the resilient inflexibility of individuation as it sustains decency and dignity in the face of indecency and indignity.

Staunch individuation appears to counteract not only indignity but the imminence of death itself in one of Turgenev's last prose narratives, "Living Relics," an addition to *A Sportsman's Sketches* that Turgenev made twenty-five years after publishing the majority of them. The protagonist, a peasant girl named simply Luker'ia, has been stricken with a physical paralysis that, unlike Tat'iana's transitory illness, will not "soon pass," but will slowly kill her. Yet Luker'ia determinedly maintains the self-possession that individuation engenders even as she slips away from life.

When first seen by the narrator, Luker'ia confidently asserts her identity, repeating the pronoun "I" three times, calling to him, when he fails to recognize her, that it is "I, yes, master—I. I—Luker'ia" (3: 328).[15] Although almost totally immobilized and thoroughly emaciated, Luker'ia firmly retains her self-command as she details her physical condition, yielding to neither self-pity nor despair. She relates the misadventure that led to her paralysis "without oh's or ah's, not in the least complaining or abjuring participation" (3: 329). And the narrator observes on Luker'ia's face as she talks a smile that "persists and will not dissolve" (3: 328), a smile that reflects Luker'ia's psychic resilience in the face of her physical disability.

Luker'ia accounts for this resilience by explaining to the narrator that she finds the passing of time painfully slow when she engages her intellect, and so "I thus taught myself not to think, and above all not to remember" (3: 331).[16] She knows that remembering how she lived in the past, beautiful, popular, and active, can only be demeaning in the present and will discourage the desire to continue living at all. Hence she avoids summoning up memories, seeking support for her identity in other sources of strength.

One of those sources is her sensory powers. She proudly tells the narrator, "I, thank God, see excellently and hear everything, everything. . . . And I can distinguish every odor, no matter how weak it is! When the buckwheat in the field or the linden tree in the garden flowers—it is not necessary to tell me: I am already the first to smell it" (3: 330). And when engrossed in such sensory explorations, she declares, "I feel that I am alive, I breathe—and all of me is here" (3: 331). In this way Luker'ia can recover the feeling of integrity that she loses when comparing past to present. Employing fully and proudly the faculties she still has, Luker'ia thus enjoys a sense of self-determination that she otherwise lacks. But she can evoke this sense only when alone; she confesses to the narrator that if she allows the thought of other, healthy people to intrude during the time she spends in sensory expeditions into the natural world, "then it occurs to me: were there other people around me, none of this would exist and I would feel nothing except my misfortune" (3: 333). Luker'ia's self-definition requires solitude to ensure its sanctity.

This self-definition will not admit of self-deception, either. Luker'ia is well aware of her physical condition as a complete cripple incapable of living a normal life. When the narrator asks her what became of the boyfriend she had been going to meet the night of the accident, Luker'ia replies that he has long since married and adds, "What sort of a girlfriend could I be?" (3: 329). Moreover, Luker'ia knows she is not only crippled but dying. When the narrator asks her age, she responds simply, "Twenty-eight... or twenty-nine... I won't make thirty" (3: 337). Certain of this, she refuses to be moved to a hospital from the peasant hut where the narrator has found her, insisting that "I will only undergo greater torment there. And where is there to go to cure me?" (3: 332). Besides, she argues, "Who can help someone else?

Who can enter someone else's spirit? Each person himself must help himself!" (3: 333). Her illness, while physically debilitating, has brought Luker'ia exemplary self-awareness and self-reliance. Paradoxical as it may be, her psychological individuation is actually increased by her loss of physical mobility.

This individuation is further evidenced by Luker'ia's response to the narrator's parting query as to whether he can perform any service for her. She begins and ends her answer with the same words: "I do not need anything; I am satisfied with everything" (3: 337). Luker'ia has become utterly sufficient unto herself; she has confronted some of the cruelest constraints circumstances can impose on an individual and has taught herself not merely to accommodate but to assimilate those circumstances into a satisfactory conception of herself and her existence. And although she does succumb to the pressures of memory briefly to regret that her illness has forced her to cut off her beautiful long hair, she regains her sublime self-acceptance before the narrator's departure. Thus Luker'ia is an especially noble representative of the virtues of individuation as Turgenev portrays them.

Whereas Dmitrii Insarov, Mar'ia Aleksandrovna, Tat'iana Petrovna, and Luker'ia embody various facets of essentially successful individuation, a number of Turgenev's other characterizations illustrate various forms of the failure to establish or sustain individuation. For instance, a veritable study in the demise—and subsequent resurrection—of individuation is provided by the characterization of Grigorii Litvinov in *Smoke*. Turgenev depicts the dissolution and reconstruction of his personality, thereby illuminating both the fragility and the resilience of individuation. At the novel's outset, Litvinov appears to be the quintessence of self-determination. First pictured while "he sat calmly and simply, like a man who would find it inconceivable that someone might notice or study him," Litvinov conveys the impression of an unselfconscious and yet "businesslike, somewhat self-assured young man" (7: 253). Litvinov's confidence evidently arises from both his past, which was "completely open and uncomplicated," and his expectations of his future, his sense that "his life distinctly and clearly lies before him, that his fate has revealed itself, and that he is proud of that fate and rejoices in it, as the work of his own hands" (7: 255). Litvinov has created an identity and a future course of life befitting past history. Conditioned but not constricted by circumstances, he entertains a self-image that fits comfortably within internal and external confines.

Yet it turns out that Litvinov has not always enjoyed such comfort; his past had been more complicated than it first seemed. As a young student in Moscow, he had fallen deeply in love with and been deeply hurt by a beautiful, ambitious girl, Irina, who broke her engagement to Litvinov to pursue a wealthier match in St. Petersburg. And although Litvinov had apparently wholly recovered from this blow to his self-esteem and subsequently become engaged to Tat'iana Petrovna, on unexpectedly meeting Irina again as he awaits Tat'iana's arrival in Baden-Baden, Litvinov immediately shows signs of an eroding self-command. After first encountering Irina, he finds his reaction to her unfathomable, in that he cannot dismiss the thought of her. He tries to read after returning to his hotel, mentally waving Irina away with the thought, "Let her enjoy herself with her generals!"—Irina has married a wealthy army officer—but he then discovers that he "was not up to reading" (7: 306). The use of a passive construction in Russian (*emu ne chitalos'*) hints that the diminution of self-control and concomitant self-awareness is well under way in Litvinov.

And indeed, continued relations with Irina overtly compromise Litvinov's integrity. After another conversation with her, Litvinov experiences "an unpleasant feeling of ever-growing internal discomfort," and becomes "thoroughly dissatisfied with himself, as if he had lost at roulette or had not kept a promise" (7: 318). Quite so. By becoming reinvolved with Irina, Litvinov is gambling with the highest possible stakes: his engagement, his future, his very identity. But the fact that he perceives his gamble only indirectly, envisioning it with a simile rather than a direct statement, suggests that Litvinov's self-awareness no longer functions reliably. His self-comforting conclusion—"of course, there can be no sort of danger here"—ironically underscores Litvinov's ignorance of Irina's power of attraction. Yet the reason for that ignorance remains ambiguous, for "Litvinov either was not able or was not willing to admit to himself to what degree Irina seemed beautiful to him and how strongly she awakened his feeling" (7: 318). In effect, the alternatives introduced by the narrator as to whether Litvinov suffers from the mental inability or the moral unwillingness to confront directly his unabated instinctual longing for Irina aptly reflect Litvinov's own psychic confusion. If Litvinov "was not able" to make such admissions, then he has lost his self-awareness; if he "was not willing" to do so, then he has lost his self-control. In either case, though, his rational individuation is inexorably deteriorating under the influence of irrational desire.

This deterioration is further signaled by the breakdown of Litvinov's psychological integration: his consciousness temporarily splits in two. He hears a conversation carried on in his own head between two voices, one urging that he and Tat'iana "have been eternally united and cannot, must not separate," while "another voice" asserts that "you don't have the right to deceive her." This latter assertion then evokes the response from the first voice that "this is all sophistry, shameful cleverness, false conscience" (7: 342). One voice is rational, the other rationalizes. Litvinov thus finds himself inclining toward subjective gratification in the guise of objective decency, and he no longer has the psychic coherence to mount any significant opposition to his own desires, or to the mental breakdown they insidiously engineer.

Deciding thereupon to confess his love for Irina to both women, Litvinov proves that what appears to be a self-centered and self-indulgent passion is actually a self-destructive one. The process of self-destruction is first evidenced viscerally, by Litvinov's experiencing "an unbearable aching and gnawing sensation of emptiness, of emptiness within his very self" (7: 347). He further senses that "a strange change had occurred within him since yesterday—in his entire appearance, in his movements, in the expression of his face; and he felt himself to be a different person" (7: 352). In Litvinov, psychological disintegration is signaled by physical alteration. And he concludes as much, declaring to Tat'iana that in the resurgence of his attraction to Irina, "I have lost myself," and that "I have perished, never to return" (7: 372).

Indeed, he goes so far as to describe himself several times as dead: he thinks that "he had cast his entire past, his entire life into a grave" (7: 383); he writes to Irina that "my 'I,' my former 'I' died and was buried yesterday. I feel, I see, I know this clearly" (7: 384). The "I" who feels, sees, and knows is not the Litvinov who believed he created and controlled his own fate. He writes further, "I myself... where am I? What am I? On the side, an observer, an observer of my own life!" (7: 384). His personality is fragmented, his consciousness relegated to the status of exterior passive observer rather than interior active participant by the force of Irina's power over him. The "former" Litvinov is thereby demolished.

But just as Litvinov's former individuation was not as thorough and stable as it appeared, neither is its demolition as total as he imagines. When Irina refuses to leave her husband and her life of monied leisure, after Litvinov has broken with Tat'iana on the strength of Irina's promise to do just that, Litvinov's energy and integrity suddenly reassert themselves. He instinctively affirms to himself, "I will not allow her to play so mercilessly with my life" (7: 391). Once again he has "will," he has a "life" on behalf of which to exercise that will. Instead of bringing Litvinov to her feet with a final maneuver to enslave him, Irina sets him back on his own psychological feet. He rediscovers the courage "to push away from himself both those memories and that enchanting image" (7: 392). And he recovers both his self-awareness and his self-control as he writes elliptically to Irina: "I cannot... that which you want. I cannot and do not want to" (7: 393). Litvinov is again able to unite capacity and morality in clearly defined action, because his self-definition, although rocked to its foundations, has revived in time.

Having returned to Russia to recuperate from his traumatic encounter, "he again began to resemble the former Litvinov, and he again began to move and to act among the living like one alive" (7: 401), although it still at times "occurred to him that he was carrying his own corpse" (7: 397). Litvinov is not in fact quite the same person he was before—his complacent self-confidence has died. He has learned that the confidence born of individuation cannot be dissociated from self-awareness and self-control. But Litvinov has also learned that, even if terribly damaged by irrational and instinctual forces, individuation can reconstitute itself, restoring the conscious rationality, equanimity, and self-satisfaction that a delimited identity can endow.

Not all of Turgenev's characters have identities durable enough to survive the onslaught of irrationality and instinct that Litvinov, though nearly devastated, manages to outlast. One who perishes from the frailty of his identity is Mar'ia Aleksandrovna's correspondent, Aleksei Petrovich. He exhibits at best alternations between self-knowledge and self-deception, self-control and self-abandon, which reflect his inability to maintain the rigorous psychic discipline required to procure and prolong individuation.

At times Aleksei Petrovich appears almost totally self-deluded. For instance, in his second letter to Mar'ia Aleksandrovna, after flatly denying that he cultivates the image of a Byronic hero—"I have never imitated Byron," he announces firmly—he nonetheless portrays himself as a Byronesque victim of Weltschmerz. He claims that he is "completely alone on earth," that he suffers from "the tendency to fantasize and a love for fantasy, rather cold blood, pride, laziness," and that, in sum, "a multitude of reasons have distanced me from the society of people" (5: 23). Such self-stylization is worthy of Byron's Corsair or Childe Harold or Manfred, all of whom are solitary, proud, alienated beings. In Aleksei Petrovich, though, these qualities are the product of a pose, not of the natural temperament he discloses in subsequent letters. Here he betrays a tendency toward the misrepresentation and misinterpretation of his own character and motives betokening an enfeebled self-definition, one that will appear in less benign form later on.

Yet Aleksei Petrovich is hardly ignorant of himself. His confession that, from youth, "one thing occupied me—my dear *I*; I took my good-natured egotism for shyness; I avoided society—and now I have horribly bored myself" (5: 23–24) rings true. Apparently vulnerable since childhood to accusations of inadequacy, he has tried to protect himself from threats to his identity presented by social expectations he fears he might not satisfy. The resultant self-absorption has led him to avoid experiences that might have added structure and substance to his self-definition. He concedes as much in observing that "I even have no memories, because I find nothing in all my past life except my own being" (5: 24). His very need to keep danger out has left him empty within. Hence he lacks the internal resources even to entertain himself.

Voicing his recognition of the extent to which he has victimized himself by his unconstructive self-obsession, he offers Mar'ia a complex metaphor:

Have you ever had occasion to free a fly from a spider? . . . You remember, you put it in the sun; its wings and legs were stuck together and gluey. . . . How awkwardly it moved, how awkwardly it tried to clean itself! After great exertions . . . it tried to adjust its wings . . . but it cannot travel as it used to. . . . At least it did not fall into the horrible net of its own will . . . but I!

I was my very own spider! (5: 26)

Aleksei Petrovich strikingly melds self-pity and self-contempt as he casts himself in the roles of both victim and victimizer. And he here shifts the locus of responsibility for his victimization from society to himself, confessing that, by contrast to a spider's innocent prey, he has deliberately entangled himself in his own web of debilitating isolation.

Before being utterly consumed by the self-loathing this confession arouses, though, his protective instincts reassert themselves, and he qualifies his utter self-condemnation with the remark that "by the way, I cannot blame myself too much." Aleksei Petrovich subsequently finds consolation in the rationale that "it is better to say that we are all to blame, or even that it is nevertheless impossible to blame us," for, he now insists, "circumstances define us; they drive us on one road or another, and then they punish us." His reasoning, or rather rationalizing, thus follows a step-by-step regression to the point of completely exonerating himself from any responsibility for developing an identity capable of resisting circumstantial pressures. Instead he concludes with the convenient generalization that "each individual has his fate" (5: 26); in other words, predetermination precludes self-determination.

Still, he again backs away from that all-embracing alibi in a more balanced rephrasing: "Each person makes his own fate, and it makes each person" (5: 26). Aleksei Petrovich thus vacillates between self-defensive excuses and self-deprecating explanations for his inability to thoroughly govern his own existence. Using the same technique, he next offers a meditation on self-consciousness by focusing particularly on the workings of the Russian mind. "Too early is consciousness awakened in us," he avers, so that "too early do we begin to observe ourselves. . . . We Russians have no other life task than time and again to rework our personality. . . . Thus we, as barely more than children . . . not having received from without any defined direction, not really desiring anything, not strongly believing in anything, willfully make of ourselves what we wish" (5: 27). Lacking any shaping external force or idea to support a consistent, well-defined self-image, Russians allow their worst instincts to create artificial, arbitrary identities unconnected to the exigencies of actuality. As a result, they remain "eternally unacquainted with the satisfaction of real action, or sincere suffering, or the sincere triumph of conviction" (5: 27). No authentic achievement can be attained, no true emotion enjoyed by those whose identity is constructed solely around the fulfillment of instinctive, narcissistic needs.

Aleksei Petrovich eventually gives himself over—literally—to such needs. Despite his firm promise not to be deterred from visiting Mar'ia Aleksandrovna by the appeal of, as he puts it, "let us say, another Ninette" (5: 43), an Italian girl with whom a friend of his has recently been in love, on the eve of his departure for the visit Aleksei Petrovich does the very thing he has said he will not do—he abandons his plan to meet Mar'ia in order to pursue his own Ninette, a dancer, around Europe. To be sure, the mere fact that he had taken the trouble to deny his susceptibility to seduction in itself suggests that he suffers from just such susceptibility; he possesses just enough self-definition to engender a self-defensive rationalization, but not enough self-control to resist gratifying instinctual desires, however demeaning the life he must therefore lead until his premature death. The example of Aleksei Petrovich thus elucidates the self-delusion and self-destruction that eventuate from insufficient individuation.

Even a temperamental inclination to develop individuation may not suffice to remedy its lack. This is the issue explored through the characterization of Elena Stakhova in *On the Eve.* Elena is generally viewed as one of Turgenev's noblest and psychologically strongest heroines, ultimately risking her life to carry on the fight of her deceased husband, Insarov, for Bulgarian independence.[17] But her portrayal actually reveals her to be far more complex and conflicted, less self-aware and self-controlled than the stereotypical martyr. Indeed, Elena demonstrates even more vividly than Aleksei Petrovich the painful consequences of being unable to achieve a self-determined identity. Her inability, though, stems not so much from self-deception as from self-ignorance.

Elena begins her romance with Insarov while experiencing vague yearnings for a new direction in her life, but, as she divulges in her diary, she is also plagued by the inability to decide for herself what would constitute an appropriate direction. She asks herself a series of questions: "What do I want? Why is my heart so heavy, so oppressed? Why do I look with envy at the birds that fly past? It seems that I would like to fly with them. . . . Isn't this wish sinful? I have a mother, father, and family here. Don't I love them?" (6: 224). Such questions betray her lack of the objective comprehension of her own temperament that would dictate the correct path for her to take in quest of fulfillment. Confused and uncertain, her attraction to the birds suggests simply a subjective longing to escape her inchoate anxieties by following a course set by others. And a subsequent diary entry, "Oh, if only someone would say to me: here is what you must do!" (6: 224), confirms Elena's lack of the self-knowledge that would enable her to discern what she "must do" by herself.

Without this self-knowledge, her own emotional life is a mystery to her. She remarks in her diary one day, "I don't know what is happening with me," and, having been told that she looks sad, records having thought "I didn't even suspect that I had a sad face" (6: 225). Elena can grasp neither the nature nor the origins of her feelings; she has no well-delineated self-image within which to place and analyze her reactions to other individuals and events. In particular, she cannot place her reaction to Insarov, noting uncomprehendingly, "I am still shy with Mr. Insarov. I don't know why," as well as "I don't understand why I think about Mr. Insarov so often," and "when he leaves I recall all his words and get annoyed with myself and even worry... I myself don't know why" (6: 224). Elena's self-ignorance prevents her from acknowledging the obvious attachment she is forming.

Only when she learns that Insarov intends to depart permanently does she find a means to achieve insight into her emotional state—she finds "a word." That word is a passive participle in Russian (*vliublena*), which Elena employs in a passive construction. Instead of actively asserting "I love Insarov," she proclaims in her diary, "The word has been found, light has dawned on me! God have mercy on me... I am in love!" (6: 228). An exact echo of Tat'iana Larina's thrice-repeated declaration of her love for Eugene Onegin in Pushkin's "novel in verse,"[18] Elena likewise resorts to a relatively indirect formulation to codify her experience. The word "has been found"; she has not found it herself.

Yet the self-comprehension Elena has found does instill some measure of confidence in herself and in her ability to act—she begins to show signs of individuation. For one, she single-mindedly pursues Insarov to his apartment and professes her love for him even before he voices his for her. In the brief exchange that follows their admission of mutual love, Elena evinces an active understanding of herself and her circumstances that she has hitherto lacked. Moreover, she expresses an unprecedented conviction in her own physical and psychological capability to face the obstacles their love entails and to overcome them:

Insarov: And you aren't deceiving yourself, you know that your parents will never agree to our marriage?

Elena: I am not deceiving myself; I know that.
Insarov: You know that I am poor, almost a beggar?
Elena: I know.
Insarov: That I am not a Russian, that I am not fated to live in Russia, that you will have to rend all your ties to your native land, to your family?
Elena: I know, I know.
Insarov: Do you also know that I have dedicated myself to a difficult, thankless task, that I... that we will have to be exposed not only to danger, but to deprivation, perhaps to humiliation?
Elena: I know, I know everything. I love you.[19] (6: 237)

Now Elena can repeat to Insarov with assurance the words "I know" instead of repeating to herself with doubt "I don't know." She has found the person she sought to give direction to her life, and she momentarily discovers what she takes to be a solid foundation for an identity—as wife, helpmate, and corevolutionary.

Yet this identity unavoidably encompasses dependence, since it originates in her connection to Insarov. Paradoxically, to gain a definite, delimited sense of self, Elena must give herself up, that is, give up the independent self she might have developed. Thus when Insarov perceives in her "a life given over to him" (6: 236), he is more correct than he perhaps knows. He accepts her assurances that she has a strength of character equal to his own, and that therefore in giving her life over to him, she actually enriches that life, just as his life is enriched by devoting himself to the cause of Bulgarian independence. But without a definite, autonomous identity, her life cannot be enriched, only diminished by becoming dependent on him for its definition. And when later on she tells an impassioned Insarov to "take" her (6: 268), her meaning carries beyond the physical realm. Any self she has she consigns to his keeping.

Hence, in his absence, her self-assurance and sense of direction rapidly begin to dissipate. She awakens one morning, while Insarov is traveling, in a mood of contemplative tranquillity as she muses on their future, but "in the course of the morning, worry gradually took control of Elena" (6: 243), and still later in the day, she realizes that "fear was taking control of her . . . and she did not soon regain control over herself" (6: 244). Once again at the mercy of irrational energies she cannot govern without a well-defined identity, Elena's nascent self-confidence is easily overwhelmed by elemental insecurities about the future.

On Insarov's return, she nevertheless marshals enough psychic wherewithal to devote herself to him, nursing him when he becomes ill, marrying him, and then leaving her family to accompany him to Italy, whence they expect to depart for Bulgaria. But when Insarov dies in Italy, Elena is thrown back on what finally prove to be her own inadequate psychological resources. In effect rejecting the possibility of establishing an autonomous existence, she declares in a final letter to her parents, "Everything is over for me . . . what will become of me I don't know" (6: 298). Reverting to her earlier stance of self-ignorance—invoking her formerly habitual "I don't know"—Elena reveals that she has lost any semblance of self-determination whatsoever. She announces that she will devote herself to Insarov's cause only because she has nothing else to do and nowhere else to go. Thus she readies her departure for Bulgaria hopelessly, not enthusiastically: "I sought happiness," she writes, "and will perhaps find death" (6: 298). Losing the person who conferred on her the essence of her own identity, she loses any sense of life-affirming, self-conserving individuation.

In closing, she summons enough self-awareness to suggest that she had never cultivated true self-control. When in her last letter she begs her parents' forgiveness for the bitter pain she caused them by her marriage and departure, she avows that "it was not in my will" (6: 298) to do otherwise. Her will, to the extent that she ever really had one at all, could engage itself only to follow another person who she believed could impart to it the shape and potency that it so desperately lacked.[20] This elemental impotence prevents Elena from selecting a satisfying course to pursue for the remainder of her existence, condemning her instead to the joyless quest of a goal to which she had merely a vicarious commitment. She never consciously devises a self-definition sufficient to impose a direction on her life of her own choosing.

Nothing further is heard from Elena because nothing of her is left. Whether she lives or dies, the chance for an independent identity has already been lost. Her portrayal therefore reveals not a self-sacrificing heroine but a selfless one in the saddest sense of the term—one who never had a complete self to sacrifice. She made an understandable but irrevocable miscalculation: she sought to overcome psychological weakness and existential emptiness not by creating and fulfilling her own identity but by attempting to assimilate the identity of someone else. This act of internalization succeeds only as long as that someone else lives; death reinstates the emptiness in magnified form. Elena's characterization therefore illustrates both the necessity and the difficulty of achieving genuine individuation for oneself and oneself alone.

Elena at least perceives the need for individuation and sincerely struggles to achieve it, even if she self-defeatingly depends on another individual in her struggle. A characterization in telling contrast is that of Varvara Pavlovna in *A Nest of Gentry*, who makes no serious effort to establish a consciously integrated identity but gladly assumes whatever identity she finds convenient at the moment. The promiscuous wife of Dmitrii Lavretskii, worthy of the appellation *femme fatale*, she is an extraordinarily attractive woman who employs physical and psychological wiles to gain power over men. In so doing, she repeatedly evinces the appearance, but not the substance, of individuation.

Varvara Pavlovna affects an air of unstudied self-confidence bespeaking a secure self-definition: when Lavretskii first meets her, she is "so calm and self-assuredly gentle that everyone in her presence at once felt at home" (6: 47). At home with herself, all others feel at home with her. But her calm comes from a well-founded faith in her physical charms: she knows that she exudes something "difficult to put into words, but that touched and aroused—and what it aroused was, of course, not shyness" (6: 47). Varvara Pavlovna thus displays a self-knowledge and self-control that are palpable and yet superficial, instinctive and yet artificial. Her public identity resides in the form of her elegant exterior, not in the essence of her decadent personality.

To be sure, Varvara Pavlovna knows what she wants and how

to get it. In accepting the naive Lavretskii's proposal of marriage, "it was well-known to Varvara Pavlovna that her fiancé was wealthy," and she puts his money to good effect, for "she had a great deal of practicality, a great deal of taste, and a very great love of comfort, along with a great ability to obtain for herself that comfort" (6: 48). She avails herself of Lavretskii's innocent malleability to impose order on their life together, as a distinct identity might impel her to do, but she imposes the order most convenient for self-indulgence, not self-delimitation. To be sure, that order provides mesmerizing comforts for Lavretskii: he is amazed at "how everything that surrounded him was thought out, foreseen, arranged for by Varvara Pavlovna" (6: 48). She knows and controls the effects of her actions well enough to convince Lavretskii that she works her magic to his benefit.

But the benefits she brings to her husband are always secondary to those she obtains for herself. Having procured in him a source of status and financial support and having rendered him well contented with her, she convinces Lavretskii to move to Paris, where she can find other men to provide the sexual and social stimulation that the unsophisticated Russian cannot. Yet it is through the very success of her self-gratifying machinations that Varvara Pavlovna's lack of true individuation begins to take its toll. Her infidelity causes Lavretskii to cast her out, and she leads an ever more scandalous life culminating, he learns, in "a tragicomic history carried with fanfare in all the newspapers, in which his wife played an unenviable role" (6: 54). Without a family or husband to impart a minimally constraining structure for her behavior, Varvara Pavlovna lapses into a disreputable way of life, the semblance of graceful self-control abandoned in favor of more immediate, if disgraceful, instinctual pleasures. The subsequent published report of her death, although false in fact, nevertheless has symbolic truth. Varvara Pavlovna has been publicly stripped of the veneer betokening a rational, civilized self, and so that false self in a sense does die; only her real self, the utterly uncivilized, irrationally unrestrained one, survives.

Yet Varvara Pavlovna salvages the veneer on returning to Russia, where she arrives at Lavretskii's estate relatively unchanged in appearance and manner. She still generates the self-command to wage a skillful campaign seeking the renewal of their marital relationship, appealing to his decency, cleverly offering no excuses for her betrayal. "I am guilty before you, deeply guilty" (6: 115), she confesses to him. And she claims to have contemplated suicide, having refrained only for the sake of their daughter, whom Lavretskii has never seen and whom Varvara Pavlovna suddenly brings forth to clinch her case for forgiveness. But, disabused of his illusions about Varvara Pavlovna, Lavretskii recognizes her actions for what they are—a premeditated, staged performance, carefully scripted and even costumed. Thus he caustically responds, "From which melodrama does this very scene come?" (6: 116). He has finally grasped that her manifestations of self-definition are merely attributes of public roles she plays in order to obtain private satisfactions; only this time, she has been "caught in the act."

Nonetheless, unphased by Lavretskii's derision, Varvara Pavlovna searches out a new audience from which to draw the supportive applause her designs require. She finds such an audience in Lavretskii's foolish aunt, Mar'ia Dmitrievna, whom Varvara Pavlovna impresses with equal measures of remorse, French clothing, and musicianship. And she finds an even more eager member of her audience in a visitor to Mar'ia Dmitrievna's home, Vladimir Panshin. Varvara Pavlovna quickly ensnares Panshin with her seductive allure: in expressing a difference of opinion with him as they chat, for instance, her words were severe but "the sound of these words caressed and fondled, and her eyes said... it was hard to say precisely what those wonderful eyes said, but their speeches were neither strict nor clear, and very sweet" (6: 132). She soon dispenses with Lavretskii and takes Panshin with her to St. Petersburg, where he meets her needs, at least temporarily: Varvara Pavlovna "worked him over, literally worked him over—no other term can express her unlimited, irrevocable, total power over him" (6: 152). Then, having finished "working him over," Varvara Pavlovna finally returns to Paris, where she musters enough self-control to organize a satisfactory mode of existence, albeit one based on mindless sentimentality and sensuality, as her main pleasures in Paris derive from "the dramas of Dumas-fils" and "a retired officer known as 'the great bull of the Ukraine'" (6: 153).

But Varvara Pavlovna's at best semi-self-awareness and quasi-self-control never provide her with complete individuation. They impart to her a certain confidence in her innate seductive skills, to be sure, but this is seduction by a vacuum that draws others in to fill its own emptiness. The identity her skills induce is shallow and spurious, rooted in dependence—her own and others—rather than in independence and integrity. She remains in Paris, where "the number of Varvara Pavlovna's admirers lessened but did not cease; several she probably will keep until the end of her life" (6: 153). Some men will always dance to her tune, but the melody can only become shopworn over time. Varvara Pavlovna therefore displays the practical advantages of a modicum of self-mastery;[21] but she demonstrates even better the hollowness of an identity that thrives on exploitation. Varvara Pavlovna is at most an individuated personality manqué.

Paradoxically, the character in Turgenev's narratives who most explicitly articulates the doctrine of individuation is one who cannot sustain his own incarnation of it. This is the father of the narrator of *First Love*, Petr Vasilevich. The very inability of this protagonist to live according to his own precepts therefore exposes the possibility that excessive individuation can be as damaging as insufficient individuation.

Petr Vasilevich, described by his son as "young and very handsome" (6: 304), appears to enjoy supreme self-possession. Having married an older woman for her wealth, he is emotionally intimate with neither his wife nor his only son. Although his son reports that his father "respected my freedom," Petr Vasilevich also insists on his own freedom as well, and therefore, so the son states, "would not let me approach him" (6: 323). The narrator can recall that "once—only once!—did he caress me with such tenderness that I almost cried... But both his gaiety and tenderness disappeared without a trace" (6: 324) shortly thereafter, so insistently does Petr Vasilevich impose a self-protective distance between himself and others.

At one point he explains to his son the philosophy that keeps him distant, telling the youth, "Take what you can, but do not put yourself into another's hands; to belong to yourself—the entire key to life lies in this" (6: 324). Here is the essence of individuation—to know what one is capable of "taking" means to comprehend one's temperament and one's environment, and to remain in one's own "hands" is to control the relation between oneself and that environment. Thus "to belong to yourself" is to attain complete autonomy, complete individuation.

Petr Vasilevich commends autonomy further in a subsequent discussion of freedom with his son, asking the adolescent, "Do you know what can give an individual freedom?," then answering his own question with the assertion, "Will, one's own will, and the power it gives, which is better than freedom. Be able to want—and you will be free and will command" (6: 324). Petr Vasilevich acknowledges the constraints placed on human freedom by such forces as nature, society, and irrationality that render total freedom illusory. And so he advocates that an individual exercise "will," and "want" only what is possible within those constraints. But he suggests that, by carefully selecting what is wanted and by directing the will in an exclusive pursuit of what is wanted, the individual can dominate the realm within those limits and can even dominate others. Petr Vasilevich thus expects to turn self-control into the control of others—a potential perversion of true individuation, which anticipates the sanctity of self-determination.

Having set forth his ideology, Petr Vasilevich proceeds to act on it. He has met the lovely Zinaida, young daughter of an impoverished princess staying in a summer home adjacent to his, has found her attractive, and has evidently decided that he "wants" her. And, true to his own teachings, he knows "how to want." He discreetly courts Zinaida, visits her mother's house, goes riding with her, and finally arranges a midnight tryst with her. As a result, though, Petr Vasilevich gets more than he "wants." For he falls in love with Zinaida, and thereby puts himself "into another's hands."

That he has succumbed to this self-abandonment is suggested on his return with his wife and son to Moscow from their sum-

mer home after the affair has been discovered. There Petr Vasilevich continues to see Zinaida, as his son learns by witnessing,
uninvited and unobserved, one such visit. He observes his father
standing outside the window of Zinaida's Moscow house looking at once "sad, serious, handsome, with an ineffable mark of
devotion, sadness, love, and some sort of despair" (6: 360). None
of these emotions bespeaks the freedom and control that he
had so confidently advocated to his son. Petr Vasilevich has
evidently lost his self-definition, his self-assurance, his self-
mastery.

This loss of mastery is further betrayed by a futile and rash
attempt to assert it anew during the visit the son witnesses,
when he hears either Zinaida or his father—he does not report
which one—say in French, "Vous devez vous séparer de cette..."
(You must separate yourself from that...) (6: 360). Then, as Zinaida holds out her hand, perhaps in farewell, the son recalls
that "suddenly before my eyes occurred an unbelievable act: my
father suddenly raised his whip, with which he brushed the dust
of the fields off his jacket, and then I heard the sound of a sharp
blow along her arm, bare to the elbow." But rather than turning
away emotionlessly, as would a ruler after punishing an errant
subordinate, "my father flung the whip to the side, and hurriedly
running up the steps of the porch, tore into the house" (6: 360).
And when the son subsequently queries his father about the
whereabouts of the whip, his father simply says, "I threw it
away" (6: 361). The whip, emblem of Petr Vasilevich's ability to
rule, to master himself and others, is cast away as is the last ves-
tige of his self-control.

Another emblem of this loss is the uncertain attribution of
the French phrase "Vous devez vous séparer de cette...." Either
Petr Vasilevich or Zinaida might have spoken the words; but the
point is that it does not matter who spoke them, since neither
one can separate from the other, or from the circumstances that
bind the one to the other. They have both lost all independence
through their commitment to an impossible love. And Petr Vasilevich knows it, as he later reveals on the very day of his death
from a stroke, writing to his son with final counsel: "Fear a
woman's love, fear this happiness, this poison" (6: 362). He ad-

mits that he overstepped the limits within self-awareness and self-control can guarantee integrity and autonomy. He knows he abandoned the dictates of individuation by believing he could control the course of a compelling physical and emotional engagement, when he actually could not. Instead, having received a letter from Zinaida most likely requesting money, he who prided himself on his self-reliance was forced, according to his son, to go "request something from my mother and, they say, even cried" (6: 361). Begging, tears—this is the behavior of a man utterly without command of himself or his circumstances.

Thus the price Petr Vasilevich pays for his transgression of the limits of individuation is particularly high. He loses all equanimity, all self-possession. In seeking satisfaction he tries to stretch the boundaries of his identity, but those boundaries break down under the excessive pressure. Although he retains some self-awareness, Petr Vasilevich ends up bereft of self-control and independence. Hence he exemplifies the necessity of zealously guarding the self, no matter how well defined, from the temptation to take individuation for granted.

Like Turgenev's characters, the characters that people Realist fiction also serve to illuminate issues of individuation. They too seek to clarify an identity and to ensure their integrity. Pierre Bezukhov, Konstantin Levin, Emma Woodhouse, Lucien Leuwen, Daniel Deronda, and Dorothea Brooke, to mention but a few, strive just as Grigorii Litvinov, Aleksei Petrovich, and Elena Stakhova do to ascertain the psychological and circumstantial limits within which they exist, and then to embrace ideas, emotions, and actions befitting that existence. But in narratives appropriately affiliated with Realism, characters successfully define themselves and defend their individuation within some communal context, be it marriage, family, or a segment of society. Left to their own devices, they tend to be misled or to mislead themselves, apart from the structures, both supportive and corrective, that continuous interaction with intimately associated fellow beings furnishes. Turgenev's characters, by contrast, generally go wrong under the influence of fellow beings, because intimacy more often than not is accompanied by the loss of autonomous identity and equanimous integrity. The characters peopling Turgenev's fiction, then, have the far harder moral task, for no community paves the way to secular salvation in Turgenev's fictional universe. In that universe, souls must save themselves by generating and defending their individuality on their own.

Conclusion:
Failed Realism and Final Affirmation

Turgenev is at his best, indeed is perhaps matchless, when his ethics and poetics marry perfectly to portray characters either autonomously redeeming themselves from myriad threats to their identity and integrity, or instructively failing. Only where Turgenev adopts some other ethical end or some other poetic means does he disappoint. Yet these disappointments only underscore the accomplishments.

And nowhere does Turgenev disappoint more conspicuously than in his final novel, *Virgin Soil*. Where most of his other narratives are taut, this one is tired; where the others set forth their ideas with provocative ambiguity, this one openly expresses a shallow ideology; where the others are carefully circumscribed, this one goes too far—at least too far for Turgenev's distinctive literary gifts. Even Turgenev's strongest critical supporters dismiss *Virgin Soil*: Garnett concedes that *Virgin Soil* "is artistically the least perfect of six great novels";[1] Freeborn entitles his chapter devoted to it "The Failure of *Virgin Soil*."[2] And *Virgin Soil* is conspicuous in other critical writings chiefly by its absence or denigration.

Yet for all of the critical consensus on the failure of *Virgin Soil*, that failure has not been satisfactorily explained. The explanation is this: whereas Turgenev's best works exemplify his unique ethics and poetics, *Virgin Soil* is as close to pure Realism as Turgenev ever gets. Employing far more extensively than in any other work images of spatial and temporal continuity, referential language, a single narrative point of view, and characters committed to collective action, Turgenev thereby informs *Virgin Soil* with poetics properly termed Realist. In so doing, he also admits to the novel an ethics of communal and political engagement as the means to individual fulfillment. During the process of introducing these relatively transparent, expansive, and socially minded poetics and ethics, though, Turgenev loses his own artistic voice; he sounds too much like too many other authors and too little like the one who prizes ambiguity, constraint, and autonomy in the pursuit of self-preservation.

By far Turgenev's longest narrative (approximately 260 pages), *Virgin Soil* allows Turgenev the latitude to loosen his typical constraints on space and time—and he forfeits the tension of ethical conflict as a result. The characters, primarily a group of proto-revolutionaries, come and go at will, confident of making steady progress over time. The poet Nezhdanov and the activist Mashurina freely leave St. Petersburg to pursue their revolutionary tasks; Nezhdanov's friend Paklin pops up on unexpected visits; the sympathizer Solomin goes wherever he pleases whenever he pleases; even the dependent Marianna faces only verbal opposition to her decision to leave the Sipiagin estate. As a result of this freedom of movement, the characters' actions, no matter how decently motivated, carry little moral weight: no existential barriers necessitating difficult choices have to be overcome in order to act.

Turgenev also generally forsakes the language of litotes in this narrative, thereby sacrificing verbal nuance and protective power. From the outset, when he employs an epigraph not from a work of literature but from "a farmer's notebook," he selects diction and rhetoric largely devoid of the ambiguity that enriches even as it obscures meaning. Litotes themselves, semi-definite terms, equivocal negations, imprecise adjectives rarely appear in the text—and "slightly" never occurs at all. Perhaps paralleling the desire voiced by Marianna to become "simplified," Turgenev strips his discourse in *Virgin Soil* down to referential simplicity—and thus denies it the beneficent obscurity that veils demoralizing detail.

For the most part, Turgenev also renounces the alterations in narrative point of view that elsewhere dramatize the virtues of maintaining a distanced perspective on events. He fixes the narration almost exclusively in the mode of apperception, switching in only a handful of lines to the mode of autonomy to interject a brief passing comment; he does not avail himself of the mode of assimilation at all. The novel retains a virtually impersonal single point of view that the realistic poetics of authors such as Flaubert would require, if not the multiple and yet consensual points of view that the Realist poetics of authors such as Eliot would mandate. By contrast to Turgenev's characteristically shifting narrative modes, this constant perspective precludes the perception of much depth or complexity. Moreover, it offers no deliberate encouragement to the reader to remain at a psychological remove from the difficulties the protagonists confront; any distance maintained is the product of uninterest rather than of an appreciation for the virtues of self-protection nurtured by Turgenev's other narratives.

To be sure, the characters in this novel are not so far removed in nature from those of his better narratives, and yet their personalities lack the psychological or moral profundity, for good or ill, of the others. They are more pale imitations of early figures: Solomin is prefigured by Insarov; Marianna combines aspects of Elena, Tat'iana, and Gemma; Nezhdanov unites the prerevolutionary Rudin, Sanin, and the narrators of "Andrei Kolosov" and "Asya." The protagonists of *Virgin Soil* do not manifest the ambivalences, the uncertainties, the self-ignorance and self-delusion that add the characterological complexity to so many of Turgenev's other creations. None of them takes advantage of the traditional Turgenevan defense mechanism—rationalization—because none has need of it: Marianna and Solomin are invariably self-confident as they invest themselves in communal life; Paklin is forthright in the admission of his treacherous betrayal of them; even Nezhdanov acknowledges from the start his lack of total commitment to the cause. And when he completely gives up on that cause, and life as well, his suicide is graphically presented, unlike the suicides of Masha in "A Quiet Place" and Susanna in "The Unhappy One," in which the moral ambiguity of their deaths is mirrored by the concealment of their final acts. Nezhdanov's suicide is utterly unambiguous in its admission of self-loathing and self-defeat—he even leaves letters of explanation, as the women do not—and therefore uses no aesthetic shield to deflect and reflect his despair. The dramatic strains engendered by true psychological and moral rifts, so often present just below the surface of Turgenev's other narratives, are markedly absent here.

The overall failure of *Virgin Soil* thus confirms the rich distinctiveness Turgenev imparts to his other narratives by virtue of his nonrealistic poetics and non-Realist ethics. Without the constraints, ambiguities, distances, and defenses that incorporate the ethical principles Turgenev espouses in those narratives, his poetics become ordinary and derivative, his characters one-dimensional, his fictional universe flat. In abandoning the ethical advocacy of self-preservation and the subtle poetics that foster it, Turgenev essentially roots *Virgin Soil* in barren ground.

Fortunately, *Virgin Soil* was not Turgenev's final literary endeavor. In failing health, he turned away from the burden of lengthy narratives and began to write the brief sketches he would collect before his death under the title *Poems in Prose.* Representing a natural culmination of his literary career—Turgenev began that career as a poet—the 51 prose poems he authorized for publication (along with 32 he chose not to release) provided more solid if occasionally uneven ground on which Turgenev could build one more small but enduring monument to his ethics and poetics.

Granted, like *Virgin Soil*, some of these pieces suffer from the abandonment of Turgenev's guiding principles, although not in the same ways as the novel. Where the novel is tediously plain, the prose poems can be overbearingly elaborate: the grandiose images of Alpine mountains exchanging occasional remarks over the course of centuries in "The Conversation," the cataclysmic tidal wave in "The End of the World," the hideous fantasies of fleshless talking heads in "The Skulls" and of a murderous flying monster in "The Insect," the apocalyptic embodiment of death in "The Old Woman"—these elements represent a complete departure from the aesthetic standards of restraint Turgenev had so consistently upheld.

In other prose poems, though, he reaffirms those standards, and he creates some of his finest artistic moments as a result. In "The Rose," for example, he intriguingly invokes a litotes, and its attendant atmosphere of ambiguity, to conclude the description of an unhappy young woman weeping as she throws a rose she had been given into the dying flames of a stove. The first-person narrator recounts her declaration that tears burn rather than cleanse, and remarks that she exclaimed "not without boldness," "Flames burn still better than tears." The narrator then simply ends with the unexplicated observation that "her beautiful eyes, still glistening with tears, laughed insolently and gaily," adding only the final line: "I understood that she too had been seared" (10: 145). No analysis of the contradictions she embodies—simultaneously crying and laughing, destroying while being psychologically destroyed—is forthcoming. The extent of the passionate upheaval she undergoes is expressed only by its ambiguous suppression.

Turgenev is never more graceful in altering narrative modes to convey an ethical message than in another prose poem, "To the Memory of Iu. P. Vrevskaia." Having portrayed in the mode of apperception the untimely death of this young woman, who had left a life of luxury to work as a war nurse, he turns to the mode of autonomy to make a general observation: "It is sad to think that no one said thank you even to her corpse—although she herself would have been embarrassed and distressed by any thanks." He then addresses her spirit, as well as the reader, with the affectionate conclusion: "May her dear shade not be offended by this belated wreath, which I dare to lay upon her grave" (10: 146). Here the reader encounters both the finality of a farewell gesture and the endurance of an artistic creation, as spatial, temporal, and psychological distances are both acknowledged and bridged.

And within the circumspectly constructed limits of the penultimate poem in prose, "The Prayer," Turgenev encapsulates his entire ethical vision. This poem's narrator begins by declaring that all prayers are requests for miracles, and are in fact variations on one request: "Almighty God, make it that two times two does not equal four." Echoing the complaint of Dostoevsky's Underground Man, that "two times two equals four" symbolizes the oppression of the human spirit by arbitrary rules of logic and laws of nature, Turgenev's narrator nonetheless shuns the Underground Man's conclusion that people should give themselves over to irrational, even self-destructive, rebellion against those rules and laws. Instead, the narrator grants that some people can be redeemed from this oppression by believing in a God capable of transcending all logical and natural limits, including that of human mortality. But then the narrator asks, "What if reason objects to such absurdity" as belief in this God? An ambiguous, Turgenevan answer follows: "We must drink and be merry—and pray" (10: 172). To whom and for what should the nonbeliever pray? The answer can only be to themselves, for self-redemption through creative acts of will that can sustain the human spirit by protecting and giving purpose to otherwise unprotected, purposeless, irredeemable lives. In other words, they should pray for secular salvation.

Thus, read anew and aright, Turgenev's narratives offer through their whitish curtains a subtle vision of effective means to master the diverse, often threatening, exigencies of everyday actuality, not only as it was known in Turgenev's times but as modern, secular human beings find it. And in this way, those narratives may speak to readers of the twentieth and twenty-first centuries as much as—and perhaps more than—they did to readers of the nineteenth century, in the heyday of Realism.

Reference Matter

Notes

Introduction

1. Ernest Renan, "Adieu à Tourguèneff," *Œuvres complètes,* ed. Calmann-Lévy (Paris, 1947), p. 869.

2. Max Nordau, *Degeneration,* trans. anon. (New York, 1895), p. 145.

3. Robert L. Jackson, "The Turgenev Question," *Sewanee Review,* 18, no. 2 (Spring 1985): 306.

4. Virginia Woolf, *Collected Essays* (New York, 1925) vol. 1, p. 248.

5. Friedrich Nietzsche, *The Birth of Tragedy,* trans. Francis Golffing (Garden City, N.Y., 1956; orig. German ed., 1872), p. 141.

6. This concept is clearly allied to Dale Peterson's notion of Turgenev's "clement vision," that is, "the capacity of human perception for deriving felt values from neutral or hurtful circumstances," which he persuasively articulates in *The Clement Vision: Poetic Realism in Turgenev and James* (Port Washington, N.Y., 1975), p. 123. This capacity, Peterson argues, places individuals in a "condition of redemptive remove" (p. 133) from difficulty. Yet Peterson affiliates Turgenev with realism, albeit a poetic realism that wraps "the commonest truths of experience" in "an exquisite envelope of poetry" (p. 134), whereas I argue that Turgenev, if necessary, ignores or denies such truths. More significantly, Peterson asserts that Turgenev's clement vision is the product of "a humane struggle to liberate the aesthetic consciousness from the oppressive guardianship of the ethical conscience" (p. 134), but I would maintain that Turgenev deems aesthetic and ethical sensibilities united in the pursuit of the blessings conferred by secular salvation.

Chapter 1

1. Letter to L. N. Tolstoy, Jan. 15/3, 1857, in I. S. Turgenev, *Pis'ma v trinadtsati tomakh,* ed. M. P. Alekseev et al. (Moscow-Leningrad, 1961–68), vol. 3, p. 75.

2. See Gary Saul Morson's comprehensive discussion, for example, of the critical reception afforded *War and Peace*, in ch. 2 of *Hidden in Plain View: Narrative and Creative Potentials in "War and Peace"* (Stanford, Calif., 1987).

3. George J. Becker names "the tenet of objectivity" as "the foundation stone" of realism, claiming that the realist author "serves no interest save that of truth; he has no preconceived view of how things should be; he observes and he states." George J. Becker, ed., *Documents of Modern Literary Realism* (Princeton, N.J., 1963), p. 29.

4. Letter to M. A. Miliutinaia, Mar. 6 / Feb. 22, 1875, in Turgenev, *Pis'ma*, vol. 11, p. 31.

5. Written in English, this is Turgenev's rephrasing of Shakespeare. The actual words from *Hamlet*, act 3, scene 2, lines 22–24, read: "To show virtue her own feature, scorn her own image, and the very age and body of the time his form and pressure."

6. Quoted by Paul Bourget, "Ivan Tourguéniev," in *Essais de psychologie contemporaine* (Paris, 1924), vol. 2, p. 212.

7. Letter to Ia. P. Polonskii, Mar. 11 / Feb. 27, 1869, in Turgenev, *Pis'ma*, vol. 7, p. 328.

8. Theodor Fontane, another author customarily identified as a realist, offers similar refinement to the conception of realism when he insists, in his 1853 essay "On Lyric and Epic Poetry Since 1848," that "realism . . . *is art*" and elsewhere argues that therefore the realist must engage in the "transfiguration" (*Verklarung*) of reality so as not to lapse into the habit of representing only "the dark side of human existence." Quoted in Gabriele A. Wittig-Davis, *Novel Associations: Theodor Fontane and George Eliot Within the Context of Nineteenth-Century Realism* (New York, 1983), p. 53.

9. Vissarion Belinskii, "Vzgliad na russkuiu literaturu 1847 goda," in K. Boneckii, ed., *Turgenev v russkoi kritike* (Moscow, 1953), pp. 102–3.

10. Guy de Maupassant, quoted in V. V. Grigorenko et al., eds., *I. S. Turgenev v vospominaniiakh sovremennikov v dvukh tomax* (Moscow, 1969), vol. 2, p. 276.

11. Henry James, "Iwan Turgeniew," *North American Review*, 118 (Jan.–Apr. 1874): 326.

12. James, p. 330.

13. V. Sakharov, "Finaly Turgenevskikh romanov," *Literaturnaia ucheba*, no. 3 (1985): 180.

14. A. P. Chudakov, "O poetike Turgeneva-prozaika (Povestvovanie—predmetnyi mir—siuzhet)," in K. N. Lomunov, A. M. Dolotova,

and S. E. Shatalov, eds., *I. S. Turgenev v sovremennom mire* (Moscow, 1987), p. 266.

15. Even the most depressing and hopeless moments of Turgenev's narratives are conceived not as "tragedies, but, on the contrary, are connected with the eternal movement of life, full of hope and faith in the positive future of Russia, its best inhabitants and social strengths, its people." Sakharov, p. 180.

16. Henri Granjard, *Ivan Tourguénev et les courants politiques et sociaux de son temps* (Paris, 1954), pp. 9–10.

17. Edmund Wilson, "Turgenev and the Life-giving Drop," in Ivan Turgenev, *Literary Reminiscences and Autobiographical Fragments*, trans. David Magarshack (New York, 1958), p. 49.

18. Ibid., p. 50.

19. Ibid., p. 24.

20. Ibid., p. 23. Hence, Wilson proclaims, when Turgenev "tries to go inside his characters, he is likely to be less satisfactory than when he is telling you merely what they say and do, how they look and what one feels about them."

21. Richard Freeborn, *Turgenev: The Novelist's Novelist* (London, 1960), p. 48.

22. Ibid., p. 49.

23. Ibid., p. 53.

24. Ibid., p. 45.

25. Ibid., p. 49.

26. Most recent studies of Turgenev echo without critically evaluating this traditional conceptualization of Turgenev's literary achievement. In *Turgenev: His Life and Times* (New York, 1978), for instance, Leonard Schapiro generally characterizes Turgenev's works as straightforward portrayals of Russian life in the realist mold. And Victor Ripp, in *Turgenev's Russia* (Ithaca, N.Y., 1980), examines Turgenev's works more closely but comes to no significantly different conclusion. Turgenev intended above all, Ripp suggests, to depict "society," "political issues," and the overall "historical situation," (p. 93) with the result that in Turgenev's narratives "even love may turn out to depend on the health of the body politic" (p. 26).

27. Osip Mandelstam, "The Noise of Time," in *The Prose of Osip Mandelstam*, trans. Clarence Brown (Princeton, N.J., 1965), p. 83.

28. Freeborn, p. 75.

29. Oscar Wilde, "The Decay of Lying," in Richard Ellman, ed., *The Artist as Critic: Critical Writings of Oscar Wilde* (New York, 1968), p. 302.

30. See Jacques Barzun's parallel discussion of the confusion engendered by the use of the adjective "romantic" to describe both "permanent elements in human nature and their periodic emphasis in history," in the comparative study *Classic, Romantic and Modern,* 2d ed. (Garden City, N.Y., 1961), pp. 7–9. Note also that it is customary for art historians to capitalize "Realism" when referring to the movement in painting. See, for example, Linda Nochlin, *Realism* (New York, 1971).

31. Carl Dahlhaus, *Realism in Nineteenth-Century Music,* trans. Mary Whittall (Cambridge, 1985), p. 16.

32. Stephan Kohl, *Realismus: Theorie und Geschichte* (Munich, 1977), p. 11.

33. C. P. Snow, *The Realists* (New York, 1978), p. v.

34. Harry Levin, *The Gates of Horn: A Study of Five Realists* (New York, 1963), p. 13.

35. George Levine, *The Realistic Imagination: English Fiction from Frankenstein to Lady Chatterley* (Chicago, 1981), p. 11.

36. Ibid., p. 22.

37. Ibid., p. 40.

38. Donald Fanger, *Dostoevsky and Romantic Realism: A Study of Dostoevsky in Relation to Balzac, Dickens, and Gogol* (Chicago, 1965), p. 3.

39. Roman Jakobson, "Realism in Art," in L. Matejka, ed. and trans., *Readings in Russian Poetics: Formalist and Structuralist Views* (Cambridge, Mass., 1971), p. 38.

40. Ibid., p. 20.

41. René Wellek, *Concepts of Criticism* (New Haven, Conn., 1963), p. 252.

42. Quoted ibid., p. 228.

43. Ibid., p. 255.

44. These descriptions come from Dahlhaus (p. 7), who too questions the validity and utility of the term, because of what he deems the endless debate over whether Realism must actually mirror reality or not, the advantage going to whichever side dominates "the state of cultural policies."

45. Wilde, p. 303.

46. Watt exemplifies this tendency when he observes that the "realism" of philosophy entertains "a view of reality diametrically opposed to that of common usage . . . that it is universals, classes or abstractions, and not the particular, concrete objects of sense-perception, which are the true 'realities.'" Ian Watt, *The Rise of the Novel: Studies in Defoe, Richardson and Fielding* (Berkeley, Calif., 1957), p. 12. He

thus finds the shared terminology on the whole "unhelpful," although he does find a certain affinity between the two, in "the general temper of philosophical realism," which has been "critical, anti-traditional, and innovating" (p. 13).

47. George Bernard Shaw, "Realism, Real and Unreal," in Stanley Weintraub, ed., *Bernard Shaw's Nondramatic Literary Criticism* (Lincoln, Neb., 1972), p. 110.

48. J. P. Stern, *On Realism* (London, 1973), p. 110.

49. Romanticism and Modernism are both more generally acknowledged to be characterized by an ideal of human existence—each one radically divergent, to be sure, from that of Realism. I am indebted to Caryl Emerson for observing that the recognition of an ideal at the core of the definition of Realism places that "-ism" on a par with the other two.

50. Stern, p. 130.

51. Levin, p. 83. Levin accepts the socially adversarial role of Realism, articulated by the brothers Goncourt in the preface to *Germinie Lacerteux*: "The public also loves vapid, bland stuff, adventures with a happy ending, fantasies that do not spoil its digestion nor disturb its peace of mind; this book with its tragedy and violence is designed to upset the public's habits and challenge its complacency." Quoted in Roland N. Stromberg, ed., *Realism, Naturalism, and Symbolism* (New York, 1968), p. 69.

52. Levine, p. 8.

53. Goethe's Faust, who feels two souls within his breast, Byron's Manfred, who deems himself half god and half dust, and Lermontov's Pechorin, who describes himself as two beings, one who acts and one who judges, are but three exemplars of the Romanticist sense of a spiritual division plaguing mankind.

54. Ferdinand Tönnies, *Community and Society*, ed. and trans. Charles P. Loomis (New York, 1957; orig. German ed., 1887). For a comprehensive review of the history of ideas about the community, see Robert A. Nisbet, *The Quest for Community* (New York, 1953; reprinted 1971). And for additional elaboration on the perceived differences between the *Gemeinschaft* and the *Gesellschaft*, see Raymond Williams, *The Country and the City* (New York, 1973).

55. Meyer Schapiro's 1941 article, "Courbet and Popular Imagery: An Essay on Realism and Naivete," explores the sources and reception of this painting, and concludes that "the consciousness of the community, awakened by the revolution of 1848, appears for the first time in a monumental painting, in all its richness of allusion." Reprinted in

Meyer Schapiro, *Modern Art: 19th and 20th Centuries. Selected Papers* (New York, 1978), p. 74.

56. George Eliot, *Adam Bede* (New York, 1981; orig. British ed. 1859), p. 175.

57. Steven Marcus, *Representations: Essays on Literature and Society* (New York, 1975), p. 198. The fulfillment of society as a whole inevitably accompanies the fulfillment of the individual, Marcus suggests, as a result of which, "the individual person is not separable from the human whole; and in turn the social whole is equally dependent on each individual person, since each contributes to the common life." He thus concludes that society and individual persons "are not separable or distinct phenomena," but are essentially "the collective and distributive aspects of the same circumstance or thing" (p. 197).

58. Marcus puts it thus: "In the centrality of the sentiment of sympathy, . . . of communion and community, society itself appears to be re-sacralized" (p. 204).

59. Quoted in Victor Brombert, *Victor Hugo and the Visionary Novel* (Cambridge, Mass., 1984), p. 124.

60. Dostoevsky may have reflected his sense of this very difference with the comment in an 1877 entry to *Diary of a Writer* that "I am terribly fond of realism in art, but there is *no moral center* in the pictures of some of our modern realists" (emphasis Dostoevsky's), for it is the "moral center" formed by the Realists' faith in community that transforms pictorially precise, realistic representations of human experience into ethically coherent presentations. Quoted in Robert Louis Jackson, *Dostoevsky's Quest for Form: A Study of His Philosophy of Art*, 2d ed. (Bloomington, Ind., 1978), p. 76.

61. Claiming that *Madame Bovary* constituted an offense against both public morals and religion, the prosecutor, Ernest Pinard, accused Flaubert's novel of immorality "not because it paints the passions: hatred, vengeance, love (the world only lives by these, and art must paint them)—but because it paints them without restraint, without bounds," and therefore "is no longer art." Quoted from the transcription of the trial, in Evelyn Gendel, trans., "The Trial of Madame Bovary," in Gustave Flaubert, *Madame Bovary*, trans. Mildred Marmur (New York, 1964; orig. French ed. 1857), p. 347. In fact, the prosecutor wrongly put his conclusion in aesthetic terms. What he actually objected to were the antisocial implications in the rendition of those emotional experiences, that is, the lack of Realist ethics in the novel.

62. Lionel Trilling, *The Opposing Self* (New York, 1955), p. 65. Trilling differentiates Tolstoy's poetics, which he claims attract the reader

to Tolstoy's fictional universe, from Flaubert's, which Trilling maintains regularly irritate and even alienate the reader. Thus in part this critic also implicitly distinguishes poetics that are "Realist," which appeal to readers, from those that are merely "realistic," which often do not.

63. Eliot, p. 403.

64. This view is articulated in several important critical studies on the novel, most notably Leo Bersani, *A Future for Astyanax: Character and Desire in Literature* (New York, 1976); George Levine, *The Realistic Imagination: English Fiction from Frankenstein to Lady Chatterley* (Chicago, 1981); and Susan Gilbert and Susan Gubar, *The Madwoman in the Attic: The Woman Writer and the Nineteenth-Century Literary Imagination* (New Haven, Conn., 1979).

65. Eva Kagan-Kans, *Hamlet and Don Quixote: Turgenev's Ambivalent Vision* (The Hague, 1975), p. 20.

66. Mikhail Gershenzon, *Mechta i mysl' I. S. Turgeneva* (Moscow, 1919; reprinted, Providence, R.I., 1970); Dale Peterson, *The Clement Vision: Poetic Realism in Turgenev and James* (Port Washington, N.Y., 1975).

67. G. B. Kurliandskaia, *Khudozhestvennyi metod Turgeneva-romanista* (Tula, 1972); Marina Ledkovsky [Astman], *The Other Turgenev: From Romanticism to Symbolism* (Würzburg, 1973); A. Walicki, "Turgenev and Schopenhauer," *Oxford Slavonic Papers*, 10 (1962): 1–17.

68. Edward Garnett, *Turgenev: A Study* (London, 1924; reprinted Port Washington, N.Y., 1966); André Maurois, *Tourguéniev* (Paris, 1952); Leonid Grossman, *Turgenev: Etiudy o Turgeneve—Teatr Turgeneva* (Moscow, 1928).

69. Walter Koschmal, *Vom Realismus zum Symbolismus: Zu Genese und Morphologie des Symbolsprache in den spaten Werken I. S. Turgenevs* (Amsterdam, 1984); Peter Brang, *I. S. Turgenev: Sein Leben und sein Werk* (Wiesbaden, 1977).

70. Victor Terras, "Turgenev's Aesthetic and Western Realism," *Comparative Literature*, 22 (1970): 19–35.

71. S. E. Shatalov, *Problemy poetiki I. S. Turgeneva* (Moscow, 1969); Nina Kauchtschischwili, *La Narrativa di Ivan S. Turgenev: Problemi di lingua e arte* (Milan, 1969); Robert Louis Jackson, "The Root and the Flower. Dostoevsky and Turgenev: A Comparative Esthetic," *Yale Review* (Winter 1974): 228–50. Kauchtschischwili holds that Turgenev subscribes to what she terms "minimalism," that is, ever-reductive aesthetic principles, in all his choices of language and narrative struc-

tures. Shatalov identifies a pervasive technique he calls "diffusion" (*diffuziia*), with which, he argues, Turgenev renders his own ideas indistinct by reflecting the personalities of characters in narrative voices.

Chapter 2

1. In his essay "Discourse in the Novel," for instance, Bakhtin does concede that although "the language and style of Turgenev's novels have the appearance of being single-languaged and pure . . . this unitary language is very far from poetic absolutism." He finds examples of "heteroglossia" and "language stratification" that render the voice of the author "relativized," not completely dominant. Nonetheless, he observes, "in Turgenev, the novelistic orchestration of the theme is concentrated in direct dialogues; the characters do not create around themselves their own extensive or densely saturated zones, and in Turgenev fully developed, complex stylistic hybrids are relatively rare." Thus Bakhtin rates Turgenev's artistic achievement lower than that of authors who make extensive use of "stylistic hybrids." Mikhail Bakhtin, *The Dialogic Imagination: Four Essays by M. M. Bakhtin*, ed. Michael Holquist, trans. Caryl Emerson and Michael Holquist (Austin, Tex., 1981), p. 316.

2. Mikhail Bakhtin, *Problems of Dostoevsky's Poetics*, ed. and trans. Caryl Emerson (Minneapolis, 1984), p. 270.

3. Ibid., p. 22. These characters, Bakhtin alleges, "seldom escape to become full *subjects*, telling their own tales. Instead they generally remain as objects *used* by the author to fulfill preordained demands" (p. xxii; emphasis Bakhtin's).

4. Ibid., p. 285.

5. Ibid., p. 191.

6. Ibid., p. 192. Bakhtin continues: "Double-voiced discourse did not turn out well in his work (consider the satiric and parodying passages in *Smoke*). For that reason he chose narrators from his own social circle. Such narrators inevitably had to speak a literary language, since they could not reliably sustain oral *skaz*." Bakhtin evidently had not read all of *A Sportsman's Sketches*, or Turgenev's short stories such as "The Dog" and "The Story of Father Aleksei," in which primary narrators display highly idiosyncratic narrative styles.

7. Ibid., p. 231.

8. A far more nuanced discussion of the overarching aesthetic and philosophical differences between the two authors is provided, for example, in Robert Louis Jackson, "The Root and the Flower. Dostoevsky

and Turgenev: A Comparative Esthetic," *Yale Review* (Winter 1974): 228–50.

9. In "The Root and the Flower," Jackson summarizes such observations in noting that "it is remarkable how consistent are the critics and commentators in identifying the final statement of Turgenev's personality, art, and outlook not with 'radical contradiction' or dissonances but with the attributes of his beloved nature: balance, measure, harmony" (p. 246).

10. Friedrich Nietzsche, *The Birth of Tragedy*, trans. Francis Golffing (Garden City, N.Y., 1956; orig. German ed., 1872), p. 20.

11. Ibid., p. 21.

12. Ibid., p. 24.

13. Ibid., p. 51.

14. Bakhtin, *Problems of Dostoevsky's Poetics*, p. 122.

15. Nietzsche, *The Birth of Tragedy*, p. 38.

16. Ibid., p. 35.

17. Bakhtin, *Problems of Dostoevsky's Poetics*, p. 122.

18. Nietzsche, *The Birth of Tragedy*, p. 21.

19. Ibid., p. 145.

20. Ibid., p. 102.

21. Ibid., p. 129.

22. Ibid., p. 28. Nietzsche argues further on that, however appealing Apollonian "charm" may be, eventually Dionysian art forces individuals to "see the struggle, the pain, the destruction of appearances, as necessary, because of the constant proliferation of forms pushing into life" that make us "realize our great good fortune in having life—not as individuals, but as part of the life force with whose procreative force we have become one" (pp. 102–3). Thus the energy of the human spirit survives through its Dionysian manifestations as it never can through Apollonian illusions.

23. Friedrich Nietzsche, *The Will to Power*, ed. Walter Kaufmann, trans. Walter Kaufmann and R. J. Hollingdale (New York, 1967; orig. German ed., 1901), p. 435.

24. Ibid., pp. 451–52. Jackson makes use of these passages in his discussion of philosophical similarities and differences between Dostoevsky and Nietzsche in "Dostoevsky and Nietzsche: Counterpoint," *The Comparatist* (May 1982): 24–34.

25. Jackson, "The Root and the Flower," p. 245.

26. Ibid., p. 235.

27. Ibid.

28. Ibid., p. 246.

29. Ibid.

30. Letter to K. N. Leontiev, Feb. 23/11, 1855, in I. S. Turgenev, *Pis'ma v trinadtsati tomakh,* ed. M. P. Alekseev et al. (Moscow-Leningrad, 1961–68), vol. 2, p. 259.

31. The mother of Vera Nikolaevna Eltsova in "Faust" responds to the narrator's claim that "reading poetic works is *both* useful *and* pleasant" with the argument that "it is necessary to choose beforehand in life: either the useful or the pleasant, and thus decide once and for all. Even I once wanted to unite them both... This was impossible and leads to death or to banality" (5: 98). Although rejecting the notion of Longinus, which others of Turgenev's characters tacitly accept, that literature has the power both to delight and to instruct, the elder Eltsova nonetheless shares with them a sense of the power of literature to affect human life; indeed, she senses it more acutely than they—and is not proven wrong. Yet had she allowed her daughter to become accustomed to the emotions engendered by literature from youth, her daughter might not have succumbed to its power so rapidly and completely as an adult.

32. Norman Holland, *The Dynamics of Literary Response* (New York, 1975), p. 68.

33. "A Strange History" is also subtitled "A Story," and although not officially subtitled, the narratives "The Inn" and "Brigadier" also have "A Story" written below the title in the original manuscripts. (See the facsimiles on 4: 275 and 8: 41.) Other narratives marked thus as fiction include "Knock... Knock... Knock!," subtitled "A Study," "*Diary* of a Superfluous Man," and "The *Story* of Father Aleksei" (emphasis mine).

34. See especially ch. 6, "Implied Authors as Friends and Pretenders," in Wayne Booth, *The Company We Keep: An Ethics of Fiction* (Berkeley, Calif., 1988), pp. 169–98. Interestingly, Booth commences the epilogue to this study with a passage from the Chekhov story "At Home," in which the moral impact of narratives is attributed to the "deceptions and delusions" that fiction promulgates but that nonetheless promote new comprehension of human experience (p. 484).

35. Oscar Mandel, "Molière and Turgenev: The Literature of No-Judgment," *Comparative Literature,* 3 (1951): 245.

36. Schapiro, for instance, qualifies his description of Turgenev's political "outlook" as "more acceptable to a Western European liberal than that of Dostoevsky, or Tolstoy," by adding that "Turgenev was no Western European liberal in the accepted sense," meaning that Turge-

nev espoused no specific liberal party program or doctrine. Leonard Schapiro, *Turgenev: His Life and Times* (New York, 1978), p. xii.

37. Richard Freeborn, *Turgenev: The Novelist's Novelist* (London, 1960), p. 16.

38. Quoted in Jackson, "The Root and the Flower," p. 247.

39. For a compelling close reading of this text, see Robert Louis Jackson, "The Ethics of Vision in Turgenev's 'Execution of Tropmann,' and Dostoevsky's View of the Matter," in *The Poetics of Ivan Turgenev*, Occasional Papers, no. 234, Kennan Institute for Advanced Russian Studies (Washington, D.C., 1989), pp. 27–43. Jackson too stresses the importance of "seeing" in the text, although he argues that Turgenev the artist "does not and cannot turn away from the beheading" when the narrator does, because numerous details of the execution are supplied. Yet Jackson notes that the interpretation of these details is left up to the reader, who has "to exercise his imagination when the narrator momentarily turns away from the actual decapitation" (p. 30). My point here is that Turgenev supplies the reader with a model of alternative imaginative behavior that creates rather than copies experience.

40. See Chapter 6 of this study for a discussion of the ways in which characters find life "too difficult," and the coping mechanisms they develop in response.

41. Sigmund Freud, *Civilization and Its Discontents*, ed. and trans. James Strachey (New York, 1961; orig. German ed., 1930), p. 25.

42. Jackson, "The Root and the Flower," pp. 231–32.

43. See Freeborn, esp. pp. 25–28, for the argument that Belinsky's influence led Turgenev to value social commitment more highly than individual fulfillment.

44. In *Smoke* the difficulty of making such a distinction is made explicit when the narrator notes that "Litvinov himself was unable or was unwilling to acknowledge to what extent Irina seemed beautiful to him and how strongly she aroused his feelings" (8: 318); in "The Unhappy One," Susanna too conflates inability and unwillingness, thereby leaving unclear which has the greater force, when she reports that in response to the kisses of the man she loves, "I could not, I did not want to receive them" (8: 110). Expressly observed in these instances, an ambiguous relation between intentional and unintentional action is repeatedly suggested at moments of moral import.

45. Friedrich Nietzsche, *On the Genealogy of Morals*, ed. Walter Kaufmann, ed. and trans. Walter Kaufmann and R. J. Hollingdale (New York, 1967; orig. German ed., 1887), p. 137. Nietzsche says: "Our ed-

ucated people of today, our 'good people,' do not tell lies—that is true; but that is *not* to their credit! A real lie, a genuine, resolute, 'honest' lie . . . would be something far too severe and potent for them: it would demand of them what one *may* not demand of them, that they should open their eyes to themselves, that they should know how to distinguish 'true' and 'false' in themselves. All they are capable of is a *dishonest* lie," that is, a self-deceptive one (emphases Nietzsche's).

46. Edward Garnett, *Turgenev: A Study* (London, 1924; reprinted Port Washington, N.Y., 1966), p. 7.

47. See Gary Saul Morson, *Hidden in Plain View: Narrative and Creative Potentials in "War and Peace"* (Stanford, Calif., 1987), esp. ch. 6, "Forms of Negative Narration," for a penetrating analysis of Tolstoy's means and ends in rejecting Beauty as a goal of narrative.

48. Quoted in Robert Louis Jackson, *Dostoevsky's Quest for Form: A Study of His Philosophy of Art,* 2d ed. (Bloomington, Ind., 1978), p. xi.

49. Jackson's masterly study of Dostoevsky's "quest for form" demonstrates the ways in which Dostoevsky reconciled the tragedies and conflicts of human existence through "faith in a higher beauty, in Christ, in moral-aesthetic perfection . . . which renders this truth of [man's fallibility] incomplete" (p. 212).

Chapter 3

1. One notable exception can be found in Gary Saul Morson's essay in honor of Joseph Frank, "Genre and Hero / *Fathers and Sons*: Intergeneric Dialogues, Generic Refugees, and the Hidden Prosaic" (forthcoming). In this wide-ranging, provocative discussion, Morson points out that Turgenev deliberately sets up conflicting images of temporality to underscore differences not only between the generations represented in the work itself, but between the work's readers of the time and future readers. I discuss some other forms of temporal conflict informing *Fathers and Sons* later in this chapter.

2. Henry James, for one, perceived a "dusky pall of fatality" in Turgenev, quoted by Dale Peterson in *The Clement Vision: Poetic Realism in Turgenev and James* (Port Washington, N.Y., 1975), p. 44. Commentators such as Mikhail Gershenzon, in *Mechta i mysl' I. S. Turgeneva* (Moscow, 1919; reprinted, Providence, R.I., 1970), and André Maurois, in *Tourguéniev* (Paris, 1952), discuss at length the fatalism that, they conclude, leads Turgenev to advocate self-transcendence in order to obviate the pain caused by human powerlessness.

3. Even the huge forest in "A Journey to the Forest" is introduced by the narrator as he observes it from one side of the river that defines its outer edge (5: 131).

4. This coy refusal to provide the town's name only affirms its separate identity, so distinctive that the narrator considers himself compelled to try to conceal that identity.

5. For example, the home of the young woman with whom Andrei Kolosov becomes involved lies on the outskirts of Moscow; the rooms rented by Asya and her half brother are perched on a hill outside the German town where the narrator encounters them; the store and residence of Gemma's family is located on "one of the insignificant streets at the edge of Frankfurt" (8: 257), and so on.

6. Bakhtin is therefore only partially right when he claims that in Dostoevsky's narratives, "absolutely nothing here ever loses touch with the threshold, there is no interior of drawing rooms, dining rooms, halls, studios, bedrooms where biographical life unfolds and where events take place in the novels of writers such as Turgenev, Tolstoy, and Goncharov." Mikhail Bakhtin, *Problems of Dostoevsky's Poetics*, ed. and trans. Caryl Emerson (Minneapolis, 1984), p. 170. The threshold is indeed far less important to Turgenev than to Dostoevsky, but interiors are far less important to Turgenev than Bakhtin thinks. One of Turgenev's more detailed descriptions of an interior, that of Anna Sergeevna's living room in *Fathers and Sons*, occupies all of six lines (7: 76); when compared to Balzac's two-page description of the sitting room of Madame Vauquer's boarding house at the beginning of *Father Goriot*— as well as to interiors portrayed by Tolstoy and Goncharov—the relative scantness of Turgenev's attention to interiors becomes apparent.

7. Freeborn has also observed that Turgenev generally confines his novels to a specific setting that "circumscribes the action of the major participants as if they were performers upon a stage." Noting a circumscription of time as well, he thus discerns a distinctly theatrical quality in Turgenev's fiction. Richard Freeborn, *Turgenev: The Novelist's Novelist* (London, 1960), p. 53. Theatricality as a distinctive feature of Turgenev's narrative technique has also been observed by Ludmila Hellgren, in *Dialogues in Turgenev's Novels: Speech-Introductory Devices* (Stockholm, 1980).

8. Irving Howe waxes positively rhapsodic over Liza, adoring her as "the most madonna-like of Turgenev's heroines. Still tied to the peasants, yet possessed of a modest cultivation, she is a figure of true moral repose, an embodiment of the idea of Russian purity to which all the

Russian writers return again and again." This purity, Howe claims, is born of unparalleled selflessness. Irving Howe, "Turgenev: The Virtues of Hesitation," *Hudson Review*, 8, no. 4 (Winter 1956): 541.

9. Liza's ultimate decision to "go back" to her cell-like room distinctly contrasts with the decision taken by the young girl in Turgenev's prose poem "The Threshold" (10: 147). Threatened explicitly by every sort of torture—physical, emotional, spiritual—she nonetheless insists on going forward across her threshold. See Ch. 6 of this study for a comparison of Elena Stakhova to the same figure.

10. Frank identifies the "spatialization of forms" primarily with modern fiction, pointing to Proust, for example, as an artist "oppressed and obsessed by a sense of the ineluctability of time and the evanescence of human life," who therefore sought, as Proust himself said, "to seize, isolate, immobilize for the duration of a lightning flash . . . a fragment of time in its pure state." Joseph Frank, *The Widening Gyre: Crisis and Mastery in Modern Literature* (Bloomington, Ind., 1963), pp. 20–21. Frank does concede that the awareness of temporal progression inherent in reading makes the devices for creating spatial forms "techniques to achieve the impossible—as much as possible" (p. 60).

11. It should be stressed that by "antiplot" is meant a certain *type* of plot, not the total absence of plot. Thus the antiplot still fulfills the definition of plot set forth, for instance, by Peter Brooks in *Reading for the Plot: Design and Intention in Narrative* (New York, 1985): "Plot as we need and want the term is hence an embracing concept for the design and intention of narrative, a structure for those meanings that are developed through temporal succession" (p. 12). An antiplot simply opposes the promotion of awareness of that temporal succession.

12. In his comparative study *Modern Fiction and Human Time* (Tampa, Fla., 1985), Wesley Kort indirectly observes the antitemporal effect of antiplots by arguing for the obverse, that "when plot does dominate, its effect is to grant time primacy" (p. 9).

13. The narrator singles out Kolosov's willingness to accept the inexorable flow of time with the rhetorical question posed to his audience: "Who among us could part on time with one's own past?" (4: 33). Kolosov is thus distinguished by this conscious, willed act of submission to temporal constraints. Another figure who mentally encompasses an integrated vision of past, present, and future is the narrator of *A Sportsman's Sketches* as he is represented in the final sketch, "Forest and Steppe." While in the midst of the forest, he finds that "impressions long asleep unexpectedly awaken," and that his "heart suddenly begins to tremble and throb, passionately casts itself forward, then irrevocably

drowns itself in memories. All one's life unrolls lightly and quickly, like a scroll." Yet he has these sensations within a moment that he experiences as virtually outside space and time: "Nothing around disturbs one—for there is neither sun, nor wind, nor sound..." (3: 358). Thus this instance of transcendent unification does not necessarily endure beyond an instant.

14. Hans Meyerhof, *Time in Literature* (Berkeley, Calif., 1955), p. 35.

15. In her persuasive discussion of fictional representations of time, Eleanor Hutchens draws the following general conclusion: "The assumption of the novel is that truth is the daughter of time. The novel avails itself of rhythm, mimesis, and of the microcosm; but its rhythms are those of time, the great action it imitates is the process of time, and its microcosmic moment renders an image not of the eternal but of a temporal macrocosm—namely, the human life-span." Just so, but for many of Turgenev's characters, forced confrontation with temporal truth entails recognition of the *brevity* of the human life-span, and therefore inspires the impulse to deny time—and hence to deny that truth—even, if necessary, by lying. Eleanor Hutchens, "An Approach Through Time," in Mark Spilka, ed., *Towards a Poetics of Fiction* (Bloomington, Ind., 1977), p. 60.

16. The morality of such investment in the present is nowhere better illustrated than in "Living Relics," one of *A Sportsman's Sketches*, as the paralyzed protagonist, Luker'ia, tells the narrator that she has trained herself "not to think, and most of all, not to remember" (3: 331). See Ch. 6 for an analysis of the moral implications of her characterization.

17. In Georges Poulet's *Studies in Human Time*, trans. Elliot Coleman (Baltimore, 1956), the author asserts that "never so much as in the nineteenth century had time appeared to be perceptible to the eyes of the spirit," because "it is conceived as an immense causal chain" (p. 32). This causal chain is manifested in Realist works through the primarily chronological representation of events.

Chapter 4

1. George Steiner, *Language and Silence: Essays on Language, Literature, and the Inhuman* (New York, 1970), p. 21.

2. Ibid., p. 52.

3. One critic, labeling Rudin "nothing more than a blabbermouth," goes so far as to call Rudin morally inferior to "the uneducated Khlestakov," Gogol's blithely amoral adopter of the eponymous role in *The Inspector General* (Vl. Zotov, "Russkaia Literatura," *S.-Peterburgskie*

vedomosti, no. 52 (Mar. 6, 1856). From the time of the novel's publication to the present day, Rudin has been identified with the tradition
in Russian literary characterization known as "the superfluous man,"
a type often seen manifested in figures such as Griboedov's Chatskii,
Pushkin's Onegin, and Lermontov's Pechorin, who display well-
developed intellects and refined verbal skills but make little or no social contribution. See Ellen Chances, *Conformity's Children: An Approach to the Superfluous Man in Russian Literature* (Columbus, Ohio,
1978), for a comprehensive survey of the critical history of the concept.

4. Henry James, for instance, admires the "characteristic precision"
of Turgenev's verbal performances, discerning in them a "vividly definite element" that makes for total verisimilitude. Henry James, "Iwan
Turgeniew," *North American Review*, 118 (Jan.–Apr. 1874): 326–56.
Likewise, Paul Bourget declares that because Turgenev "considers himself solely a mirror responsible for showing us the greatest possible
number of objects without deforming them," he employs a language of
the purest possible "objectivity" and exactitude. Paul Bourget, "Ivan
Tourguéniev," in *Essais de psychologie contemporaine* (Paris, 1924),
vol. 2, p. 213. The typical Soviet view of Turgenev's language as an epitome of exactitude is represented, for instance, in A. Kuprenskii, "Iazyk
i stil' Turgeneva," *Literaturnaia ucheba*, no. 1 (1940): 41–65.

5. William Empson, *Seven Types of Ambiguity*, 2d ed. (New York,
1970), p. 1.

6. Ibid., p. 247.

7. The entry on litotes in *The Princeton Encyclopedia of Poetry and
Poetics* (1974) observes that litotes are used to convey irony so often in
Beowulf as to become "a distinguishing mark of that literature," but
also observes the fact that "the irony in the litotes is not total, but only
gradual" (p. 459).

8. This novel is rife with litotes, appropriately enough for a work
whose title invokes an elemental agent of ambiguity, since smoke be-
clouds and thus precludes a clear view of anything. In addition to the
litotes included in the earlier list are these: Litvinov's mother is said to
be "not without a strong personality" (7: 253); Litvinov participates in
local elections "not without unpleasantnesses" (7: 254); the youthful
relationship between Litvinov and Irina "did not proceed without certain misunderstandings and shocks" (7: 285); after seeing Irina again in
Baden-Baden, Litvinov answers a knock at his door "not without a certain shudder," and Potugin, who has knocked, receives Litvinov's ensuing greeting "not without faltering" (7: 308); etc.

9. I am indebted to William M. Todd III for his suggestion that en-

countering the language of litotes in Turgenev's works sets off in the reader what Leo Spitzer terms a "philological click," that is, a characteristic response of recognition indicating that "detail and whole have found a common denominator." Leo Spitzer, *Linguistics and Literary History: Essays in Stylistics* (Princeton, N.J., 1948), p. 27.

10. Wolfgang Iser's distinction between negation and negativity has resonance here. Iser observes that the latter provides not merely rejection of some concept but the introduction of an "unwritten base" in narratives that "does not negate the formulations of the text, but—via blanks and negations—conditions them," that is, negativity creates a background of unarticulated significance. The negations of Turgenev's language of litotes serve precisely this purpose. Wolfgang Iser, *The Act of Reading: A Theory of Aesthetic Reponse* (Baltimore, 1980) pp. 225–29.

11. Another example appears in "Faust," when the protagonist who writes the letters that constitute it, Pavel Aleksandrovich, asks permission to marry the daughter of a neighboring widow, only to have his suit rejected with the explanation that "not such a husband as this is needed" (5: 100). And no description of the "sort of husband" that *is* "needed" is ever forthcoming. Deeply attached to and protective of her daughter, the widow may in fact think that no man would make a satisfactory match, but she would not want to reveal publicly the intensity of her opposition to any marriage for fear of appearing excessively and unnaturally possessive. With this ambiguous mode of expression, then, the mother can intimate that she indeed has the "necessary" criteria in mind for an acceptable son-in-law, but simply prefers avoiding potentially protracted and painful debate over Pavel Aleksandrovich's particular qualifications. This negative phrase thus enables the preservation of the courteous demeanor a well-bred woman expects of herself, while nonetheless suggesting the possibly limitless contempt in which she holds this—and perhaps any—man.

12. Nonetheless, the single most powerful instance of negative ambiguity arguably occurs in one of *A Sportsman's Sketches*, "My Neighbor Radilov." This brief narrative includes a dizzying, literally negative description of the reclusive landowner: "I could not discover in him any passion, not for wine, not for hunting, not for Kursk nightingales, not for doves suffering from falling sickness, not for Russian literature, not for strolls, not for card or billiard games, not for evenings of dancing, not for trips to regional and capital cities, not for paper factories and beet sugar plants, not for painted pavilions, not for tea, not for horses run to exhaustion, not even for fat coachmen" (3: 54). This veritable

cyclone of negated possibilities perfectly embodies the thoroughgoing negativity of Radilov, who is utterly hostile to his own mode of existence. Indeed, the pounding repetition of the words "not for"— as Turgenev makes use of the rhetorical device of repeated negation known as *recusatio*—leaves unclear whether Radilov actually has a "passion" for anything or anyone at all, and is merely concealing it, or whether he has been consumed by his own negativity to such an extent that he has rendered himself passionless, nearly devoid of personality. Perhaps this personality is merely inscrutable to the somewhat ingenuous narrator, but perhaps there is nothing left to scrutinize. By emphasizing at such length and so absolutely what this elusive figure does *not* care about, Turgenev leaves in ambiguity whether Radilov involuntarily *can*not or voluntarily *will* not care about ordinary actuality.

13. There are literally hundreds more negatives in the narrative; they appear beginning in the very first sentence, when the narrator announces that his recollections of the unhappy one are so painful, "I would not want to revive them in my memory" (8: 61). One more set of examples should be presented because they reveal the extent of Susanna's reliance on negatives: she uses them to describe one of the few *positive* experiences in her life, the moment when Michel acknowledged his love for her. She reports in her diary: "He knew that Semen Matveich would *not* ever give him permission to marry me, and he did *not* hide this from me. I myself did *not* doubt this, and I rejoiced *not* that Michel did *not* lie—he was *not* capable of lying—but that he did *not* try to deceive himself. I myself did *not* demand anything" (8: 110; emphases mine).

14. See Empson, pp. 133–54, for a discussion of this type of ambiguity.

15. In fact, the narrator also employs the term in reference to another major protagonist, Lavretskii, noting that one evening while Lavretskii wandered alone in the Kalitin garden, "he thought of nothing, waited for nothing" (6: 104). Yet he is waiting for something, the opportunity to confess his love for Liza. Lavretskii's feelings are thus shown still to be inchoate, undefined, and inaccessible to him.

16. As though to emphasize the importance of the term, Lemm adds the complaint that would normally be translated "but he [Panshin] cannot understand anything." Yet since Russian employs double negation, an alternative literal translation would read "but he cannot understand nothing" (*no on ne mozhet nichego ponimat'*). The special meaning of "nothing" for Lemm might well justify the unconventional translation.

17. Kurliandskaia remarks the prevalence of such terms, which she

more traditionally labels "indefinite pronouns," in her discussion of Turgenev's language. Yet the bulk of her discussion is addressed to the precision of that language; she lauds Turgenev for widening "the descriptive capacity" of Russian by composing new compound adjectives and putting established adjectives to new uses. G. B. Kurliandskaia, *Khudozhestvennyi metod Turgeneva-romanista* (Tula, 1972), pp. 131–61.

18. This prevalence of semi-definite terms is re-created in a passage in *The Devils*, in which Dostoevsky parodies Turgenev's narrative style. The novel's narrator describes a writer named Karmazinov, a caricature of Turgenev, addressing an audience thus: "This was some sort of account of some sorts of impressions, of some sorts of reminiscences." F. M. Dostoevsky, *Sobranie sochinenii v dvenadtsati tomakh* (Moscow, 1982; orig. Russian ed., 1871–72), p. 21. Although intended to lampoon Turgenev's vagueness, this parody nonetheless indirectly confirms the typicality of semi-definite terms in Turgenev's prose. I am indebted to Gary Saul Morson for reminding me of this passage.

19. An equally marked but morally much less suspect incidence of "something" occurs in "The Unhappy One," as the narrator recounts his reaction to Susanna's malevolent guardian. He notes that "in this man, I felt it, there was something that repelled me, that frightened me. And this 'something' was expressed not by words, but in his eyes" (8: 105). Here the semi-definite term indicates the evil buried within the guardian that the narrator senses but has not yet witnessed in overt action.

20. In *Spring Torrents*, see 8: 269, 278, 293, 296, 307, 310, 321, 329, 347,353, 359, 366. In "The Unhappy One," see 8: 70 (twice), 77, 87, 96, 107, 109, 110, 113 (twice), 120, 122. There are dozens of instances of "slightly" in the novels, particularly, as we will see, in *Fathers and Sons*, and in *A Nest of Gentry* and *Smoke*, as well.

21. The translation of *nel'zia* as "cannot" is the one sanctioned by Progress Publications, the official Soviet translation bureau. See Ivan Turgenev, *Stories and Poems in Prose* (Moscow, 1982), p. 415.

22. Donald Fanger, *Dostoevsky and Romantic Realism: A Study of Dostoevsky in Relation to Balzac, Dickens, and Gogol* (Chicago, 1965), p. 6.

23. Ibid., p. 7.

24. Ian Watt, *The Rise of the Novel: Studies in Defoe, Richardson and Fielding* (Berkeley, Calif., 1957), p. 30.

25. George Levine, *The Realistic Imagination: English Fiction from Frankenstein to Lady Chatterley* (Chicago, 1981), p. 22. Levine also

qualifies this contention, though, by noting that "the world beyond words" may instead be "merely monstrous and mechanical, beyond the control of human meaning."

Chapter 5

1. Percy Lubbock, *The Craft of Fiction* (London, 1929), p. 121. Bakhtin quotes Boris Eikhenbaum's similar assessment of Turgenev's narrative style: "Extremely widespread is that form, authorially motivated, which introduces a special narrator to whom the narration is entrusted. But very often this form has a completely conventional character (as in Maupassant or Turgenev), testifying to no more than the vitality of the tradition of a narrator as a special personage in the story. In such cases the narrator remains the author, and the motivation for introducing this narrator plays the role of a simple introduction." Boris Eikhenbaum, *Literatura* (Leningrad, 1927), p. 217; quoted in Bakhtin, *Problems of Dostoevsky's Poetics*, ed. and trans. Caryl Emerson (Minneapolis, 1984), p. 266 n2.

2. Richard Freeborn, *Turgenev: The Novelist's Novelist* (London, 1960), p. 70. An underlying reason for this impression is suggested by Watt's remark that "a patent selectiveness of vision destroys our belief in the reality of the report, or at least diverts our attention from the content of the report to the skill of the reporter." Ian Watt, *The Rise of the Novel: Studies in Defoe, Richardson and Fielding* (Berkeley, Calif., 1957), p. 30. Since Freeborn takes Turgenev to be the quintessential Realist, he would not expect Turgenev to engage in any narrative act that would undermine the reader's "belief in the reality of the report." To be sure, Freeborn does acknowledge as well what is taken to be the alternative Turgenevan narrative style: "When Turgenev addresses himself to the reader, it is Turgenev who is addressing us and we need never have any doubts about his role" (p. 48).

3. M. A. Rybnikova, "Odin iz kompozitsionnykh priemov I. S. Turgeneva," in N. Brodskii, ed., *Tvorcheskii put' Turgeneva* (Petrograd, 1923), pp. 52–101.

4. S. E. Shatalov, *Problemy poetiki I. S. Turgeneva* (Moscow, 1969), pp. 272–73.

5. Shatalov argues that Turgenev designs his narrative style primarily to reflect the consciousness of the hero, when actually this is only one of the manipulations of point of view in which Turgenev engages. See Shatalov's central chapter, "The Structure of Turgenev's Narratives," *ibid.*, pp. 37–130.

6. Wayne Booth has devoted a significant portion of his critical ca-

reer to the observation and analysis of the moral implications of variations in narrative voice. Most recently, in *The Company We Keep: An Ethics of Fiction* (Berkeley, Calif., 1988), Booth employs the terms of "friendship," false and true, to describe the moral tenor of the relationship between narrator, reader, and text conveyed by an author—or, as Booth qualifies it, an implied author. Turgenev's evident mistrust of friendship unfortunately renders such terminology inappropriate here.

7. The Russian reads as follows: "Spokoina i samouverenno-laskova, chto vsiakii v ee prisutstvii totchas chuvstvoval sebia kak by doma; pritom ot vsego ee plenitel'nogo tela, ot ulybavshikhsia glaz, ot nevinno-pokatykh plechei i bledno-rozovykh ruk, ot legkoi i v to zhe vremia kak by ustaloi pokhodki, ot samogo zvuka ee golosa, zamedlennogo, sladkogo—veialo neulovimoi, kak tonkii zapakh, vkradchivoi prelest'iu."

8. For a painstakingly elaborate and impressive analysis of the various capacities of narrative point of view, see Susan Lanser, *The Narrative Act: Point of View in Prose Fiction* (Princeton, N.J., 1981). The schematic breakdown of categories applicable to the point of view provided on p. 224 (fig. 21) is invaluable to any student of the subject, even if her technical terminology is a bit ponderous.

9. Surely no author manipulates narrative point of view more expertly than one of Turgenev's greatest admirers, Henry James. Consider the single sentence opening chapter 24 of *Portrait of a Lady*, in which James conflates at least three perspectives on Isabella's decision to call on Gilbert Osmond—what Isabella should have perceived, what Isabella did perceive, and why Isabella did not perceive what she should have perceived: "It would certainly have been hard to see what injury could arise to her from the visit she presently paid to Mr. Osmond's hilltop." Henry James, *The Portrait of a Lady* (New York, 1963; orig. pub., 1880), p. 234.

10. The protective instincts at work here are set in clear relief when compared to the changes Dostoevsky effects in his narratives in order to confront and challenge rather than to screen and support the reader. Robin Feuer Miller's *Dostoevsky and The Idiot: Author, Narrator, and Reader* (Cambridge, Mass., 1981) persuasively demonstrates this, analyzing Dostoevsky's narrative style to show how at times it is deliberately constructed to antagonize the reader.

11. For a comprehensive survey of both the formal and the substantive achievements of this collection of narratives, see S. E. Shatalov, *"Zapiski okhotnika" I. S. Turgeneva* (Stalinabad, 1960).

12. This utterance constitutes the first remark that the sportsman

expressly directs to the reader. In subsequent sketches he abandons socially formal terms of address, though, in favor of those acknowledging the literary basis of the relationship. Thus he apostrophizes the reader as just that, "reader."

13. The inhumane treatment of helpless peasants observed in the third sketch, "Raspberry Water," for example, inspires no private response in the narrator, or at least none that he articulates.

14. It should be stressed that these differences do not always redound to the sportsman's credit. In "Death," for instance, the narrator's inability to participate in the deathwatch for a terminally burned peasant is unflatteringly compared to the peasant's stoic resignation to his fate (3: 200–201).

15. Gary Saul Morson provides an incisive analysis of the narratorial use of the pronoun "you" in Tolstoy's *Sevastopol Tales*, in his article "The Reader as Voyeur: Tolstoi and the Poetics of Didactic Fiction," *Canadian-American Slavic Studies*, 12, no. 4 (Winter 1978): 465–80.

16. He employs the second-person form of narrative address throughout "Forest and Steppe" equally evocatively (3: 354–60). Thus the sportsman particularly favors this form to draw the reader into woodland settings.

17. Many of Turgenev's works of the 1870's, including the so-called "supernatural tales" such as "Knock... Knock... Knock!," "The Watch," "The Dream," and "Klara Milich" might best be understood as exercises in the mode of assimilation as well, since Turgenev repeatedly permits the consciousness of one character tacitly to assume control over a formally impersonal narration.

18. For example, Sanin insists to Gemma, "To embark in marriage with you, Gemma, to be your husband—I know no greater blessing!" (8: 326).

19. Boris Uspensky, *A Poetics of Composition: The Structure of the Artistic Text and a Typology of a Compositional Form*, trans. Valentina Zavarin and Susan Wittig (Berkeley, Calif., 1973), p. 137.

20. In the process of making this introduction, Uspensky notes, the framing narrative achieves "the transition from the real world to the world of representation (i.e., the world of art)," p. 137.

21. In the prologue to *Don Quixote*, for instance, the narrator turns to his "kind reader" and tells him, "You yourself will be relieved at the straightforward and uncomplicated nature of the history of the famous Don Quixote de la Mancha, who, in the opinion of all the inhabitants of the district around the plain of Montiel, was the chastest lover and the most valiant knight seen in those parts for many a year." Miguel de

Cervantes Saavedra, *The Adventures of Don Quixote*, trans. J. M. Cohen (Baltimore, 1950; orig. Spanish ed., 1605), p. 30. The reader is thus doubly drawn into the realm of the novel's art: he is apostrophized by the narrator, and he is told that the characters of the novel have existed in the reader's own, real world and have been encountered by other inhabitants of that world.

22. See, for example, Robert Alter's discussion of the narrative structure of *Don Quixote*, in *Partial Magic: The Novel as a Self-Conscious Genre* (Berkeley, Calif., 1975), pp. 1–29.

23. Robert Darnton, *The Great Cat Massacre and Other Episodes in French Cultural History* (New York, 1984), p. 234. Darnton reports that "a certain Mme Du Verger," for one, wrote "from an obscure outpost in the provinces" begging to know, "Is Saint-Preux still alive? What country on this earth does he inhabit? Claire, sweet Claire, did she follow her dear friend [Julie] to the grave?" (p. 245).

24. Erving Goffman, *Frame Analysis: An Essay on the Organization of Experience* (New York, 1974), p. 45.

25. In *Problemy poetiki I. S. Turgeneva*, pp. 63–73, Shatalov discusses in particular the use of the assimilative mode, although he describes it in other terms, concluding that "the style of the narrative . . . constantly departs from the author's own tone and approaches the intonation, the voice of the hero whose point of view the author is bringing forth at the given moment" (p. 73). Compare this conclusion to Bakhtin's assertion that, "when introducing a narrator, Turgenev in most instances makes no attempt to stylize *another person's* distinctly individual and social manner of storytelling. The story in 'Andrei Kolosov,' for example, is narrated by an intelligent and literary man of Turgenev's own circle. Thus would Turgenev himself have spoken, and spoken of the most serious matters in his own life." Mikhail Bakhtin, *Problems of Dostoevsky's Poetics*, ed. and trans. Caryl Emerson (Minneapolis, 1984), p. 191; emphasis Bakhtin's.

26. Indeed, they may be responsible for leading David Lowe, in his insightful study of *Fathers and Sons*, to assert that "the narration in *Fathers and Sons* is inconsistent: the narrator wavers between authorial omniscience and the limited first-person point of view of a faceless participant in the novel." Lowe concludes that there are in effect "two narrative *personae*" in the novel. David Lowe, *Turgenev's "Fathers and Sons"* (Ann Arbor, Mich., 1983), p. 33.

27. Granted, Turgenev did write to M. M. Stasiulevich that he regretted publishing "Enough" "not because I consider it bad, but because in it are expressed such *personal* memories and impressions, which

there was no need to share with the public." Letter to M. M. Stasiulevich, May 20/8, 1878, in I. S. Turgenev, *Pis'ma v trinadtsati tomakh*, ed. M. P. Alekseev et al. (Moscow-Leningrad, 1961–68), vol. 27:1, p. 322; emphasis Turgenev's. Nonetheless, critics have accepted this claim too readily, taking as a given that this narrative constitutes "a distinctive intimately-philosophical confession of the author, pervaded by a deeply pessimistic conception of the history of human society, nature, art" (vol. 7, p. 491).

28. Erich Auerbach goes so far as to exclude Tolstoy and Dostoevsky from the realm of Realism on the grounds that they allow narrators to obtrude themselves in the narration in violation of impersonal verisimilitude. Erich Auerbach, *Mimesis: The Representation of Reality in Western Literature*, trans. Willard R. Trask (Princeton, N.J., 1953; orig. German ed., 1946), pp. 521–24.

29. Elizabeth Ermarth, *Realism and Consensus in the English Novel* (Princeton, N.J., 1983), pp. ix–x.

30. Ibid., p. x.

Chapter 6

1. Friedrich Nietzsche, *The Birth of Tragedy*, trans. Francis Golffing (Garden City, N.Y., 1956; orig. German ed., 1872), p. 65.

2. Ibid., p. 33.

3. Ibid., p. 132.

4. Ibid., p. 52.

5. It should be noted that Turgenev concludes the essay by remarking that he has described "two elemental directions of the human spirit" (5: 348). Thus, although he initially refers to the Hamletic and the Quixotic as different character types, he also implies that a single spirit can encompass both directions. Hence Turgenev suggests a more complex conception of human nature than one of pure typological divisions.

6. Eva Kagan-Kans, *Hamlet and Don Quixote: Turgenev's Ambivalent Vision* (The Hague, 1975), p. 11. There are really only two positions of measurements, though, on this characterological yardstick: the Hamletic character, whose "basic traits are his egotism, lack of faith and the self-analysis which inevitably accompanies these attitudes," and the Quixotic character, who "burns with enthusiasm" and "is fearless, patient, devoid of egotism, determined and full of confidence" (p. 10).

7. Ibid., p. 12. Kagan-Kans does discern some variations or subtypes, such as the heroic villain (p. 31) and the vampire woman (p. 52).

8. René Wellek, *A History of Modern Criticism*, vol. 4 (New Haven, Conn., 1965), p. 142.

9. For a discussion of the similarities and differences between Schopenhauer's and Turgenev's treatments of self-transcendence, see A. Walicki, "Turgenev and Schopenhauer," *Oxford Slavonic Papers*, 10 (1962): 1–17.

10. Garnett, for one, argues that Turgenev admired and embodied characters who, like Don Quixote, represent "self-sacrifice, disregard of one's own interest, and forgetfulness of the 'I.'" Edward Garnett, *Turgenev: A Study* (London, 1924; reprinted Port Washington, New York, 1966), p. 192. In support of the claim that Turgenev espouses self-transcendence, Kagan-Kans (p. 99) turns to the conclusion of "Faust," where the narrator declares, "Renunciation, constant renunciation—this is [life's] secret meaning, its resolution: not the fulfillment of favorite notions and dreams, however elevated they may be, but the fulfillment of duty, this is what the individual should be concerned with" (5: 129). Yet the narrator does not explain how "dreams" and "duty" are defined; therefore the nature of individual obligation remains less precise than has traditionally been assumed.

11. Indeed, Freeborn finds Insarov so selfless as to be utterly empty of substance altogether, asserting that he "appears to have no inner world of his own, no existence beyond what he says and does," as a result of which, "the figure of Insarov, on whose characterization Turgenev has expended so little art, pales in comparison [to Elena]." Richard Freeborn, *Turgenev: The Novelist's Novelist* (London, 1960), pp. 65–66.

12. How appropriate, though, that Mar'ia Aleksandrovna should be associated with a woman who strove so consciously to create a distinctive, autonomous identity.

13. Curiously, Henry James perceives no redeeming strength of character in Mar'ia Aleksandrovna. Labeling "The Correspondence" "a polished piece of misery," James deems both protagonists equally weak-willed, subjected to unhappiness by Aleksei Petrovich's inability to control his instinctual urges. Henry James, *French Poets and Novelists* (New York, 1964; orig. pub. 1878), pp. 245–52. For an explanation of James's reaction, see Dale Peterson, *The Clement Vision: Poetic Realism in Turgenev and James* (Port Washington, N.Y., 1975), pp. 44–45.

14. The eminently pragmatic Tat'iana thus shares with the idealist Iakov Pasynkov the ability to prevent deep disappointment from perverting love and turning it into the bitterness of self-pity. Yet Tat'iana does not seem to partake of Pasynkov's devotion to "the word I singled

out long ago: resignation" (5: 77; the original text used the French *résignation*). Her individuation calls for active confrontation with painful realities in order to control their effects; his entails uncomplaining withdrawal from what he cannot control. Each thus adopts a psychic stance appropriate to their nature, and each thereby sustains their individuation.

15. Robert Louis Jackson points out that the last syllable of Luker'ia's name—ia—is also the Russian word for "I," and therefore only reinforces her self-affirmative response in Russian: "Ia, da, barin—ia. Ia—Luker'ia."

16. Luker'ia thus illustrates the virtues of attempting to isolate oneself from a sense of time's passage. Like Andrei Kolosov, she has accepted without question the truth of Pushkin's line from *The Gypsies* (which Kolosov quotes): "That which was will not be again" (4: 25). Therefore there is no need to dwell on the past.

17. The novelist Evgeniia Tur even entered into a polemical debate over Elena's right to sacrifice herself, by rhetorically asking a critic who had alleged the immorality of Elena's behavior, "Is it possible to throw stones at Elena because she, . . . having fallen in love with the unattractive, poor, and awkward Insarov, has followed him to the ends of the earth" while knowing that his life "belonged indivisibly to the liberation of his fatherland, so that nothing is left to her? In this consciousness is already encompassed self-renunciation, the complete absence of egotistical feeling." Evgeniia Tur, "Neskol'ko slov po povodu stat'i 'Russkoi zhenshchiny,'" *Moskovskie vedomosti*, no. 85 (Apr. 17, 1860), quoted in I. S. Turgenev, *Pis'ma v trinadtsati tomakh*, ed. M. P. Alekseev et al. (Moscow-Leningrad, 1961–68), vol. 6, p. 459.

18. Aleksandr Pushkin, *Evgenii Onegin*, ch. 3, ll. 19–20, in *Polnoe sobranie sochinenii i pisem*, ed. B. V. Tomashevskii and A. I. Korchagina (Moscow, 1956), vol. 5, p. 64.

19. The similarity between this dialogue and one in Turgenev's prose poem "The Threshold" is striking. There a nameless girl is anonymously interrogated as she prepares to enter an enormous building:

—"O you, who wishes to cross this threshold, do you know what awaits you?"
—"I know," answers the girl.
—"Cold, hunger, hatred, scorn, disgust, insult, prison, illness, and death itself?"
—"I know."
—"Total alienation, isolation?"
—"I know. I am ready. I will endure all suffering, all blows."
—"Not only from enemies, but from relatives as well, from friends?"

—"Yes... even from them."

—"Very well. Are you ready for sacrifice?"

—"Yes." (10: 147)

Finally answering all the questions satisfactorily, the girl is allowed to enter, as the exclamations "Fool!" and "Saint!" echo behind her (10: 148). Neither term aptly applies to Elena, though—she does not intend to cross any dangerous threshold alone.

20. Another character who seeks self-definition by attempting to fill roles defined by others is the narrator of "Andrei Kolosov." First trying to fill the role of Kolosov's treasured friend Gavrilov, who has recently died, and then trying to supplant Kolosov in the affections of a young woman Kolosov has forsaken, the narrator fails in each performance. Unlike Elena, though, over time he consciously realizes the futility of trying to fulfill himself by filling roles alien to his nature.

21. Perhaps for this reason Varvara Pavlovna avoids the more dire fates of other femmes fatales upon whom nature has bestowed greater gifts but also exacted a greater toll. Compare her with Zola's eponymous Nana, for instance, who, once the most desirable woman in Paris, dies hideously disfigured by syphilis: "What lay on the pillow was a charnel-house, a heap of pus and blood, a shovelful of putrid flesh. . . . And around this grotesque and horrible mask of death, the hair, the beautiful hair, still blazed like sunlight and flowed in a stream of gold. Venus was decomposing." Emile Zola, *Nana*, trans. George Holden (London, 1972; orig. French ed., 1880), p. 470. By comparison, Varvara Pavlovna escapes relatively unscathed.

Conclusion

1. Edward Garnett, *Turgenev: A Study* (London, 1924; reprinted Port Washington, N.Y., 1966), p. 140.

2. Richard Freeborn, *Turgenev: The Novelist's Novelist* (London, 1960), pp. 162–78.

Index

In this index an "f" after a number indicates a separate reference on the next page, and an "ff" indicates separate references on the next two pages. A continuous discussion over two or more pages is indicated by a span of page numbers, e.g., "pp. 57–58." *Passim* is used for a cluster of references in close but not continuous sequence.

Library of Congress Cataloging-in-Publication Data

Allen, Elizabeth Cheresh, 1951–
    Beyond realism : Turgenev's poetics of secular salvation /
Elizabeth Cheresh Allen.
        p.   cm.
    Includes bibliographical references (p.   ) and index.
    ISBN 0-8047-1873-3 (alk. paper) :
        1. Turgenev, Ivan Sergeevich, 1818–1883—Criticism and
interpretation.   1. Title.
PG3443.A47   1992
891.73'3—dc20
91-19405

    ∞ This book is printed on acid-free paper.